THE BATTLE
FOR
LEYTE GULF

THE BATTLE FOR LEYTE GULF

The Incredible Story of World War II's Largest Naval Battle

C. Vann Woodward

Foreword by
Evan Thomas

Skyhorse Publishing

Skyhorse Publishing books may be purchased in bulk at
special discounts for sales promotion, corporate gifts, fund-
raising, or educational purposes. Special editions can also be
created to specifications. For details, contact the Special Sales
Department, Skyhorse Publishing, 555 Eighth Avenue, Suite
903, New York, NY 10018 or info@skyhorsepublishing.com.

www.skyhorsepublishing.com

10 9 8 7 6 5 4 3 2

ISBN-13: 978-1-60239-194-9
ISBN-10: 1-60239-194-7

Library of Congress Cataloging-in-Publication-Data is
available on file.

Printed in Canada

FOR PETER

CONTENTS

SYMBOLS
AND
ABBREVIATIONS

1. U.S. Navy Ships

BB	Battleship	DD	Destroyer
CA	Heavy Cruiser	DE	Destroyer Escort
CL	Light Cruiser	LCI	Landing Craft, Infantry
CLAA	Light Cruiser (Antiaircraft)	LCM	Landing Craft, Mechanized
CV	Aircraft Carrier	LCT	Landing Craft, Tank
CVL	Light Carrier	LST	Landing Ship, Tank
CVE	Escort Carrier	PC	Submarine Chaser
		PT	Motor Torpedo Boat

2. Command Designations

FIF Flagship of the fleet commander
FF Flagship of the task force commander
GF Flagship of the task group commander

3. Designations of U.S. Naval Aircraft

Model	Class	Name
F6F	Fighter	Hellcat
SB2C	Dive Bomber	Helldiver
SBD	Dive Bomber	Dauntless
TBM	Torpedo Bomber	Avenger
PBY	Patrol Bomber	Catalina
PBM	Patrol Bomber	Mariner

FOREWORD

By Evan Thomas, author of *Sea of Thunder: Four Commanders and the Last Great Naval Campaign, 1941–1945*

If, as the British essayist and statesman Isaiah Berlin once wrote, historians can be divided into hedgehogs and foxes, C. Vann Woodward was a hedgehog. He could see the big picture; he could find and give resonance to the broad themes of history. A much-honored professor at Johns Hopkins and Yale in the '50s and '60s, Woodward was known as the premier historian of the American South and its troubled racial heritage. In person, the soft-spoken Woodward was given to "quizzical understatement," his old friend and fellow Southern bard, the columnist Ed Yoder, once told me. But on the page, Woodward was, as Yoder put it, a writer of "ringing words."

The big picture is out of fashion among academics these days. That's too bad, because the art of story telling with a broad sweep has been too often lost in all the attention to minute sociological detail. Woodward was a great storyteller, and his talents are amply displayed in *The Battle for Leyte Gulf*. During World War II, Woodward served on the navy's history staff (under the greatest of all naval historians, Samuel Eliot Morison), where he pored over ship's logs and after-action reports and the interrogation transcripts of officers of the Imperial Japanese Navy. First published only two years after the war's end, Woodward's account of the greatest naval battle ever fought holds up remarkably well—not just as a factual analysis of a complex engagement but as a timeless depiction of men under stress. (The battle raged for over three days. The Japanese commander, Admiral Takeo Kurita, whose flagship was sunk on the first day, did not sleep the entire time.)

With his eye for human drama, Woodward grasped the tragic aspect of the conflict. The Battle of Leyte Gulf, or as it is sometimes called The Second Battle of the Philippine Sea, spelled the end of the Imperial Japanese Navy as a fighting force at sea. Many of the combatants showed imagination and daring. Nonetheless, the battle was something of a botch by the commanders on both sides. An epic failure of communication allowed the Japanese main battle fleet to slip behind Admiral William F. Halsey's fast carriers and battle ships and attack the smaller auxiliary or "jeep" carriers supporting General Douglas MacArthur's invasion of the Philippines. The bugaboo of divided command was partly to blame, as well as wireless telegraph technology that was more early-than late-twentieth century, but personality and character also contributed to the blundering. "Bull" Halsey of the Third Fleet was a colorful sea dog. "I believe in violating the rules," Halsey once said. "We do the unexpected . . . Most important, whatever we do, we do fast!" When the Japanese wildly exaggerated the impact of air strikes on Halsey's fleet in mid-October 1944, Halsey broke radio silence with the remark that his sunken ships had been salvaged and were "retiring at high speed towards the Japanese fleet." By contrast, Admiral Thomas C. Kinkaid of the Seventh Fleet (MacArthur's Navy, handling the amphibious assault) was taciturn and suspicious of showboaters like Halsey. "Please don't say that I made any dramatic statements," he told reporters after his fleet mauled the Japanese at Surigao Strait. "You know I am incapable of that."

The failure of the two men to understand each other at the crucial moment—as the Americans and Japanese maneuvered on the second day of battle, October 24—could have precipitated one of the great disasters of U.S. naval history. But the Americans were saved when the Japanese commander, Admiral Kurita, turned around his fleet just as it seemed on the verge of annihilating an American task force left undefended by Halsey's wild goose chase in the wrong direction on the night of October 24–25. Although ordered by the top brass in

Tokyo to forge ahead "trusting in Divine guidance," Kurita sailed in circles for a time and finally withdrew. Woodward uses Shakespeare to help understand Kurita. He compares the Japanese fleet commander to Hamlet, brooding and indecisive. "What was needed on the flagship of the Yamato on the morning of the 25th was not a Hamlet but a Hotspur—a Japanese Halsey instead of a Kurita," wrote Woodward in a characteristic grace note.

Though a hedgehog, Woodward knew when to play the fox. He was a master of telling detail. His description of the courage of the men of the besieged American destroyers and carriers of the task force Taffy Three is at once thrilling and moving. After the small carrier *Suwannee* was hit by a kamikaze plane, Woodward writes, "an enlisted man, William S. Brooks, Chief Ship's Fitter, crawled forward along the hangar deck until he was knocked unconscious and injured in the abdomen by explosions. Regaining consciousness, he crawled under the planes to the valves controlling the water curtain and sprinkler system and opened them, thus preventing the fire from igniting the gas-filled planes on the hangar deck, which probably would have made the fires uncontrollable and doomed the ship. Brooks had performed the same duty the previous day," Woodward notes, "under similar circumstances." The Americans may not have been as careless of life as the Japanese, but they were no cowards.

So turn the page and read on as the Japanese fleet catches Taffy Three by surprise on the morning of October 25. ("Through a long glass a signalman aboard the *Kitkun Bay* watched in dismay as the pagoda masts of Japanese battleships and cruisers loomed slowly above the horizon.") Feel the fear that must have gripped the men of the destroyer escort *Samuel B. Roberts* as they heard their captain, Lieutenant Commander Robert W. Copeland, announce through a bullhorn that they were entering "a fight against overwhelming odds from which survival cannot be expected." And experince the giddy relief among the survivors of Taffy Three when Admiral Kurita's fleet suddenly breaks off and retreats. ("Oh hell, they got away!" cried a seaman aboard one of the carriers, with the kind of insouciance that from time to time relieved moments of mortal peril among young American sailors.) There may never be another naval battle on the scale of the Battle of Leyte Gulf; there will certainly never be such a brilliant retelling as the one Woodward gives us here.

PREFACE

A list of those to whom I am indebted for information and assistance in writing this book would approximate in length the roster of a heavy cruiser. Such a list would include high and low in military rank—regular and reserve, officers and enlisted, army and navy. Among them are scores who took part in the Battle for Leyte Gulf, both in the Third Fleet and in the Seventh Fleet. They were especially helpful and eager to "get the story straight." To them and to all hands I wish to express my sincere appreciation. Particularly do I feel an indebtedness to my fellow officers and former colleagues in the Office of Naval Intelligence and the Naval Office of Public Information. For the interrogations of Japanese naval officers I am indebted to the capable and intelligent staff of the Naval Analysis Division of the United States Strategic Bombing Survey.

C. V. W.

INTRODUCTION

The Battle of Leyte Gulf was the greatest naval battle of the Second World War and the largest engagement ever fought on the high seas. It was composed of four separate yet closely interrelated actions, each of which involved forces comparable in size with those engaged in any previous battle of the Pacific War. The four battles, two of them fought simultaneously, were joined in three different bodies of water separated by as much as 500 miles. Yet all four were fought between dawn of one day and dusk of the next, and all were waged in the repulse of a single, huge Japanese operation.

For the Japanese the battle represented the supreme naval effort of the war. They committed to action virtually every operational fighting ship on the lists of the Imperial Navy, which at that time still commanded a formidable surface force. Among the nine enemy battleships present were the two new leviathans of the *Yamato* class, which were designed as the most powerful warships in the world and far outweighed our heaviest ships. These forces, organized in three fleets, were hurled at our newly established beachhead in the Philippines from three directions.

They were guided by a master plan drawn up in Tokyo two months before our landing and known by the code name *Sho* Plan. It was a bold and complicated plan calling for reckless sacrifice and the use of cleverly conceived diversion. As an afterthought the suicidal Kamikaze campaign was inaugurated in connection with the plan. Altogether the operation was the most desperate attempted by any naval power during the war—and there were moments, several of them in fact, when it seemed to be approaching dangerously near to success.

Unlike the majority of Pacific naval battles that preceded it, the Battle of Leyte Gulf was not limited to an exchange of air strikes between widely separated carrier forces, although

1

it involved action of that kind. It also included surface and subsurface action between virtually all types of fighting craft from motor torpedo boats to battleships, at ranges varying from point-blank to fifteen miles, with weapons ranging from machine guns to great rifles of 18-inch bore, fired "in anger" by the Japanese for the first time in this battle. Whether or not the Battle of Leyte Gulf will be the last of its kind fought upon the high seas, it may be said to have brought to its maximum development the tendency of an era toward heavy ordnance and armor.

The major phase of the battle opened in the Sibuyan Sea with strikes by our carrier-based aircraft against the largest Japanese surface force. The enemy replied with land-based and carrier-based air strikes against our carriers. The next phase was a night surface battle between two other forces in Surigao Strait, entirely devoid of air action but including the largest torpedo attack of the war and one of the heaviest gunnery actions. On the following day at dawn two new battles opened. The one off Cape Engaño to the north was a one-sided carrier aircraft action against a Japanese carrier-battleship force. That to the south off Samar Island was fought between two of the most oddly matched forces which ever joined action—the heaviest enemy surface ships in existence against our light escort carriers. The engagement had not been contemplated by either side, and came as a complete surprise to both.

In order to understand the scale upon which the Battle of Leyte Gulf was fought, it might be well to draw a few comparisons with forces involved in an earlier Pacific engagement. In the Battle of Midway, one of the most important actions of the war, our forces entered the engagement with three aircraft carriers. At Leyte Gulf we used eight carriers, eight light carriers, and sixteen escort carriers—thirty-two in all. This is not to say that the latter action was ten times the size or importance of the earlier, but that the scale of air action had increased in something like that proportion. At Midway, of course, there was no surface action and our force contained no battleships.

In our two fleets participating in the Philippines battle we had twelve battleships to the enemy's nine.

To extend comparisons to the precarrier era of naval warfare is difficult and likely to be deceptive. The Battle of Jutland, however, has become a bench mark against which subsequent battles are almost inevitably measured, and a few cautious comparisons need not be misleading. The concept of standard tonnage displacement is a refinement of the naval treaties following the First World War and was not employed in the estimate of tonnage at the time of Jutland. Methods of computing displacement at that time tend to increase estimates about ten percent above those arrived at by present methods. Even without allowance for this difference, however, it is clear that the tonnage of ships engaged in the Battle of Jutland was considerably less than that of ships taking part in the Battle of Leyte Gulf. The figures, arrived at by different standards of measurement, are 1,616,836 tons of combatant ships at Jutland and approximately 2,014,890 tons at Leyte. Without counting the American ships present in the area but not in the task forces engaging the enemy, the number of ships in the Leyte battle on both sides was 244 as compared with 254 at Jutland.

The disparity of tonnage lost in the two battles is even greater than that of tonnage present, the losses at Leyte being about twice the tonnage of losses at Jutland. The Japanese losses were about five times those of the Germans at Jutland. The total figures, again using different standards of measurement, are twenty-five ships and 172,000 tons lost at Jutland and thirty-two ships of approximately 342,000 tons sunk at Leyte. No comparison of aircraft losses can be made, of course, but some four hundred planes were destroyed at Leyte.

A full comparison of casualties is impossible because of lack of complete Japanese statistics. The number of Japanese killed was reported as 7,475, and while no report is available on the number of wounded, it may be presumed that there were as many injured as killed. When it is considered that the *Musashi* lost more than half of her 2,400 personnel and that there were very few survivors of the two battleships which sank in Surigao Strait, the official figure of 7,475 seems remarkably low. The total of Japanese casualties will probably never be known with any exactness, but it seems not improbable that they were more numerous than the total casualties sustained by both Germans and British at Jutland, the number of which was 9,826. Our own forces in the Battle off Samar suffered 2,803 casualties.

In the greatest naval battle of the First World War the total superiority of British over German surface forces was, in terms of tonnage, about eight to five; that of American over Japanese forces at Leyte was somewhat less than two to one (approximately 1,316,360 to 698,530 tons). It should be pointed out, however, that while Admiral Jellicoe's Grand Fleet fought its classic engagement within a few hours' steaming of English bases, and some of his commanders played tennis on English courts the afternoon before the battle, our fleet at Leyte Gulf fought the Japanese more than 7,000 miles from the nearest continental home base. While American superiority in carrier-based planes was overwhelming, it should be recalled that this battle was fought within range of nearly a hundred enemy air-fields and without a single field which the United States forces, army or navy, could use effectively for direct land-based air support.

One question that was debated with regard to Jutland can never be raised in connection with Leyte—the question of who was the victor. Rarely in all naval history has a power staked so much upon one operation as the Japanese did in this, and rarely has any power suffered such an overwhelming defeat. Leyte Gulf was the last surface battle and the last naval engagement of any size in the war. In its decisiveness it is more readily comparable with the Battle of Tsushima, where the Japanese annihilated the Russian fleet, than with Jutland, where decisiveness was lacking. After Leyte Gulf our command of the sea was undisputed, save by land-based planes.

In the course of a battle which resulted in an overwhelming victory the victor appeared to be faced with the threat of a military disaster of incalculable proportions. This is only one aspect of the struggle at Leyte which will make the battle a subject of enduring interest and extensive study.

This essay is not to be regarded as definitive. For the first time, however, it is possible to fill in the important features of the Japanese side of the story and at the same time round out the American side without the inevitable restraint of wartime regulations.

United States naval missions have carried out intensive investigations in Japan since the war, unearthing mounds of technical information, tactical data, and historical documents. Elaborate interrogations of surviving Japanese officers who exercised command in the Battle of Leyte Gulf have cleared up many mysteries. Until this was done there were hundreds of unanswered questions and numerous enigmas surrounding the enemy's conduct of the battle. Until very recently his command relationships, his fleet organization, his basic intentions in the operation, his losses, and finally the reasons for his most important tactical decisions have remained in large measure matters of speculation.

The new information naturally results in some extensive alteration and revision in the earlier accounts of the battle. Some details remain to be filled in, and as additional Japanese documents come to light and admirals begin to publish their memoirs the picture will undergo some further alteration. Over the many controversial points argument will be endless. It is believed, however, that the basic information is now at hand and that in its fundamental aspects the picture will not be greatly changed in the future.

I

SORTIE OF THE IMPERIAL FLEET

Only once in the two years that had passed since the hard-pressed, bitterly fought days of Coral Sea, Midway, and Guadalcanal had the Japanese Fleet ventured out in strength to offer battle. Even in the critical actions of 1942 nothing like full scale commitments had been made on either side, and while the Battle of the Philippine Sea brought out a large part of the enemy fleet the engagement had been confined to air action. None of our many landing operations in 1943 and, with the single exception of the Marianas, none in the following year had been challenged by major forces of the Japanese Navy.

The westward sweep of our Pacific offensive had by the fall of 1944 converged in two mighty thrusts aimed at the Philippine Islands, flanking them from the east and south. On September 15 simultaneous landings were made on Peleliu Island of the Palau Group and on Morotai in the Moluccas. The Peleliu landing brought the Central Pacific Forces, under the command of Admiral Chester W. Nimitz, to the Western Caroline Islands within five hundred miles east of Mindanao. The path of their advance had been westward from the Gilbert Islands through the Marshalls and Marianas. By the landing on Morotai General Douglas MacArthur advanced the frontier of his Southwest Pacific Forces, which had pushed northwest along the coast of New Guinea, to within three hundred miles southeast of Mindanao. The Philippines lay ahead as the next great objective.

Would the landing in the Philippines precipitate the long-awaited event? Would the Imperial Japanese Navy at last be tempted to risk a full scale action with our fleet? In spite of its inferior strength and its long period of hiding, there was reason to believe that the enemy fleet would resist our next assault with an all-out attack. Only a month before the landing took place, Navy Minister Admiral Mitsumasa Yonai told the Japanese Diet that the Combined Fleet remained intact and that the officers and men under Admiral Soemu Toyoda were "imbued with a burning fighting spirit to crush the enemy at the earliest opportunity." He also observed that "the nearer the enemy approaches the inner line of our solid national defense, the greater will become the difficulties and weaknesses of the enemy."

These were not altogether idle words of Admiral Yonai. The Japanese Fleet was by no means impotent at this time, and general strategic factors were heavily in the enemy's favor. While our lines of communication and supply were being stretched to tremendous distances his were being materially shortened. He would fight, moreover, within easy range of scores of his own airfields. The assault upon the Philippines would be unlike any of our landings on the tiny atolls and islands to the eastward, and different from our jungle-locked beachheads in New Guinea. In those operations it had been possible to neutralize enemy airfields. The airfields and emergency strips in the Philippines, some seventy of them operational, would be too numerous to be effectively neutralized and too close to Formosa and the Empire to be cut off from reinforcement. On the other hand, we would be fighting 500 miles from our nearest airfield, entirely dependent upon carrier-based planes for cover and under grave strategic disadvantages. The winding passages through the Philippines, presumably mined and covered by land-based planes, were denied to our forces, while they remained open to those of the enemy.

So impressed was our high command with these disadvantages that as late as mid-September our closely guarded plans for future operations called for three amphibious operations in addition to the two on the 15th before the landing on Leyte Island was to be attempted. The first of these was a landing on Yap Island as a continuation of the Western Carolines campaign by the Central Pacific Forces. This was set for

September 26. MacArthur's forces were to move on to Talaud Island, northwest of Morotai, on October 15, and from that stepping-stone they were to leap to southern Mindanao on November 15. The landing in Leyte Gulf was not scheduled until December 20. In prospect the Philippines campaign therefore assumed somewhat the shape of the long struggle for the Solomons and New Guinea. Plans and preparations were made accordingly.

Then came a sudden and dramatic change in the whole concept and strategy of the campaign. A week before the Morotai-Peleliu landings the Third Fleet, under the command of Admiral William F. Halsey, Jr., began a series of air strikes which lasted until the 15th and had as their purpose the neutralization of enemy airfields which might interfere with the landings of that date. These attacks revealed much unexpected weakness of the enemy in that area. One of Halsey's grounded pilots made his way back to the fleet with the aid of Filipino guerrillas bringing information that confirmed this weakness. Halsey's staff, which had developed the strategy of bypassing in the Solomons, had already discussed the possibility of adapting the same strategy to the Philippines campaign. With the new information in hand, Halsey recommended in a message sent in the early morning hours of the 13th* that all intermediary and preparatory landings and operations be dispensed with and that the assault on Leyte Gulf be carried out as soon as possible.

The landings of the 15th went forward as scheduled, but Admiral Nimitz and General MacArthur concurred in Halsey's recommendations for the abandonment of additional landings and promptly forwarded them for approval to the Joint Chiefs of Staff, then attending an inter-Allied conference at the Château Frontenac in Quebec. Called hastily from a dinner party, the admirals and generals of the Joint Chiefs quickly approved the change in plans and the proposed target date of October 20 for the Leyte landing. The new plan, which promised

---

* All dates and times, unless otherwise indicated, will be those of the Philippine Islands. In military parlance—"Item Zone."

to shorten the war by several months, went into effect on the same day, in fact within a few hours of the time it was proposed.

There was now only a little more than one month instead of more than three months in which to prepare for the great offensive in the Philippines. With a gigantic grinding of gears and applying of brakes many vast operations were pulled to a sudden halt and the huge Pacific war machine was reorganized and turned in a new direction.

A large part of the task force intended for the seizure of Yap Island had already departed from Hawaii combat-loaded, while the remainder was embarked and ready to sail the following morning. These ships and troops were at once diverted to the Southwest Pacific by Admiral Nimitz and put under the command of General MacArthur. Later Nimitz placed Vice Admiral Theodore S. Wilkinson and the Third Amphibious Force at the disposal of MacArthur for the Leyte operation and greatly augmented the naval forces of Vice Admiral Thomas C. Kinkaid, commander of the Seventh Fleet, which was part of MacArthur's command. Large numbers of transport vessels as well as escort carriers, battleships, cruisers, and destroyers were transferred to the Seventh Fleet.

The speed with which the supreme army and navy commands, which had heretofore operated independently, coordinated their plans and forces for this operation was one of the greatest achievements of the Pacific War. All resources of supply, intelligence, ordnance, and all other military services from Washington to Hollandia were set to work at top speed planning, coordinating, administering, training, loading, fueling, and arming in preparation for the great offensive. In the steaming sweat of the New Guinea tropics the operation known by the code name "KING TWO" was mounted.

To add to the complications and difficulties, there occurred in October what Admiral Nimitz pronounced "the greatest change in supply lines of any month in the war up to that time." This was occasioned by the advancing of the main base of the Pacific Fleet more than a thousand miles westward from Eniwetok, the previous base, to Ulithi, which was seized without opposition on September 21. The stepping up of the Leyte invasion schedule upset carefully balanced logistic scales and caused unexpected shortages. Nature added its contribution in the form of a typhoon which slashed through Ulithi lagoon spreading destruction on October 3. The strategic advantages of this base, however, justified all its shortcomings. Ulithi represented an inescapable challenge to Japanese naval power.

While our base was being advanced westward to Eniwetok and thence a thousand miles to Ulithi, the Japanese base was being withdrawn from Truk all the way to Brunei Bay on the western side of Borneo. For many months the Japanese press and radio had been minimizing the seriousness of the long series of reverses Japan had suffered in the loss of her island empire to the eastward. This propaganda was accompanied by repeated prophecies of the complete destruction of our fleet once it was lured farther west. Speaking in Tokyo of the approaching struggle, Admiral Nobumasa Suetsugu, a prewar commander of the Japanese Combined Fleet, said that it was to be regarded "not as a mere battle for the Philippines but one which will decide whether Japan can maintain or is to be cut off from her communication with the vital resources of the southern regions. For that reason," he continued, "the outcome of the Philippine operations will be of such a far-reaching nature as to decide the general war situation, and I am certain it will be the greatest and most decisive battle fought." When the right moment came, he predicted, Japanese forces would "deal the final smashing blow to the enemy." The bluff was now to be called, and the time was approaching when the boast would have to be made good.

Japanese documents of the highest authenticity, captured before the end of the war, reveal in remarkable detail and clarity the development of Japanese naval strategy and organization after the Battle of the Philippine Sea as well as the background of the fateful decision of the High Command which led to the Battle for Leyte Gulf.

For some time after the Battle of the Philippine Sea, fought on June 19–20, the extent and character of Japanese losses remained unknown in spite of the efforts of our intelligence. Eventually it was learned that three carriers were sunk, the *Hiyo* by carrier planes and the *Shokaku* and *Taiho* by submarines, and that approximately 400 planes were destroyed. Even more important than the loss of the three carriers was the almost complete destruction of the air groups of three enemy carrier divisions. Only about forty planes and one hundred pilots remained aboard the surviving Japanese carriers at the end of the battle.

Japanese fleet organization underwent extensive changes between June and October of 1944. These changes involved the tacit admission that the backbone of Japan's carrier-based air power had been all but broken in the Philippine Sea by the Fifth Fleet under the command of Vice Admiral Raymond A. Spruance. While the enemy set to work at once to rebuild his carrier air groups, he had to start practically from scratch, and the handicap proved too great. In the meantime, Admiral Toyoda, commander in chief of the Combined Fleet, regrouped his forces with one object plainly in mind: the strengthening of forces available for *surface* action in the Western Pacific. Carrier action remained, perforce, hypothetical.

Prior to the action in the Philippine Sea the two principal task forces of the Combined Fleet were the Third Fleet, made up of three carrier divisions with screening cruisers and destroyers, under the command of Vice Admiral Tokusaburo Ozawa, and the Second Fleet, consisting of the two new, powerful battleships *Yamato* and *Musashi*, each with nine 18-inch guns, the modernized *Nagato* with eight 16-inch guns, the two old battleships *Kongo* and *Haruna*, with 14-inch guns, three cruiser divisions consisting of ten heavy cruisers, and a squadron of twelve destroyers and one light cruiser. The Second Fleet was commanded by Vice Admiral Takeo Kurita. To all intents and purposes this arrangement left three Japanese area fleets, consisting of cruisers and destroyers, and a training force of two battleships, a light cruiser, and eight destroyers separated both physically and tactically from the main fighting force of the Combined Fleet and unavailable for a fleet action in the Western Pacific.

The regrouping of these fleets made them all available for a fleet action under a new organization called the "Striking Force," placed at first under the command of Admiral Ozawa. The Striking Force was divided into two task forces, the Main Body, containing the remaining carrier strength, and No. 1 Diversion Attack Force, which included the main gun power of the fleet. The latter force consisted of the Second Fleet strengthened by the two battleships *Fuso* and *Yamashiro*, and a division of four cruisers and one of six destroyers. Although called a "diversion" force, it constituted the chief instrument of the enemy's new strategy of surface action. The so-called "Main Body," likewise confusingly named, contained most of the old Third Fleet as the "A" Force and a No. 2 Diversion Attack Force embracing Vice Admiral Shima's Fifth Fleet and a newly organized carrier division composed of the *Ise* and *Hyuga*, two hybrid battleships with flight decks aft, the first carrier-battleships in naval history. In effect the new organization was as follows:

The base of operations for Admiral Kurita's No. 1 Diversion Attack Force was designated as Lingga Anchorage, near Singapore, from which, when invasion threatened, it was to advance to Borneo or to the Philippines. The Main Body would remain based temporarily in the Inland Sea of the Empire. Actually the High Command would have preferred to keep the entire fleet based in the Empire, but scarcity of fuel made the transfer of Kurita's force to Singapore a necessity. Kurita arrived at Lingga toward the end of July and began intensive training for operations against landing forces—the attack of ships at anchorage, the conduct of night battles, the use of radar and star shells, and perhaps most important of all, antiaircraft fire. Admiral Ozawa remained in the Empire with his crippled carrier force to expedite the repair of his ships and the training of new pilots and air groups. Japanese intelligence at that time estimated that the next major American landing would probably not come before the first of November. Ozawa hoped that before that time he could complete his preparations, rebuild his air groups, join forces with Kurita to

COMBINED FLEET
(Admiral Toyoda)

STRIKING FORCE (Vice Admiral Ozawa)

MAIN BODY (Vice Admiral Ozawa)

"A" Force (Vice Admiral Ozawa)	No. 2 DIVERSION ATTACK FORCE (Vice Admiral Shima)	No. 1 DIVERSION ATTACK FORCE (Vice Admiral Kurita)
Carrier Division 3	*Fifth Fleet*	*Second Fleet*
1 large carrier	2 heavy cruisers	5 battleships
3 light carriers	3 light cruisers	10 heavy cruisers
Des. Squadron 11	5 destroyers	1 light cruiser
1 light cruiser	*Carrier Division 4*	12 destroyers
6 destroyers	Ise	Fuso
Cruiser Mogami	Hyuga	Yamashiro
Des. Squadron 10	*Destroyer Squadron*	*Cruiser Division 16*
6 destroyers	6 destroyers	1 heavy cruiser
		3 light cruisers
		Destroyer Squadron
		6 destroyers

the south, and operate with him against the coming American offensive. Ozawa was racing against time.

It remained to specify the circumstances under which the reorganized fleet would give battle. This was determined by the High Command, which, in effect, drew an imaginary line from Honshu, main island of the Empire, down through Shikoku, Kyushu, the Nansei Shoto (which includes Okinawa), Formosa, and the Philippines. The full force of the Japanese fleet would be thrown at any Allied invasion thrust against this line. Palau and Truk were to be left virtually without hope of naval support, while an invasion of Hokkaido, northernmost island of the Empire, and the Bonin Islands was to be countered only under favorable circumstances. Four sets of operational plans were drawn up, one for each of four areas under threat of invasion. Our concern is with the first only, which was the plan for the naval defense of the Philippines, known as the *Sho* Plan.

This plan provided that Kurita's No. 1 Diversion Attack Force sortie from Singapore and proceed toward Brunei Bay or the north central Philippines as soon as the enemy plans were ascertained, and attempt to reach the beachhead during the progress of the landing. It would then "cooperate with our land-based air forces in an all-out attack." "Avoiding the attack of the [planes of the] enemy task force," continued the plan, "it will push forward and engage in a decisive battle with the surface force which tries to stop it. After annihilating this force, it will then attack and wipe out the enemy convoy and troops at the landing point."

The so-called Main Body, based in the Inland Sea, was given as its principal duty the unhappy assignment of acting as a decoy to lure off our fast carrier covering force to permit the battleships to slip through and destroy our invasion shipping. "It will facilitate penetration by No. 1 Diversion Attack Force," said the plan, "by diverting the enemy [carrier] task force to the northeast and will join in the attack against the flank of the enemy task force." The impotent state of the Japanese carrier air groups was indicated by several other significant admissions. It was expected that carrier planes would normally return to land bases rather than to their carriers and that carrier air groups might be shore-based under the various base air forces. Under certain circumstances carriers with no planes aboard might serve as decoys. "Although the strength of the Main Force includes the combined strength of most of the Third Fleet, Fifth Fleet and other units, it is not sufficient for carrying out a simultaneous air and surface battle," confessed the Japanese plan. "Even with battleships and heavy cruisers included, it is not strong enough to screen the carriers." Clearly the carriers were expendable.

After certain important alterations in command discussed below, this daring plan laid down in August was, in its general strategy, carried out in the following October. In his comments on the *Sho* Plan, Admiral Toyoda's Chief of Staff wrote that the task force assigned the mission "may be called our last line of home defense." "It must make a desperate effort to defeat the enemy," he wrote. "The mission of the task force is truly great."

In order to understand the state of mind of the Japanese at the time the final decision was made to commit their fleet in this desperate enterprise, even after the evidence of the overwhelming superiority of our naval forces was in, it is necessary to examine their curious propaganda during and after the strikes made by the Third Fleet on Formosa and Luzon from October 11 to 16. Carrier aircraft from Admiral Halsey's ships conducted this series of strikes to obtain information of enemy installations and to destroy air and surface strength which might interfere with our landing on Leyte. Begun with a surprise strike at Okinawa on the 10th, these attacks continued almost daily up to and beyond the invasion date. On the 11th a diversionary attack was made on northern Luzon. Then on the two following days carrier aircraft for the first time swept down upon Formosa, the enemy's strongest and best developed permanent base south of Japan proper. On October 14 and 15 one of the task groups of Task Force 38 attacked Luzon targets to reduce opposition emanating from that source. Thereafter the Third Fleet forces proceeded southward to give more direct support to the Leyte and preliminary landings.

In the five days of operations in the Formosa area, nearly 1,000 airborne enemy aircraft were engaged, and approximately 43 percent of them were encountered en route to or near our task force. With the possible exception of the Battle of the Philippine Sea, according to Admiral Nimitz, "this was the heaviest series of air attacks ever launched by the enemy against our naval forces."

During the period October 11 to 16 the fast carrier forces destroyed 807 enemy aircraft and 26 ships, and substantially reduced all enemy aviation facilities in the Formosa area. From the viewpoint of destruction of enemy air power, these operations were pronounced by Admiral Nimitz "one of the most successful weeks since the war began." From the strategic standpoint they proved that our fast carriers could approach the strongest enemy air base outside Japan, overwhelm the greatest aerial opposition the enemy could muster there, and stand off the heaviest counterattacks he could mount against our ships.

Our own air losses were not inconsiderable: seventy-six planes in combat, thirteen in operations, and a total of sixty-four aircraft personnel. Two of our ships were seriously damaged in the all-out enemy air attacks. At dusk on the 13th the heavy cruiser *Canberra* was hit by an aerial torpedo eighty-five miles off Formosa. After a debate as to whether she should be sunk and the task force withdrawn, it was decided to save her, and while she was towed away at slow speed the entire task force remained near by to protect her. On the following evening at dusk the light cruiser *Houston* was hit by a torpedo and also taken in tow. The carriers *Franklin, Hancock,* and *Hornet* as well as the cruiser *Reno* sustained minor damage. No vessel was sunk during the operation.

On the 15th a task group consisting of twenty-four vessels under the command of Rear Admiral Laurence T. DuBose was formed to escort the two crippled cruisers to safety. On the following day an enemy air raid, reported by intercepting fighters to consist of sixty to seventy-five planes, attacked the retiring group and scored a second torpedo hit on the *Houston.* This hit was called by one action report "probably the most expensive ever scored by a Jap plane," since it cost the enemy more than forty planes shot down during the attack. The task group escorting the two cruisers had by this time become known in Japanese reports as "the crippled remnants of the Third Fleet." In the Third Fleet the action was sometimes dubbed "The Battle of the Streamlined Bait," for by withdrawing the bulk of the fleet temporarily beyond sight it was hoped that the cripples and their escort would lure the enemy into sending his fleet to sea.

The Japanese propaganda between October 12 and 18 has been called "a campaign of mendacity unprecedented since Napoleon proclaimed the destruction of Nelson's fleet at Trafalgar." It would, in fact, provide the basis for a fascinating study of national psychology, for it seems to have involved a whole people in the toils of self-deception. The fears with which they had long lived—the penetration of our Pacific Fleet into what the Japanese themselves described as the "Essential Sea Area"—had now materialized, and their reaction can only be described as the pathology of fear. Japanese authorities announced that in the course of an action lasting six days the Imperial Navy had destroyed "60 percent of America's effective naval strength," sunk "over 500,000 tons," and sent "an estimated 26,000 American seamen to their deaths." Admiral Halsey's Third Fleet was claimed to be so badly shot up that it had "ceased to be an organized striking force," while Vice Admiral Mitscher's task force had been "completely wiped out." The Emperor himself was directly involved in these fabrications. A special session of the Japanese cabinet met to draw up a report to the Emperor "advising him on the glorious victory," and the Emperor received the cabinet delegation with an imperial rescript of commendation, assuring the world that "the army and naval forces acting in close cooperation have intercepted the enemy fleet and after valiant fighting have greatly damaged it." On October 15 imperial headquarters announced a total of fifty-three American vessels sunk or damaged, sixteen of which were said to be carriers.

Any exploration of the causes of the enemy's conduct in this regard is beyond the limits of this narrative. The extent to which the Japanese naval command was infected by the epidemic of self-deception, however, has an important bearing on the momentous strategic decisions of the next few days. Certainly the Imperial Navy's two chief official spokesmen, Captains Kurihara and Matsushima, were implicated. It is not improbable, as Admiral Halsey and others have suggested, that the enemy was misled by the extravagant claims of his own pilots returning from their strikes against the Third Fleet. Captured documents reveal a general tendency toward consistency of exaggerations not so much by the Japanese propaganda machine as by local commanders on the spot. It is possible that Admiral Toyoda, while not taken in by extreme claims, might have concluded that the often-predicted thing had occurred—that land-based planes had so impaired the strength of our carrier force that the Imperial Fleet now had an opportunity for an all-out surface action in which it might enjoy some greater degree of parity.

Whatever the reasoning of the high command, there occurred on the 15th an abortive sortie of Japanese naval forces, which indicates something of the navy's reaction. At midnight of October 14–15, Vice Admiral Shima's Fifth Fleet, consisting of two heavy cruisers, one light cruiser and four destroyers, sortied from the Inland Sea. According to the testimony of Comdr. Kokichi Mori, a member of Shima's staff, taken after the war, the admiral left the Inland Sea "to find a remnant of American force and center attack on weak points. We expected that there must be quite a number of damaged vessels." Enemy search planes located two of the four task groups composing our forces, and the reports of what they saw were evidently sufficient to sober the headiest expectations. At any rate, the enemy ships hastily withdrew on the afternoon of the 16th before they were brought under attack.

The inflation of Japanese propaganda claims continued, however, and reached new heights after this episode. By the 19th, the day before the target date for Leyte, imperial headquarters had raised the score of ships sunk or damaged to fifty-seven, of which nineteen were said to be carriers. The Formosa "victory" was said to be "as great as the blow dealt the Czarist Russian fleet in the battle of the Japan Sea forty years ago." On the 21st the naval spokesman Kurihara told the press that it was a victory which "far surpasses Pearl Harbor or the action off the coast of Malaya." It is not improbable that two days later, when the entire Imperial Fleet made its last historic sortie, visions of Japanese naval triumphs of the past were still obscuring the realities of the present.

Lest it be too hastily assumed that the popular delusions were guiding high naval strategy, however, it would be well to listen to the postwar testimony of Admiral Kurita. When asked by an admiral of the United States Navy what influence the report of American losses off Formosa had upon Japanese operation plans, he replied: "We got the report, but [I] don't think that the intelligence affected future plans too seriously."* There was some suggestion from another source that an all-out naval effort was a political need of the moment: "While it would not be accurate to say that we were influenced by public opinion," testified Admiral Toyoda, "questions were beginning to be asked at home as to what the navy was doing after loss of one point after another down south. . . . " But there were more basic considerations behind Toyoda's decision. "Should we lose in the Philippines operations," he explained, "even though the fleet should be left, the shipping lane to the south would be completely cut off so that the fleet, if it should come back to Japanese waters, could not obtain its fuel supply. If it should remain in southern waters, it could not receive supplies of ammunition and arms. There would be no sense in saving the fleet at the expense of the loss of the Philippines."

Admiral Kurita viewed the strategic decision in the same light. "The first point is," he said, "that if you seized the Philippines it would cut off all fuel supply to the Empire and that, all supply of fuel being severed, the war in all areas south of the Empire must end. *The Philippines were vital to the continuation of the war.*"† Granting such an assumption, one need not seek further justification for committing a fleet—even against odds. Other Japanese sources reveal that at the higher command levels, at least, the enemy was pretty well informed

---

* In his official action report on the Battle for Leyte Gulf, however, Kurita wrote that "a dozen or more enemy carriers and many other of his ships were sunk or damaged" between October 10 and 17.

† Italics supplied.

of the size and strength of the American naval forces he was going up against, and under no delusions regarding the preponderance of American power.

Of the many Japanese naval officers of high rank interrogated in Tokyo after the war by our naval mission, Vice Admiral Ozawa probably made the most favorable impression. Unusually tall for a Japanese, the admiral bore himself with dignity and composure. Although he was elderly and at the time of the interrogation infirm, his mind remained keen and he was well informed. It was from Ozawa that we learned of several of the important changes in the *Sho* Plan that took place shortly before the Battle for Leyte Gulf.

"We made every effort to try to get ready in time," Ozawa said, "but with every effort we couldn't do it before the 1st of November; we were hoping that would be in time. . . . In early October the repair of the carriers and also the replacement of the pilots was not progressing so smoothly." Since it became clear that he would not be able to join up with Kurita and take command of both forces before our invasion, Ozawa recommended to Admiral Toyoda that the two fleets operate separately, his own from the Empire instead of from the south.

Admiral Toyoda not only removed Kurita from Ozawa's command, but when Halsey struck at Formosa in the middle of October, he deprived Ozawa's carrier force of more than half its partially trained pilots and some 150 planes and sent them to operate from land bases in the defense of Formosa and the Philippines. It was believed that these pilots were "insufficiently trained for sea operations" anyway, "but trained well enough for land operations." "My force of carrier planes became very much weakened," said Ozawa; "it was not my intention to send reinforcement to Formosa, but it was by order of Toyoda." As a result of the order "the operation was changed to use land-based planes more frequently instead of carrier planes," and Ozawa's entire carrier force was thrown into the battle as a diversionary force that would seek to draw off our task force and permit Kurita to reach Leyte Gulf and carry out his mission.

While the ultimate use of Ozawa's carriers may have been foreseen, there is evidence of hasty reshuffling of commands and complete lack of detailed planning for several phases of the operation. "I myself telephoned to headquarters," said Captain Toshikazu Ohmae, Ozawa's Chief of Staff, referring to the final decision regarding the carrier force. "By telephone we decided. It was planned on the spur of the moment." At the same time Admiral Shima's Fifth Fleet, which had been originally assigned the diversionary mission in cooperation with the two carrier-battleships, was ordered to cooperate with Kurita in an attack on Leyte Gulf from the south. Shima had been based in the Empire and knew none of the details of Kurita's plans. Vice Admiral Nishimura, with the battle-ships *Fuso* and *Yamashiro*, was hastily dispatched south to join Kurita's force at Singapore.

The revised plan for the *Sho* Operation created a command situation of amazing complexity. There were now three fleets, each under an independent command, Kurita's, Ozawa's, and Shima's. Moreover, Kurita's force was divided into two parts which were to operate in widely dispersed areas, and Shima's force was under orders to cooperate with a part of Kurita's force without knowledge of its plans. Shima was under the Southwest Area Command, Kurita and Ozawa directly under Toyoda. In addition, the naval land-based planes in the Philippines, upon which the operation was heavily dependent, were under the Southwest Area Command. Each of these commands was directly or indirectly under Admiral Toyoda in Tokyo, the only common superior the four Japanese forces acknowledged.

In addition to the lack of a coordinating naval command in the theater of operations, Japanese naval officers complained of lack of satisfactory liaison with army aircraft in the Philippines. Kurita confessed that he did not know whether there were any available army aircraft in the islands, and apparently the navy did not expect to get assistance from the army air force. "They were to cooperate as much as possible," testified another Japanese naval officer, "but cooperation between army and navy was very poor. This had a great effect on operations. . . . The army and navy always had a row with each other. In theory they were supposed to cooperate and on the higher levels it would work, but personalities were the trouble."

On the other side, General Tomoyuki Yamashita, commander of Japanese army forces in the Philippines, with headquarters in Manila at the time of the Battle for Leyte Gulf, complained after the war that he was informed of the intended Japanese naval strike at Leyte Gulf only five days before it took place; he professed ignorance of details of navy plans. The general also complained that the army air forces in the area were run by Field Marshal Terauchi from Saigon, Indo-China, while the fleet was commanded from Tokyo.

The American command situation, while it could not approach the Japanese for complexity, was not without certain complications. One peculiarity in the organization of our naval forces for the Leyte operation gave rise to a division of command that was unique in the history of the Pacific War up to that time. Previous to the Philippines campaign, naval command had been unified within clearly defined zones or "areas." In the two great converging thrusts at the Philippines the supreme command had been separate and distinct. In the Central Pacific drive from the Gilbert Islands, through the Marshalls, the Mariannas, and the Western Carolines naval and amphibious forces had been under the command of Admiral Nimitz, commander-in-chief of the Pacific Fleet and Pacific Ocean Areas. In the drive up from the Southwest Pacific, naval and amphibious forces were under naval command responsible to General MacArthur, commander-in-chief of the Southwest Pacific Area. Nimitz had sent ships to cover certain smaller landing operations in MacArthur's area on previous occasions, but naval action had been of limited scope and divided command had not been a serious problem. The Philippines operation would be another matter. Here two huge fleets would be required to coordinate their movements closely in an intensive action.

The two fleets involved in the Leyte operation were the Third Fleet and Western Pacific Task Forces, under Admiral Halsey, and the Seventh Fleet and Central Philippines Attack Force, under Vice Admiral Kinkaid. The immediate superior of Admiral Halsey was Admiral Nimitz, at Pearl Harbor; Vice Admiral Kinkaid's was General MacArthur. The two fleets, though operating in support of the same landing, therefore, had no common superior short of the Joint Chiefs of Staff in Washington, more than 10,000 miles from the Philippines.

The disadvantages, not to say dangers, inherent in this division of command were recognized, but it was hoped that by consultation between Admiral Halsey and Admiral Kinkaid the difficulties of coordination could be overcome. To mention only one disadvantage of the command situation, there was the matter of communications—vital in all operations but especially so in one of this huge scale where two fleets were operating over wide areas. The volume of radio traffic and the number of circuits to be guarded would naturally be greatly increased. Divided command also resulted in separate operation orders and increased the opportunity for divergent interpretations of instructions, different conceptions of basic missions, and other misunderstandings of a serious character. Coordination of the movements and tactics of the two fleets would have been difficult enough in an operation against a single enemy force, but the Third and Seventh Fleets would have to deal with three forces to which several courses of approach were open.

The Seventh Fleet alone, greatly augmented by ships which normally operated in the Pacific Ocean Area under Admiral Nimitz, comprised a total of 738 vessels. Of these, 157 were combatant ships, 420 were amphibious craft, 84 were patrol, minesweeping, and hydrographic types, and 73 were service vessels. These vessels were organized in three task forces: (1) the Covering and Support Force, including the heavy bombardment, fire support, and escort carrier vessels, all directly under Vice Admiral Kinkaid; (2) the Northern Attack Force under Rear Admiral Daniel E. Barbey, and (3) the Southern

Attack Force under Vice Admiral Theodore S. Wilkinson. Both of the latter were amphibious forces. Of the combatant vessels composing the Covering and Support Force, six were the old battleships *Mississippi, Maryland, West Virginia, Tennessee, California,* and *Pennsylvania,* five of which were salvaged casualties of the attack on Pearl Harbor; there were also five heavy cruisers, six light cruisers, eighteen escort carriers, eighty-six destroyers, twenty-five destroyer escorts, and eleven frigates. Included among these ships were elements of the Royal Australian Navy which had served in the Southwest Pacific under Kinkaid's command.

With the Third Fleet were eight aircraft carriers (CV's), eight light carriers (CVL's), six new, fast battleships with 16-inch guns (BB's), six heavy cruisers (CA's), nine light cruisers (CL's) and fifty-eight destroyers (DD's). At the outset of this operation all these vessels were organized as Task Force 38, under the command of Vice Admiral Marc A. Mitscher, who was responsible directly to Admiral Halsey. The task force was in turn divided into four task groups, the first under Vice Admiral John S. McCain, in the *Wasp,* the second under Rear Admiral Gerald F. Bogan in the *Intrepid,* the third under Rear Admiral Frederick C. Sherman, in the *Essex,* and the fourth under Rear Admiral Ralph E. Davison, in the *Franklin.* Halsey's flagship was the battleship *New Jersey,* that of Mitscher the carrier *Lexington.* Task Force 38 represented the preponderance of striking force of the United States Fleet, greater fire power than had ever been assembled on the high seas under one tactical command, capable alone of dealing with any combination of forces that could be brought together by the enemy. In regular cruising formation this force stretched over a sea area some forty miles in length and nine miles from flank to flank.

It is obvious that the Japanese Navy had little chance in an action in which it was compelled to match its weight against that of the combined forces of the Third and Seventh Fleet. What chance the enemy had lay in following up the advantages at his command. These advantages included land-based air power and a strategically favorable geography. Formosa, Luzon, Palawan, and Borneo formed an almost continuous enemy-held barrier from the Empire to Malaysia behind which the enemy could maneuver, service, and concentrate his surface forces without fear of interference except from our submarines. Utilizing these advantages, and also taking advantage of the distance separating the Seventh and Third Fleets, as well as their divided command (a factor of which he is reported to have been aware), the enemy might contrive to concentrate all or a major portion of his power and achieve a surprise attack upon one of our fleets, or a part of either, with hope of success.

Vice Admiral Kinkaid's operation plan for "King Two" contained, besides the elaborate details for the amphibious operation, a tentative battle plan. In the event of a threatened attack by major enemy naval forces, he intended to order Rear Admiral Jesse B. Oldendorf, commander of his Bombardment and Fire Support Group, with the possible assistance of the cruisers and destroyers of the Close Covering Group, to interpose his heavy gun power between our amphibious forces and the enemy and destroy the latter. If conditions permitted, he would order the Escort Carrier Group to launch air strikes against the enemy force. His battle plan made three assumptions: (1) that any enemy naval forces approaching from the north would be intercepted and attacked by the Third Fleet, (2) that enemy surface units might approach the landing area from the Sulu and Celebes Seas and through San Bernardino Strait, and (3) that the enemy might attempt "Tokyo Express" runs to reinforce or evacuate, and to harass or interfere with our operations.

The basic orders under which the Third Fleet operated were contained in the operation plan of Admiral Nimitz. The commander of these forces was directed to "cover and support forces of the Southwest Pacific in order to assist in the seizure and occupation of objectives in the central Philippines." He was to "destroy enemy naval and air forces in or threatening the Philippine area," and to "protect air and sea communications along the Central Pacific axis." However, "In case opportunity for destruction of [a] major portion of the enemy fleet offer or can be created, such destruction becomes the primary task." Admiral Halsey was to operate through "the established chain of command," remaining responsible to Admiral Nimitz, but "necessary measures for detailed coordination of operations between the Western Pacific task forces [Third Fleet] and forces of the Southwest Pacific [Seventh Fleet] will be arranged by their respective commanders." It was agreed that the Third Fleet would conduct carrier air strikes on the northern and central Philippines beginning on A-minus-4 day and continuing through A-day, and that thereafter it would continue "in strategic support of the operation, effecting strikes as the situation at that time requires."

The two men in command of the fleets participating in the Battle for Leyte Gulf, Admiral Halsey and Vice Admiral Kinkaid, were of equally distinguished records in the Pacific naval war. For a period of several months in the toughest actions of the Solomon Islands campaign, when Admiral Halsey was in command of the South Pacific area, the two officers were fighting together. Those were the days of Stewart Island, Santa Cruz Island, and Guadalcanal. Early in January 1943 their ways parted, Halsey remaining in command of the South Pacific area and Kinkaid transferring to the opposite pole of operations to become commander of the North Pacific area.

In temperament, as then in areas of command, the two men were in some aspects antipodal. While one was volatile and spectacular by nature, the other was inclined to restraint and reserve. The colorful pronouncements of the carrier admiral are eminently quotable. "I believe in violating the rules," he once said. "We violate them every day. We do the unexpected—we expose ourselves to shore-based planes. We don't stay behind the battle with our carriers. But, most important, whatever we do—we do fast!" The admiral was not averse to counterpropaganda of a striking type. Of his famous prediction of victory in 1943 he said after the war: "I knew my statement could not possibly be true. I wanted to exaggerate as the Japanese exaggerate, to break down their morale." While the enemy was proclaiming the destruction of his fleet after the Formosa strikes, he broke radio silence with the remark that his sunken ships had been salvaged and were "retiring at high speed toward the Japanese fleet." Vice Admiral Kinkaid was transferred in November 1943, after the Aleutians campaign, from the arctic to the tropics to assume command of the Seventh Fleet. After the spectacular success of his forces in the Battle of Surigao Strait, the admiral made a request of correspondents interviewing him: "Please don't say I made any dramatic statements. You know I am incapable of that."

Admiral Halsey had been with the fast carrier force for only two months at the time of the Battle for Leyte Gulf. When he came aboard his flagship *New Jersey* and assumed command of the Third Fleet on August 24, the admiral had not exercised a command at sea for two and a quarter years. His identification with the carrier war had arisen in the public mind from his command of the small-scale raids against the Gilbert Islands, the Marshalls, Wake, and Marcus during the first six months of the war. He gave up this seagoing command in May 1942 shortly before the Battle of Midway. The following September he assumed command of the South Pacific area and from then until the middle of 1944 he directed the Solomons campaign from a desk in Noumea—a long, hard campaign successfully waged. It was a tedious assignment, however, for a seagoing admiral chafing for a command afloat.

In the series of classic actions of the fast carriers, from the Battle of Midway in June 1942 to the Battle of the Philippine Sea in June 1944, Admiral Halsey had played no part. They were the work of Admiral Spruance and his subordinate, Admiral Mitscher. Mitscher remained with the fast carriers until after the Leyte action, serving as commander of Task Force 38 under Halsey. To those who found reason to criticise Spruance for lack of aggressiveness in such actions as Midway and Philippine Sea, "Bull" Halsey was the answer. His popularity in some parts of the Pacific was remarkable.

To thousands of men who had never seen him, he was "The Bull," the incarnation of aggressiveness, the very symbol of the fighting man. If there were any occasion for criticism of the fast carriers in the future, it would be for some other failing than want of aggressiveness. Halsey was spoiling for a fight.

In a dispatch to Admiral Nimitz, sent two or three days before the Battle for Leyte Gulf, Admiral Halsey indicated that he felt restricted by the necessity for covering the Southwest Pacific Forces in the Leyte area, and that he was considering operating in the China Sea. Admiral Nimitz replied very positively that there was no change in the tasks assigned the Third Fleet in his operation plan, previously quoted, and that any restrictions imposed by covering the Southwest Pacific Forces were unavoidable.

In the midst of a storm of typhoon intensity on October 16 our attack and support forces arrived off Leyte Gulf for preliminary landings. Ominously bad weather prevented air activity from the carriers over that area until 0530 on the 18th. In spite of high seas and low overcast, preliminary operations went forward with the seizure of Suluan, Dinagat, and Homonhon Islands, which command the approaches to Leyte Gulf and Surigao Strait. Minesweepers and underwater demolition teams worked furiously under mortar fire from ashore, while light fire support units raked the beaches with harassing fire. By the 19th the way was cleared for the main landing, with the loss of only one vessel, an LCI, and damage to a seaplane tender and two destroyers.

On schedule at dawn of the 20th the great bombardment of the beaches on northern Leyte opened up in preparation for the main landings. Battleships fired for two hours and other ships for longer periods. Simultaneously planes from the escort carrier groups swept in for scheduled air strikes. During the fifteen minutes preceding H-hour LCI's delivered a devastating rocket and mortar barrage, and at exactly 1000, H-hour, the first landing wave hit the beaches at four points along the western side of Leyte Gulf. A half an hour earlier another landing had been made on both sides of Panaon Strait to the southward. The troops were provided by the Sixth United States Army, under the command of Lieutenant General Walter Krueger.

Besides the air support of carrier-based planes, the operation enjoyed strategic support from army air forces in China which made reconnaissance flights along the China coast and bombed Formosa. Land-based army planes from the Southwest Pacific also flew supporting missions, heavily pounding enemy airfields and strips on Mindanao Island. Chief air support throughout the landing phase and for a month thereafter, however, was derived from carrier planes. Those of the Third Fleet, in the course of strikes against airfields on Luzon on the 17th and 18th, destroyed more than 200 enemy planes, and in attacks on Cebu, Negros, Panay, and northern Mindanao in the days that followed, destroyed some eighty-five additional planes. The air squadrons of the Escort Carrier Group of the Seventh Fleet made two daily sweeps of enemy fields in the Visayan Islands and proved their worth by destroying some sixty-six enemy aircraft in close support of the landings.

As a result of the navy's effective air and surface bombardments, the landings were but lightly opposed by gunfire, which damaged several LST's and caused seventy-five casualties. Only light enemy air attacks were made during the unloading phase. The light cruiser *Honolulu* took an aerial torpedo, the heavy cruiser HMAS *Australia* was struck on the bridge by the first suicide plane of the operation, and the escort carrier *Sangamon* was damaged by a 550-pound bomb.

In spite of typhoon, high seas, and the thousand other unforeseeable difficulties which arise to plague any operation of such huge proportions as this, the Leyte Gulf beachhead was established by the end of A-day.* By the end of the following day 103,000 troops of the XXIV Corps and X Corps were safely landed. No previous amphibious operation in the Pacific had brought together so many targets to tempt and bait an enemy surface attack. The ramps of 151 LST's yawned open to the beaches, while 58 transports, 221 LCT's, 79 LCI's,

* Used in this operation instead of the more familiar "D-Day".

and hundreds of other vessels steamed in and out or lay anchored in the Gulf.

West, southwest, and northeast of the Leyte beachhead, deep in enemy territory, were posted hundreds of eyes and ears, human and mechanical, waiting for the first indication of a sortie of the Japanese fleet. Chief reliance for an early warning was placed in the large force of submarines of the Southwest Pacific Area and the Pacific Ocean Area commands, which were maintaining strong patrols in Makassar Strait, in the western entrances to the Celebes and Sulu Seas, and to the north off Hainan and Luzon. For warning of the approach of hostile forces from east of the Philippines, air searches from the carriers of the Third Fleet and land-based planes from Palau and Saipan were relied upon.

Some early signs of a reaction of Japanese naval forces were revealed by sightings of oilers and a few other auxiliary vessels between North Borneo and the area of Mindoro. But A-day and A-plus-1 day went by and A-plus-2 day came on without any reported sighting that would indicate a major effort. Perhaps, as Seventh Fleet intelligence officers had estimated in planning the operation, long before the current enemy propaganda claims that the Third Fleet had been destroyed, the enemy would not commit his fleet.

Then, in the early hours of the 22nd, a dispatch was received from the submarine *Darter,* which with the *Dace* was assigned to cover the southern entrance to Palawan Passage west of the Philippines. The *Darter* reported contact with three large vessels, thought to be cruisers, northwest of Borneo in position latitude 07° 31′ N., longitude 115° 22′ E., course 020°. The two submarines gave chase, but lost contact before dawn without gaining position for attack. In spite of extensive and prolonged air searches the following day no sightings were reported by aircraft. Three cruisers in this area meant something was afoot, to be sure, but no bigger game was yet reported.

At midnight the *Darter* and *Dace* were lying to, surfaced a few yards apart and "speaking" to each other by megaphone. At 0016 of the 23rd, Comdr. David H. McClintock, skipper of the *Darter*, suddenly interrupted the conference with the shout, "We have radar contact! Let's go!" The contact was located in latitude 08° 18′ N., longitude 116° 22′ E., some fifty miles northeast of the position of the initial contact of the previous night. This time it was evidently something much bigger. The two submarines closed at full power, the *Darter* taking up position ahead of the port column of enemy ships and the *Dace* ahead of the starboard column. The targets were headed up Palawan Passage, which lay between Palawan Island and the "Dangerous Ground" to the west.

Although Comdr. McClintock did not know it and consistently underestimated the size of the force, he had made contact with Admiral Kurita's No. 1 Diversion Attack force, which at that time consisted of five battleships, ten heavy cruisers, two light cruisers, and fifteen destroyers. This fleet, which in these pages shall be identified as the Central Force, was organized as follows:

BATTLESHIPS	HEAVY CRUISERS	DESTROYERS
Division 1	*Division 4*	*Squadron 2*
Yamato	Atago (F1F)	Kishinami
Musashi	Maya	Okinami
Nagato	Takao	Hayashimo
	Chokai	Akishimo
Division 2		Hamanami
Kongo	*Division 5*	Fujinami
Haruna	Myoko	Shimakaze
	Haguro	
LIGHT CRUISERS		*Squadron 10*
Noshiro	*Division 7*	Nowake
Yahagi	Kumano	Urakaze
	Suzuya	Isokaze
	Tone	Yukikaze
	Chikuma	Naganami
		Asashimo
		Hamakaze
		Kiyoshimo

"We are about to fight a battle which will decide the fate of the Empire," Admiral Kurita told his men upon the outset of the mission. "We expected that more than half of our ships would be lost," the admiral admitted to an American naval officer after the war.

At 0809 on 17 October, actually a few minutes before our Rangers made their first landing on one of the outlying islands in Leyte Gulf, Kurita had received from Admiral Toyoda the message which initiated the huge operation. It read simply, "Alert for the *Sho* Operation," and was addressed to the commanding officers of all fleets and squadrons and all naval and guard districts. Detailed instructions followed later in the day, and at 0145 the following morning the fleet made its sortie from Lingga Harbor near Singapore. Kurita was headed first for Brunei Bay on the northwest coast of Borneo, where he would refuel from tankers.

Accompanying Kurita as far as Brunei Bay was Vice Admiral Shoji Nishimura with what the Japanese designated as the "C" Force and what will be identified in this narrative as a part of the Southern Force. Nishimura's group consisted of the two 30,000-ton battleships *Fuso* and *Yamashiro*, each with twelve 14-inch guns, the heavy cruiser *Mogami*, and four destroyers. The *Mogami* will be remembered from the famous picture taken of her after the Battle of Midway, her superstructure a shambles, torpedo tubes dangling from her sides, and water pouring from seams and portholes. She survived to take a great deal more punishment. Nishimura's force, under Kurita's command, was to cooperate with him by attacking Leyte Gulf through Surigao Strait.

Kurita arrived at Brunei Bay in the early afternoon of the 20th, refueled, and left at 0805 on the 22nd. Leaving Nishimura at Brunei, and dividing his own force into two groups, Kurita was bound for Leyte Gulf via the Sibuyan Sea and San Bernardino Strait when our submarines picked him up shortly after midnight on the 23rd.

An attack under cover of darkness would have been safer, but Comdr. McClintock, in command of the submarine team, considered it essential to see and identify the elements of the task force, since it was probably headed for Leyte Gulf, and exact information was vital. Three contact reports were sent off during the hours of darkness, estimating the task force to consist of eleven heavy vessels. It was impossible to make out their types until dawn. In the meantime the submarines continued up Palawan Passage ahead of the task force, pacing the two enemy columns like two unseen dolphins. For a time the enemy speeded up and it seemed that it would be impossible to maintain an attack position. Then the force slowed below the maximum submarine speed, and toward dawn the submarines submerged to periscope level and maneuvered for a coordinated attack. The *Darter* was to attack the port column first, then the *Dace* five miles ahead was to attack the starboard column from the west in the half light of dawn. The radar plot then showed two columns of heavy ships, with 5,000 yards distance between columns, and destroyers flanking them.

At 0532, the *Darter* fired all ten of her bow tubes at the leading cruiser of the port column, "roaring by so close that we couldn't miss," then swung hard left to bring her stern tubes to bear on the second cruiser in column. While firing at the second target, Comdr. McClintock counted five hits on the first. Whipping his periscope back to it, he saw what he described as "the sight of a lifetime." So close that the whole ship could not be seen at one time, the cruiser was "a mass of bellowing black smoke from No. 1 turret to the stern. . . . Bright orange flames shot out from the side along the main deck from the bow to the after turret." The ship was already down by the bow, with her decks awash. Four hits were then counted on the second target, but the *Darter* had started a deep dive and was unable to witness the results.

Counting the hits of the *Darter*, Comdr. B. D. Claggett of the *Dace*, to the northeast, could see two cruisers aflame and a huge pall of smoke, behind which were dim shapes. He passed up the first two ships in the starboard column, since they were, as he said, "only heavy cruisers," and took as his target what he believed to be a battleship to their rear. The

Dace fired six of her bow tubes at 0554 and two minutes later counted four hits.

From deep below the surface the crews of the two submarines felt their craft shake with two tremendous explosions from above. A sound-man of the *Dace* said that it was "like the bottom of the ocean blowing up." These were thought to be magazines exploding. There followed "gruesome breaking-up noises" that made Comdr. Claggett think his target was "coming down on top of us." His target was a heavy cruiser instead of a battleship. It sank almost immediately with great loss of life. The screws of four destroyers were soon heard above, and depth charges began exploding. A total of thirty-six charges, the larger part of them apparently aimed at the *Dace*, were counted, but no damage was done.

The *Darter* was officially credited later with sinking the heavy cruiser *Atago* and seriously damaging the heavy cruiser *Takao*, and the *Dace* with sinking the heavy cruiser *Maya*. The Commander Submarines, Seventh Fleet, pronounced this "one of the most successful coordinated [submarine] attacks on record."

It was even a better night's work than was suspected at the time, for the *Atago* was the flagship of the Japanese No. 1 Diversion Attack Force and also of the Second Fleet and of her cruiser division. Vice Admiral Kurita's three-star flag made the first of the hurried shifts necessitated during the ensuing battle. The admiral and other survivors of the flagship were hastily transferred to the destroyer *Kishinami* from the sinking *Atago*, which went down in less than twenty minutes. The *Maya* sank in four minutes, with heavy loss of life. Half of the communications personnel of the flagship *Atago* was reported to have been killed in the torpedo attack. Communication proved to be one of the most serious difficulties of the Imperial Fleet during the battle that followed, and lack of key personnel lost with the *Atago* probably contributed to this failure. Later in the day, at about 1630, Kurita and his staff were transferred to the battleship *Yamato*, which remained the flagship during the battle. Lookouts were so jittery after the submarine attack that several depth charge attacks were conducted against floating bamboo poles which were reported as periscopes.

Surfacing cautiously three hours after the attack, the *Darter* saw the *Takao* dead in the water, protected by destroyers and planes. Unable to attack under these handicaps, she submerged to await a better opportunity. That night, while pursuing the slowly retiring cruiser for an attack, the *Darter* ran aground on Bombay Shoals and was left "high and dry" by the receding tide. Her entire crew was rescued, without casualties, by the *Dace,* but the grounded *Darter* had to be destroyed by torpedo and gunfire.

While the *Darter* and *Dace* were pursuing their targets prior to their attack on the early morning of the 23rd, the *Bream* was patroling the waters off Manila Bay some four hundred miles to the northeast. At 0240 she made contact with a force of one heavy cruiser, one light cruiser, and two destroyers. From her attack position close aboard the targets, she could see men running to their battle stations. At 0325 she fired six torpedoes, one of which struck the target and produced a tremendous flash. The *Bream* was later credited with one hit on the heavy cruiser *Aoba.* It is now known that the *Aoba* was part of a small group detached from Kurita's force earlier to carry out a troop transportation movement for the army.

That night, shortly after dark, the submarine *Angler,* patroling waters off the northern end of the Palawan chain in hope of picking up the battleship force which the *Darter* and *Dace* had attacked that morning, made radar contact with the task force. The *Angler* was unable to launch an attack, but tracked the fleet on a northeasterly course and sent off contact reports indicating a course toward Mindoro Strait. The *Guitarro* picked up the force after midnight and tracked it after it had turned southeast. It was clear that the task force was now committed to passage of Mindoro Strait, the nearest route to San Bernardino Strait— and Leyte Gulf.

By nightfall of the 23rd we had sighted only one of the four enemy surface forces which by that time were well on their way toward their objectives, steaming from four different directions. After the departure of Kurita's force from Brunei Bay, Borneo, Admiral Nishimura's battleship group departed independently and also proceeded northeast. While our guarding submarines were preoccupied with Kurita's force Nishimura slipped past them through Balabac Strait, between Borneo and Palawan, and headed first to the northeast to clear our submarine and aircraft patrol, then east across Sulu Sea toward Surigao Strait, still unobserved.

In the meantime Admiral Shima's Fifth Fleet, consisting of cruisers and destroyers, had sortied from Bako, the principal port in the Pescadores off the western coast of Formosa, and steamed south under orders to cooperate with Kurita by attacking Leyte Gulf from the south. When he left Bako, Shima apparently believed that he was expected to force Surigao Strait alone. He learned of Nishimura's intentions on his way south. He arrived at Coron Bay before dusk of the 23rd, and finding no tankers as he had hoped, refueled his destroyers from his cruisers, and about 0200 the following morning headed southeast across Sulu Sea, on the way to Surigao.

About noon on the 20th Admiral Ozawa's Northern Force of four carriers, two carrier battleships, three light cruisers, and ten destroyers had sortied from the Inland Sea of the Empire and sailed southwest toward the northern tip of Luzon. On the 22nd and 23rd nine search planes were sent out to locate the American task force, but no contact was made. For the first three days after their sortie the ships were under orders to maintain radio silence; then, according to Ozawa, "We opened up on the radio for purpose of luring."*

Nothing so bold as this plan had ever before been ventured by the Imperial Fleet. Japanese naval strategy had been, generally speaking, characterized heretofore by caution and piecemeal commitments. In the *Sho* Operation the enemy had committed nine battleships, one large and three light carriers, fourteen heavy cruisers, six light cruisers, and thirty-three destroyers—virtually the entire operational strength of the Japanese Navy. In addition the navy had transferred

---

* The approach courses of the Japanese fleets are indicated in Chart 1 on page 44.

the full force of the First and Second Air Fleets to the Philippines. Based mainly at Clark Field, these fleets together had approximately 400 planes, two-thirds of them operational. The Japanese Army had about 200 planes operational in the islands. When it is remembered that some of the officers of the forces of Nishimura and Shima considered their mission suicidal, that Ozawa was prepared to sacrifice his entire force, and that Kurita expected to lose half the ships of the main Japanese task force, the revolutionary character of the strategy becomes apparent. The *Sho* Operation was the most daring, not to say the most desperate, attempted by any naval power during the war.

What the enemy hoped to accomplish by the attack was indicated in a general way by the *Sho* Plan. A more pertinent question is: What effect could the operation actually have had upon the Allied landing in the Philippines? It is doubtful that enemy Intelligence was informed of the real situation at Leyte Gulf. In the first place, the greater part of assault shipping had been "combat-loaded" at Pearl Harbor for the attack on Yap Island and the cargoes cut to correspond to the needs of that relatively small operation. When the Yap operation was abandoned at the last minute these ships were diverted to the King Two operation, with only very minor adjustments in the cargo of some vessels and none at all in others. Leyte Island, with the support of bases and air strips throughout the Philippines, was an objective vastly different from the tiny island of Yap. The result of the use of the Yap assault shipping and the speedup of the landing schedule was a critical shortage of certain supplies, especially motor vehicles, and a narrow margin of supplies of all kinds. On A-plus-5 day, the day Kurita and Nishimura planned to enter Leyte Gulf, the majority of our troops on Leyte had supplies ashore for only a few days' operations. Interruption of the flow of supplies, even for a short period, would have created an extremely critical situation.

One bit of information which would have interested Japanese gunnery officers was the fact that the three American army headquarters, located at Dulga, Palo, and San Jose, lay practically on the beaches, within easy range of the secondary batteries of ships in the Gulf. More important was the absence of land-based air support on Leyte. Army operation plans called for the establishment of land-based air support by A-plus-5 day. Because of torrential rains and other misfortunes, however, air strips were not in condition to provide air support except that of a few P-38's for another month. Had our CVE's been destroyed or withdrawn, our troops would have been without air support and almost entirely at the mercy of enemy planes.

Should Kurita succeed in carrying out his mission and come through with even half his ships, he could isolate our troops on Leyte and, at his leisure, destroy the shipping, aircraft, and supplies that were vital to the operation. The effect would have been a disaster of incalculable proportions.

Aboard Admiral Kinkaid's flagship *Wasatch* in Leyte Gulf, Naval Intelligence officers were piecing together the submarine and other reports that had begun to flow in after the initial contact in the early hours of the 22nd. Not enough pieces of the puzzle were assembled at this time to round out the full picture of the composition and intention of the gathering enemy forces, but there were enough at hand to indicate a full-scale Japanese naval effort, probably aimed at Leyte Gulf. On the strength of this information, and before it was all in, Admiral Kinkaid informed Admiral Halsey that he believed the surface forces sighted would concentrate with others from Formosa and the Empire at Coron Bay, at the northwestern end of the Palawan Island chain, refuel there and move against our expeditionary forces at Leyte Gulf.

The only one of the approaching Japanese forces known to our commanders on the night of the 23rd, Kurita's Central Force, could not be expected to come within range of our surface vessels for at least another twenty-four hours. The Central Force, however, would come within striking distance of carrier-based planes early the following morning.

The first blood had been drawn by our submarines. The 24th would be the day for Mitscher's carrier planes.

II

THE BATTLE OF
THE SIBUYAN SEA

On the eve of the Battle for Leyte Gulf the men who manned the ships and planes of the Third Fleet carrier groups had almost completed two months of grueling action of which Admiral Mitscher wrote: "No other period of the Pacific War has included as much intensive operating." During the two previous weeks of strikes on Luzon, Formosa, and Okinawa fighter pilots and ships' crews had stood off the heaviest series of air attacks the enemy had launched against our naval forces up to that time. These strikes came at the end of a period of ten months of operations in the tropics throughout which men had been living between steel decks and bulkheads, under constant pressure, and in large part under actual combat conditions. Shore leave, except for a few hours on some barren atoll, was very rare. "Probably 10,000 men have never put a foot on shore during this period of ten months," reported Mitscher. "No other force in the world has been subjected to such a period of constant operation without rest or rehabilitation."

While all four task groups needed rearming, the primary need was rest for everyone—from flag plot to engine room, from admirals to mess boys. Ships' medical officers commented on the symptoms of fatigue in their reports. "The spirit of these ships is commendable," said Mitscher. "However, the reactions of their crews are slowed down. The result is that they are not completely effective against attack." Yet the ships of Task Force 38 were about to face their severest test.

The composition of the Third Fleet had altered from time to time as units were detached for repair and new ships joined. On the evening of 23 October, however, the fleet was organized as shown on page 42.

THIRD FLEET
Admiral William F. Halsey, in the New Jersey
TASK FORCE 38
Vice Admiral Marc A. Mitscher, in the Lexington

TASK GROUP 38.1
Vice Adm. John S. McCain

Carriers
Wasp (CV) (GF)*
Hornet (CV)
Hancock (CV)
Monterey (CVL)
Cowpens (CVL)

Cruisers
Chester (CA)
Pensacola (CA)
Salt Lake City (CA)
Boston (CA)
San Diego (CLAA)
Oakland (CLAA)

14 Destroyers

TASK GROUP 38.2
Rear Adm. Gerald F. Boganss

Carriers
Intrepid (CV) (GF)
Cabot (CVL)
Independence (CVL)

Battleships and Cruisers
Iowa (BB)
Biloxi (CL)
New Jersey (BB) (FIF)
Vincennes (CL)
Miami (CL)

16 Destroyers

TASK GROUP 38.3
Rear Adm. Frederick C. Sherman

Carriers
Lexington (CV) (FF)
Essex (CV) (GF)
Princeton (CVL)
Langley (CVL)

Battleships and Cruisers
Massachusetts (BB)
South Dakota (BB)
Santa Fe (CL)
Birmingham (CL)
Mobile (CL)
Reno (CL)

13 Destroyers

TASK GROUP 38.4
Rear Adm. Ralph E. Davison

Carriers
Enterprise (CV)
Franklin (CV) (GF)
San Jacinto (CVL)
Belleau Wood (CVL)

Battleships and Cruisers
Washington (BB)
Alabama (BB)
Wichita (CA)
New Orleans (CA)

15 Destroyers

* See page viii for explanation of symbols.

Not all of these groups were present and available for the strikes of the 24th, for at 2230 on the 22nd Admiral Halsey had ordered Admiral McCain's task group to retire to Ulithi for rest, reprovisioning, and rearming. It was unfortunate that this group, which contained more carriers and planes than any other in the fleet, would not be able to participate in the attack on the 24th. The group departed under instructions to deliver a strike on Yap Island on its way out. The three remaining groups of Task Force 38 were steaming some 300 miles east of Luzon on the night of October 22–23, with Davison's task group scheduled to proceed to Ulithi the following day.

The electrifying contact reports from our submarines west of Palawan that night changed all plans and took precedence over all other missions. The primary mission of the Third Fleet had always been the destruction of the Japanese fleet. Within the next twenty-four hours, therefore, it might have the opportunity it had unsuccessfully sought for months. All thought of rest and replenishment was put aside once more, and the orders sending Davison's task group to Ulithi were canceled. Admiral McCain's group, however, now steaming eastward, continued toward Ulithi.

At dawn on the 23rd the task groups made rendezvous with tankers in longitude 130°, some 280 miles northeast of Samar, and were refueled. Admiral Halsey then ordered the three groups to move independently toward the Philippine coast, fanning out on a broad front to gain positions for the launching of planes to search the inland seas on the morning of the 24th. While the formations steamed westward during the night the enemy tried with some success to keep in touch. Single Japanese "snoopers" hovered in the vicinity of the northernmost task group, that of Admiral Sherman almost constantly, so that night fighters had to be kept in the air to hold them at a distance. One snooper was "splashed" at 0227, but at the approach of dawn there were still five of them indicated on the radar screens at widely separated bearings. Evidently the enemy was well aware of the movements of one group though apparently not of the other two.

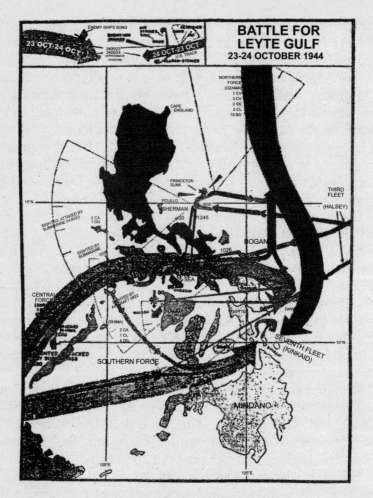

CHART 1.

By daylight of the 24th the three task groups had reached their assigned positions about 125 miles apart in a line stretching northwest and southeast along the east coast of the Philippines. To the north Sherman's group was east of central Luzon about sixty miles off Polillo Island, a position from which his search planes were to cover the sea areas well to the west of Luzon from Lingayen Gulf on the north to Mindoro

Strait on the south. In the central position, Admiral Bogan's group approached to within fifty miles of San Bernardino Strait; its search was to extend north as far as Manila Bay and south into the Sulu Sea. The southernmost position was taken by the task group of Admiral Davison, who was sixty miles off the southern tip of Samar Island, and whose search area extended west of Panay and Negros Islands into the Sulu Sea. No search to the north or northeast of Luzon was ordered, an omission which was later the cause of much concern.*

Shortly after 0600 the search planes were launched, each carrier group sending out a reinforced team of bombers as well as fighters, Helldivers, and Hellcats, one team to every ten degrees of the arc of search assigned the group. The three overlapping arcs extended to a radius of more than 300 miles to the west of the launching points and covered all possible channels penetrating the islands. Fighters were stationed at 100 and 200 miles from their bases to relay reports. In addition, a twenty-plane fighter sweep was launched by Sherman's northern group to attack enemy aircraft in the vicinity of the Manila airfields. Flying weather was excellent for the most part, with visibility over the inland area practically unlimited during the early morning, worse later on.

The background of a naval engagement is usually a monotonous expanse of water where one wave is pretty much like the next. This was certainly untrue of the scenery over which the search planes were flying and against the background of which the naval air battles of the 24th were fought. The inland waters of Tablas Strait and the Sibuyan Sea are bounded by steep-to, rugged coasts with occasional fringes of coconut palm from which volcanic peaks tower dramatically to heights of 8,000 and 9,000 feet. Irregular masses of hills and mountains and low cordillera, densely wooded with tropical growth, break up the horizon in nearly all directions. Against the brilliant blue waters of the inland seas are set islands of coral or volcanic origin.

---

* For locations and search sectors of the three groups, see Chart I on page 44.

Two fighters and one bomber covered each of the six ten-degree sectors assigned the middle group. At 0746, Lt. (jg) Max Adams, pilot of a Helldiver from the *Intrepid*, covering the third sector, which ran south of Mindoro Island, reported to his two fighter teammates that he had radar contact at a distance of twenty-five miles. Course was altered in that direction and from an altitude of 9,000 feet the search planes sighted the wakes of two large groups of ships moving on an easterly course eight miles below the southern tip of Mindoro Island.

Having no doubt that this represented the greater part of the Japanese force reported by our submarines, the search planes sent off an emergency contact report to the relay team, which forwarded it. They then circled and shadowed the contact, identifying in the leading enemy group two battleships, four heavy cruisers, one light cruiser, and seven destroyers, and four miles behind it a second group consisting of two battleships, four heavy cruisers and one light cruiser, and six destroyers, a total of twenty-seven ships. The composition and size of the force was variously reported later, and the first estimate was not entirely accurate since there was a fifth battleship present that was not mentioned. Their speed was reported to be between ten and twelve knots, course 030°. The force sighted was Admiral Kurita's No. 1 Diversion Attack Force, minus three heavy cruisers and other lighter units. It included the enemy's Battleship Division 1, composed of the new fast ships, *Yamato, Musashi,* and *Nagato,* and Division 3, the *Haruna* and *Kongo,* in addition to seven of the ten original heavy cruisers, two light cruisers, and some twelve destroyers.

The greatest interest was excited by the appearance of the mysterious new battleships *Yamato* and *Musashi.* Few Americans had even seen them, much less attacked them, and neither of them had been brought to action before. They were suspected of mounting a larger main battery than any of our heavy ships, but little was known about them. A postwar investigation revealed some remarkable information concerning the two leviathans, nearly everything about which the enemy considered top-secret. The Japanese admitted that the ships were built for world conquest and that few restrictions were placed upon their designers other than the simple instruction to produce the most powerful warships in the world. Completed after the war opened, the *Yamato*-class ships were the heaviest afloat, displacing some 63,000 tons, standard, or half again the weight of our heaviest battleships. The main battery consisted of nine guns with a bore of more than 18 inches, the largest in any navy. The barrel of one of these guns alone weighed 180 tons.

The contact report was relayed to Admiral Halsey, reaching him about 0820. It was clear to him that this force represented a major threat to the Leyte landing, since from its reported position it could easily cover the distance to Leyte Gulf through San Bernardino Strait by way of numerous interisland channels and reach the Gulf by daylight of the 25th. It was out of the question for the Third Fleet to leave its covering position and enter San Bernardino Strait to engage the enemy in the Sibuyan Sea. In the first place, the Japanese carrier force was yet to be accounted for and might be expected to put in an inconvenient appearance. Then the interisland channels were assumed to be mined and known to be covered by land-based planes. It was the obvious mission of the Third Fleet to stop the enemy Central Force by air strikes before dark that day.

Admiral Halsey's flagship *New Jersey* was in Bogan's task group, off San Bernardino Strait, the group nearest to the enemy and his line of approach. Shortly before 0830 Halsey sent out an urgent message ordering Davison's task group, which was off Surigao Strait, and Sherman's task group off Luzon, to concentrate toward the middle group off San Bernardino at best speed and to launch air strikes against the enemy force. He also directed McCain's group, then on the way to Ulithi and more than six hundred miles east of the coast of Samar Island, to put about and proceed toward a fueling rendezvous in longitude 130°.

In the meanwhile additional contact reports came in from the search planes, though only one of comparable importance.

At 0745 another search team from the *Intrepid* located a light cruiser, later identified as the *Kinu,* and a destroyer between Corregidor and Bataan and claimed a hit with a 1,000-pound bomb on the cruiser's bow. The same vessel was also strafed by fighters from the *Essex* about the same time, and two hours later four planes from the *Essex* inflicted more damage on what was apparently the same target. *Lexington* planes encountered strong air opposition in the Manila area, where they shot down some thirty-five planes. They also sighted the damaged cruiser *Aoba* and attacked three cargo vessels in Manila Bay. Three enemy destroyers steaming south along the west coast of Panay were discovered about 0800 by a search team from the *Franklin* of the southernmost task group. Two search teams, combining to attack this group with rockets and bombs, scored two direct hits and one near miss with 500-pound bombs on one of the destroyers and left it nearly dead in the water and smoking extensively. A special strike of eleven fighters and an equal number of bombers launched by the *Franklin* to continue this attack found only two destroyers remaining afloat, and left one of them burning aft. The initial attack was credited with sinking the destroyer *Wakaba,* which a returning search team from the *Intrepid* saw go down.

Overshadowing these two contacts in importance was the one made by the search group from the *Enterprise.* One search team had flown about 320 miles on its 325-mile sector over the Sulu Sea and was on the point of turning back at 0820 when Lieut. Raymond E. Moore sighted tell-tale white wakes farther west. He sent out a "tally-ho" and waited for the other *Enterprise* planes, twenty-six in all, to join up for a coordinated attack. From a high altitude the pilots looked down on the battleships *Fuso* and *Yamashiro,* the heavy cruiser *Mogami,* and four new destroyers. They were steaming westward through the Sulu Sea southwest of Negros Island at a speed of about twenty knots. This was Admiral Nishimura's force.

As the *Enterprise* planes circled to gain altitude for attack, the battleships opened heavy and surprisingly accurate anti-aircraft fire with their main batteries at a range of ten miles.

The ships were in a tight formation, with the battleships and cruiser almost in tandem and destroyers on both flanks. Our fighters led the bombers in out of the sun, pushing over at about 10,000 feet, strafing from 8,000 feet, and firing rockets at 4,000, diving through extremely heavy fire. The bombers followed closely, making dives on both the *Fuso* and *Yamashiro*. Seven rocket hits were claimed on the battleships, the cruiser, and two destroyers, and pilots believed they scored three hits on each battleship with 500-pound bombs. Antiaircraft fire was too heavy, however, to permit accurate observation. It was later learned that the *Fuso* was hit on her catapult by one bomb which destroyed her planes and started a fire that raged for an hour, and the destroyer *Shigure* took one bomb which penetrated and exploded in her No. 1 turret. Neither hit affected speed or navigation, nor was the force slowed down.

Our first air blow of the Battle for Leyte Gulf was struck at the cost of one plane, that of Comdr. Fred E. Bukatis, leader of the fighter squadron. His plane was hit in the engine and he was forced to make a water landing within sight of the enemy ships. Planes of his squadron circled above him under heavy and very accurate fire until he climbed out and made his way to a large life raft which one of the bombers dropped. Bukatis later paddled ashore, where friendly Filipinos helped him find his way back to our lines.

The report of this contact in the Sulu Sea was the first knowledge our command had of a southern flank to the enemy attack. Like the enemy's Central Force, sighted an hour before in Mindoro Strait moving eastward through the Sibuyan Sea toward San Bernardino Strait, his Southern Force could easily reach our Leyte beachhead by dawn of the 25th, though it would likely proceed through Mindanao Sea and Surigao Strait. Admiral Halsey's order directing his northern and southern task groups to concentrate toward him off San Bernardino Strait would take the *Enterprise* and Davison's task group out of striking range of the enemy Southern Force and prevent further attack. Nevertheless, the commander of the Third Fleet adhered to his earlier decision and determined to throw all his weight against the more powerful Japanese Central Force. Later in the morning a plane reported a force of two heavy cruisers, one light cruiser and several destroyers in Sulu Sea to the northwest of the battleship force that had been attacked. This was Admiral Shima's Fifth Fleet, though we assumed that it was part of Nishimura's force. Shima was not brought under attack and was not aware that he had been sighted.

Realizing that the Southern Force would have to be stopped by the Seventh Fleet, Vice Admiral Kinkaid made his plans accordingly. Planes of the Fifth Army Air Force sighted Nishimura's group steaming east toward Mindanao Sea at 0950. There was little doubt that these ships were headed for Leyte Gulf.

While the search planes were returning to their bases, every effort was being made aboard the carriers to prepare for launching strikes against the Japanese Central Force. Until late in the morning, however, they succeeded in launching only one strike. This was sent off at 0910 by the *Intrepid* and *Cabot* of Bogan's group, which was nearest the targets and was not delayed by any other mission. Throughout the day it fell to the lot of this group to carry the major burden of the strikes, although it had only three carriers, two of which were light, and the smallest number of planes available.

The northernmost task group, under Sherman, had launched twenty fighters for a special sweep of the Manila airfields in addition to a large group for the dawn search and was left with barely enough fighters to maintain combat air patrol over the group and to escort the deck-load strike which was ready to go as soon as the search planes reported contact. The report of the *Intrepid* planes was intercepted shortly before 0800, and preparations were rushed to launch the deck-load. Before it could take off, however, a large raid of about forty enemy planes was discovered approaching from the west, and a second group was soon reported to be closing behind the first. A few minutes later a third, the largest of all, appeared on the radar screen, bearing 240°, at a distance of sixty miles.

At that time the group had a combat air patrol of only twelve fighters overhead and an antisubmarine patrol of four fighters and four bombers. Since this was not adequate to deal with a major air attack, twelve additional fighters were scrambled from the *Langley,* twelve from the *Princeton,* and seven from the *Essex,* and when the third raid developed the *Lexington* was ordered at 0831 to launch her eleven remaining fighters. It had been the intention of Admiral Sherman to send off the strike against the enemy fleet before the raids got too close, but he was now without sufficient fighters to escort the strike, and the ships had to conduct such radical maneuvers to avoid the oncoming air attack that launching would be difficult. The strike therefore had to be postponed. The task group took refuge under nearby rain squalls, remaining under them while enemy planes were in the vicinity, and emerged to the edge of the squalls only when it was necessary to launch additional planes or to land those that had run out of gas or ammunition. The attack kept the task group pretty thoroughly occupied for several hours.

The first fighters scrambled from the *Essex* after the warning of the oncoming raid were seven Hellcats led by Comdr. David McCampbell, whose plane happened to be spotted on the catapult, standing by for the first strike against the Japanese fleet. The fighter director vectored this flight northwest then north to a point about thirty miles from the base* where it intercepted the enemy at 0833. The largest of the three, this raid consisted of some sixty planes, about half of them fighters, with many fighters above at about 14,000 feet and torpedo planes and bombers which they were escorting flying at a lower altitude.

McCampbell directed one combat team to dive into the group below while he climbed to attack from the top down. Because of a misunderstanding of orders, five of his fighters went down, leaving only the leader and his wingman,

* The "base" of a carrier aircraft is its carrier.

Lt. (jg) R. W. Rushing, topside. The Japanese formation then reversed course, and the lower group, after a few passes from our planes, dived through the overcast and lost contact with their escort, which maneuvered to defend themselves rather than their bombers. After gaining an altitude of 25,000 feet, McCampbell and Rushing dived out of the sun repeatedly at straggling divisions of Zeke fighters. Between them they had knocked down seven when the Japanese started orbiting in a great circle for mutual protection. Unable to penetrate this defense, the two *Essex* pilots climbed back to 23,000 feet "to light a cigarette and await further developments." The formation would eventually have to break up and head for home when fuel ran low. McCampbell, after he and his wingman had shot down five planes, began keeping the "box score" on his instrument panel with a pencil. After several circles were completed, the Zekes broke formation and strung out for Luzon. For the next hour McCampbell and Rushing, later joined by a third fighter, relentlessly pursued the weaving Zekes, picking off one straggler after another. "It was simply a question of watching for an opening," said McCampbell, "knocking them down, converting into altitude the speed we had obtained in the dive, and then waiting for a couple more to lay themselves open!" Unable to reach his own ship for want of gas, McCampbell landed aboard the *Langley* after an hour and thirty-five minutes of combat with exactly two rounds of ammunition left in his guns, ten gallons of fuel in his tanks, and nine pencil marks on his instrument panel—nine planes which he personally shot down, an all-time record! He did not count numerous targets that smoked and dived, but only sure kills. Rushing had a score of six destroyed, and the five remaining pilots got nine, among them—a total of twenty-four. No planes from this raid reached our ships, and all seven fighters returned, damaged only by flying debris from their targets.

Impressive shooting records were run up by flights which intercepted the other raids. *Princeton* planes alone claimed a score of thirty-four planes destroyed in the melee. The *Lexington* fighters shot down thirteen planes, seven of which were dive bombers, while a division of four fighters from the *Langley* reported splashing at least five planes. The fighters had scattered and thoroughly demoralized the three raids, so that no organized group of enemy planes reached the task group. Many scattered remnants and single snoopers kept popping up on the radar screen, however, at widely varying altitudes and bearings. It became almost impossible to distinguish them from our fighters, which were busily mopping up. The log keeper of the *Essex* combat information center was pushed to keep up: "Splash 1 Betty. Splash 2 Jills. Splash 1 Zeke."

The screen was relatively clear, with no enemy plane within twenty-five miles, when at about 0900 the formation turned into the wind, course 065°, and emerged from the edge of a rain squall to recover fighters in need of fuel and ammunition. In order to clear her flight deck, the *Princeton* had moved six Avengers, armed with torpedoes and ready for the deck-load strike, to the hangar deck. She had recovered ten fighters, which the gasoline detail was busy refueling, and was about to land two more. Suddenly, "out of nowhere," a Japanese bomber of the Judy type was sighted by lookouts at 0938 diving through a low cloud at the *Princeton.* It was taken under fire by several ships but kept on coming, dropped its bomb, pulled out of the dive at 1,000 feet, leveled off over the *Princeton,* passed astern apparently undamaged, and then was quickly shot down by a *Langley* plane.

The Judy scored a direct hit with a 550-pound bomb which penetrated the *Princeton*'s flight deck seventy-five feet forward of her after elevator near the center line and exploded between the main deck and second deck. Many ships had taken worse hits and survived, and Capt. W. H. Buracker's first thought was of "slapping on a patch in a hurry and resuming operations." The explosion, however, ignited the gasoline of the six TBM's in the hangar, all of which were fitted with full auxiliary wing tanks in addition to their normal gasoline load, and all were loaded with torpedoes. Thick black smoke immediately began pouring out the sides, rendering all hangar deck stations untenable, including those for damage control and fire fighting. Choking, badly burned men began reeling topside from the hangar, while personnel in the smoke-filled engine rooms and firerooms continued to operate most of the engineering plant in gas masks for twenty minutes until they were also ordered topside after securing the machinery. Although fueling of planes was in progress at the time of the attack, the gasoline detail succeeded in flooding the system with carbon dioxide and preventing it from igniting. Water pressure and electrical power began to fail in several parts of the ship, however, while intense fires raged and low detonations were heard below. Fire on the flight deck made it necessary to push five fighter planes over the side. In order to prevent the fire from being carried aft, Buracker ordered the *Princeton* turned out of the wind on a course which took her out of the group formation; whereupon Admiral Sherman instructed the light cruiser *Reno* and the destroyers *Gatling, Irwin,* and *Cassin Young* to stay with the burning ship for air protection.

Suddenly, at 1002, a huge explosion in the hangar split the flight deck open between the elevators twisting and bulging the deck, throwing the after elevator in the air, and turning it over on its back. Another and another, then a series of terrific explosions followed, sending a huge column of thick black smoke 1,000 feet in the air. Many men were blown or driven into the water, and three were seen hanging from the radio antenna boom. The destroyers closed astern to pick up men from the water, and the light cruiser *Birmingham* was ordered to stand by the *Princeton* for further assistance.

In the midst of the confusion and explosions an enemy air raid bore down on the stricken *Princeton*. A division of *Langley* fighters intercepted and shot down four torpedo planes, which were on the point of launching their projectiles, while the *Reno* knocked down two more with her main battery. The *Langley*, assisted in one case by fighters, shot down two Judys which were attempting to carry out a dive bombing attack on her. The raid was broken up before it caused any damage, and no further air attack developed during the morning.

When the fire mains aboard the *Princeton* failed completely at 1010, Capt. Buracker gave the order for "Salvage Control, Phase I," which called for all but 490 men to abandon ship. All the wounded and many others were evacuated directly to the forecastle of the *Irwin*, which had come alongside the carrier, now dead in the water. Some AA ammunition began exploding, and at 1020 another very heavy explosion shook the vessel. The captain then ordered "Salvage Control, Phase II," which called for the evacuation of all gun crews, though many hands mistook the order for "abandon ship," and the executive officer had to order all evacuation stopped. This order was instantly obeyed.

In spite of the explosions and fires, the *Princeton* had remained on an even keel. The *Irwin* managed to pump considerable water into the fire areas, though she took a heavy pounding against the carrier and sustained some damage topside. The destroyer withdrew and was relieved by the *Birmingham*, which was joined later by the *Reno* and the destroyer *Morrison*, all of which took a hand in the fire fighting. Fair progress was being made in quenching the fire, and there was even some discussion of taking a towline. The *Princeton's* situation was by no means hopeless at this time. Destroyers were busy picking up more than a thousand of the carrier's hands from the water. The group formation was maneuvered to keep in supporting range of the crippled ship, and was therefore unable to move southeastward to join Bogan's carriers.

In the exchange of preliminary air blows so far delivered, the Japanese forces had come off somewhat the better. The enemy, on the other hand, had not yet felt the weight of a major strike from our carrier decks, whereas he seems to have thrown the full weight of his planes into his first strike— and to have drawn back a severely wounded air arm. One ominous thing about the enemy's air attacks had been the appearance of carrier-type planes. As yet no carriers had been located, and if they were in the vicinity, they would have to await their turn. Sherman's carrier group had been held up and prevented by the air raids from launching any strike until

1055, when its first strike was sent out against the large battleship task force last reported south of Mindoro Island.

The biggest surprise for our airmen was the absence of air cover and fighter protection over the Japanese Central Force. As a matter of fact it was apparently an unpleasant, though not entirely unanticipated, surprise for the Japanese themselves. At least Admiral Kurita seems to have hoped for land-based fighter cover for the task force in the inland sea areas. According to the admiral, "The plan was, first the navy planes from land bases were to attack the American task force and then to shift south to act as cover for our force; but the size of the American task force made it necessary for all land-based plane activity to center on that part, namely the American task force, leaving the Second Fleet without the expected cover." Kurita himself requested fighter protection from the commander of the Japanese First Air Fleet in Luzon, but the fighters never appeared. "No request was made of the army," he said; "I do not know whether there were any army planes there or not."

In anticipation of operating without air cover, Kurita had especially stressed antiaircraft exercises during the training period at Singapore and had greatly augmented the AA batteries of the task force. "To offset the shortage of fighters," said Rear Admiral Tomiji Koyanagi, Kurita's Chief of Staff, "we had increased the number of machine guns on the ships by about 120 machine guns on each battleship on an average, ninety on heavy cruisers, thirty to forty on destroyers." These were light 25-mm guns, but the Japanese had also developed a technique of turning their heaviest batteries skyward. The increase and change in character of flak was at once noticed by our flyers.

The first strike to reach the Japanese Central Force was that launched by Bogan's carriers, *Intrepid* and *Cabot*, off San Bernardino Strait at 0910. This group, consisting of nineteen fighters, twelve bombers, and thirteen torpedo planes, sighted the enemy fleet at about 1020 east of Mindoro Island moving northeast through Tablas Strait toward the Sibuyan

Sea. Flying weather in the area was perfect. The ships were now closed up, with a screen of some twelve destroyers surrounding two columns of cruisers and a column of battleships between led by the *Yamato* and *Musashi*. The air group was directed by Comdr. William E. Ellis to take positions on all sides of the fleet disposition for a coordinated attack.

The planes were met at very long range by "everything they had" in the way of AA, including salvos from the main batteries. "The cumulative effect was terrific," according to the air group commander's report. There were bursts of pink with streamers, purple bursts with white tracers, an abundance of white phosphorus, and a new shell which burst and ejected silver pellets. Two Avengers were hit and forced to make water landings, although their crews escaped in boats. One fighter went down in flames.

The Avengers from the *Intrepid* approached at 250 to 290 knots for their runs and believed they saw two torpedo hits on a *Yamato*-class battleship and one on a heavy cruiser. The *Cabot* torpedo planes could not see the results of their drops on the battleships, but did witness one hit on a heavy cruiser. The bombers, armed with 1,000-pound bombs, believed they scored two hits on a *Kongo* battleship, possibly another, and possibly one on a *Yamato*. The intensity of AA fire made observation difficult and uncertain throughout these attacks. No evasive maneuvers were taken by the targets, except for a slow turn executed by the leading battleship.

The enemy formation seems to have taken the first attack in its stride, for when it was again sighted about 1245, by a second strike from the *Intrepid*, it had advanced some thirty miles—an average speed of eighteen knots—and had now traversed Tablas Strait and was entering the Sibuyan Sea southeast of Marinduque Island. It had split up into two groups about five miles apart, with *Yamato*, *Musashi*, *Nagato*, two cruisers, and seven destroyers in the northern group, and two battleships, five heavy cruisers, one light cruiser, and five destroyers in the other, a total of twenty-five ships. The *Intrepid*'s second strike, made up of fourteen Hellcats, twelve Helldivers, and nine Avengers, chose the northern group as the target and came in at high speed from 15,000 feet. This time the enemy ships turned and twisted in radical evasive maneuvers and once more sent up a heavy AA barrage, including 16-inch shells. In a split torpedo attack upon the easternmost *Yamato* battleship, the Avengers scored three hits which seem fairly well confirmed by photographs. The bombers put two 1,000-pound bombs in the same target and reported one in the *Nagato*, while the fighters expended more than 3,000 rounds of 50-caliber ammunition on various ships. One of our torpedo planes was forced down, but while fighters circled overhead the pilot and two crewmen were "almost immediately" picked up by Filipino guerrillas.

Three or four minutes after the attack, while the planes were making rendezvous for the return flight, a large explosion was seen amidships the *Yamato*-class ship which had taken the worst punishment.

Our planes were out of touch with Japanese Central Force for the next hour, until the first strike from Admiral Sherman's task group located the enemy at 1330. The bad luck that had prevented that group from launching its strike until late in the morning seemed to follow in the slip stream of the planes. Although it was the largest strike group of the day—thirty-two torpedo planes, sixteen fighters, and twenty bombers, divided equally by types between the *Lexington* and *Essex*—the flight ran into foul weather over Luzon which slowed it up. Five *Lexington* torpedo planes became separated from the group and returned to their base, and five bombers from the same ship also returned for various reasons. Another misfortune was that, despite the protest of the air group commander, all the torpedo planes and part of the bombers of the *Lexington* had been loaded with 500-pound general purpose bombs, which are ineffective against heavy ships.*

---

* The ship's captain forbade the rearming of the planes with torpedoes on the ground that the formation was in danger of air attack and that to open up the ship's magazines would jeopardize her safety.

After a considerable search, fighter planes located the enemy fleet, which had again shifted its formation. The *Yamato*-class battleship was left behind southeast of Marinduque Island in about the same waters in which the previous strike had found it. It was streaming oil and steaming along on a northwesterly course. This target was passed up in order to attack the two large groups discovered twenty and twenty-five miles to the southeast, each with two battleships, and all the lighter vessels originally sighted distributed between the two groups. The force was still pushing toward San Bernardino Strait and was now halfway across the Sibuyan Sea.

The westernmost group was assigned by Comdr. Theodore H. Winters, Jr., strike coordinator, to the *Essex* planes. A terrific barrage of flak and a broken overcast made identification of targets and assessment of hits somewhat uncertain. The best estimate of the pilots who returned was three torpedo hits and several 1,000-pound bomb hits on the *Yamato*-class battleship, two torpedo hits on a battleship of the *Kongo* class, four bomb hits on the *Nagato*, one on an *Atago*-class cruiser, two torpedo hits on a *Nachi* and two on an *Atago*-class cruiser. Several vessels were strafed.

Thick and unbroken clouds handicapped the attack of the *Lexington* group, whose ill luck followed them into their dives. Since few planes were armed with anything heavier than 500-pound bombs, the majority selected lighter vessels as targets. One 1,000-pound hit on a *Kongo* battleship was claimed, however, in addition to two bomb hits on a heavy cruiser, one hit on each of three heavy cruisers, and one on a light cruiser. The cost of the strike was the loss of three torpedo planes shot down by flak and two bombers forced to make water landings near their bases.

This strike represented the halfway mark in the day's air effort to stop the Japanese Central Force, and it was the heavier half in number of planes and in weight of ammunition expended. Pilots reported serious damage inflicted on several ships and believed that one of the *Yamatos* was dead in the water and down at the bow after the last attack. Yet not one ship in the force was claimed as sunk so far. This fleet was still intact, still a powerful menace, and it was still headed for the San Bernardino Strait. It seemed to be another demonstration of the ruggedness of Japanese ship construction, as well as of the determination of the Japanese naval command, once it was committed to a plan.

"If this was to be an all-out attack by the Japanese fleet," remarked Admiral Halsey, "there was one piece missing in the puzzle—the carriers." Intense concern was felt regarding this missing piece, not only at Flag Plot in the *New Jersey,* but among Admiral Mitscher's staff aboard the *Lexington,* which had additional reason for concern in the fact that the northern group had been under attack by carrier planes. These might, of course, have been land-based, since most of them were coming from the direction of Luzon. The Japanese carriers were believed to be in the Empire area, though our intelligence about them was limited and it was not known how many of them were operational. Although our submarines stationed in Empire waters had sighted no carrier force, other intelligence sources had revealed that replenishment measures might have been taken for some important movement from Empire waters. While Admiral Halsey was convinced that the Japanese Navy was making a major effort, he was not sure whether it was a direct attack, a covering movement for transporting troops, or both. It stood to reason, however, that, as the admiral observed, carriers were "sure to be employed in some manner in any operation as great as that revealed on the morning of the 24th."

At 1155 Mitscher directed Sherman to launch a search to the north consisting of two fighters and one bomber in each ten-degree sector between bearings 350° and 040°. These planes, as well as a second deck-load strike at the Central Force, were about to be launched when at 1245 another large air raid was reported at a distance of 105 miles, bearing 035°. Admiral Sherman launched the deck-load strike in spite of this report, but in order to intercept the new raid with sufficient strength it was necessary to scramble the *Lexington* fighters which were prepared to conduct the search for the carrier force. The search therefore had to be postponed. Additional cause for regretting this necessary postponement was furnished by a report that the new raid was made up of carrier planes.

A combat air patrol of four fighters from the *Langley* and two divisions from the *Essex* was vectored out at an altitude of 24,000 feet and intercepted a group of more than thirty planes of various types some forty-five miles northeast of the task group. They dived into a formation of Zekes, dispersed them, and shot down many. The raid was broken up and easily scattered by fighters that arrived later. While the dogfight was still in progress, another large raid was reported coming in at ninety miles, bearing 040°, and still more fighters had to be scrambled. For the next hour the air surrounding the task group, and sometimes overhead, was a melee of swirling dogfights, with planes crashing at various bearings and at times near the ships themselves.

A mistaken vector attributed to heavy clouds which obscured the position of our fighters caused the combat patrol sent out against the second raid to miss an interception. The raid kept boring in: 64 miles, 46 miles, 29, 20, and still no "Tally-ho." The fighter director gave a "Hey Rube!," the emergency call for help, to all unengaged fighters, and the *Lexington* recalled seven of her fighters operating to the north and sent them against the approaching raid. The *Lexington* fighters intercepted the enemy planes only fifteen miles from the task group and shot down nine in rapid succession, and other fighters destroyed more of them. Some six or eight dive bombers of the Judy type kept coming, however, and suddenly burst out of the cloud cover and started dives on the carriers. The screening vessels as well as all other ships of the formation opened fire, but so determined was the attack of the dive bombers that some officers believed that they were suicide planes, though there was no proof of this. Three of the Judys were shot down by gunfire and crashed in the sea. One scored a near miss with a bomb on the *Essex*, another dropped a large bomb within fifty feet of the starboard side of the

Lexington without causing any damage, and a third and fourth caused minor damage to the *Langley* with two near misses. No ship was hit, and gun crews ceased firing at 1353.

There followed a lull in the air attacks which lasted about an hour, although combat patrols continued to pursue scattered enemy planes. During this period the carriers maneuvered to take aboard the returning planes of the first strike against the Central Force, while destroyers picked up several pilots who were forced to make water landings near the formation.

The search to the north for enemy carriers ordered at 1155 had still not been launched. Since all the fighters of the task group had been utilized in intercepting the enemy attacks, none was available to accompany the bomber search planes. Realizing that additional delay would be necessary before a fighter escort would be ready, the task group commander requested permission from Admiral Mitscher to launch the bombers on single-plane search missions, unaccompanied by fighters. Since the mission was of vital importance and haste was essential, permission was granted. The search planes were finally launched from the *Lexington* at 1405. "We were fighting again on a shoestring," remarked Mitscher's Chief of Staff, Commodore Arleigh A. Burke, who had fought under those conditions before.

While the task force was standing off air attacks, the *Princeton* and the group of destroyers and cruisers assisting her at some distance from the formation were continuing their efforts to save the damaged ship. Two and a half hours of heroic fire fighting was apparently accomplishing what had seemed impossible, for the fires in the forward part of the carrier were almost extinguished and those aft were nearly under control. The tradition of not giving up the ship, however, was followed at great cost and ultimate tragedy.

Capt. Thomas B. Inglis of the *Birmingham*, now in command of the group, had maneuvered his ship to the windward and port side of the *Princeton* and made fast. Fourteen streams of water were soon playing on the fires from the cruiser's mains, and a party of thirty-eight volunteers under the command of

Lt. Alan Reed was put aboard the carrier to assist in fighting fires. An 18-knot wind and a choppy sea combined with heavy beam swells smashed the two ships together several times, putting two of the cruiser's 5-inch guns out of commission and doing other structural damage topside. As the fires forward subsided, the cruiser cast off and maneuvered aft to bring hoses to bear on other flames.

Capt. Buracker of the *Princeton* was calling for assistance against fires on his starboard side. Although skeptical of the possibility of fighting fires on the leeward side, Capt. Inglis directed any vessels to undertake the task if they found it possible. Unfortunately, because the conditional clause was not transmitted, the *Reno, Morrison, Irwin,* and *Cassin Young* responded immediately as to a definite order. They soon found the heat so intense and smoke so blinding on the leeward side, that they had to abandon the attempt, though not before all had received damage of various sorts. The *Reno* managed to furnish aid from astern and later from the windward side.

Comdr. W. H. Price of the *Morrison* persisted in coming alongside and getting hoses over to the carrier in spite of the hazardous position in which this maneuver placed his ship. The destroyer's superstructure became firmly wedged between the Number 2 and Number 3 stacks of the *Princeton,* which protruded from the side. There she stuck for the better part of an hour, unable to move forward or aft, while her topside was torn apart and badly smashed. She lost her foremast and forward fire director; her stacks were crushed, her searchlight platform smashed, and the port side of her bridge bashed in. A tractor and a jeep fell from the carrier's flight deck and crashed into the bridge and from there to the deck of the destroyer. She proved of great assistance to the fire fighters, however, before she finally wrenched loose.

While the *Morrison* was pinned to the side of the *Princeton,* the *Cassin Young* reported sound contact on a submarine, and at the same time radar screens indicated enemy aircraft closing the group. Fire fighting was reluctantly abandoned under this double threat while the screening vessels, including the *Birmingham*, formed up and began circling the carrier. The submarine contact proved false, but at 1404 a single Zeke fighter swept in over the circle and was taken under fire by the *Reno* without results, while the combat air patrol shot down several planes and drove away the others.

Capt. Inglis got off a report to Admiral Sherman that the fires on the carrier were confined to her after portions centered about the bomb magazine, and that "prospects were very good now." Capt. Buracker was gravely concerned over a number of bombs which, for want of space in the magazines, were stowed aft of the hangar on the main deck in the torpedo stowage. Since fires had ranged in that area for several hours, however, he believed that if an explosion were possible there it would already have taken place. There had been no heavy explosions for nearly five hours. At 1455 he suggested that the *Reno* come alongside to put out the remaining fires and that the *Birmingham* prepare to take the carrier in tow. Capt. Inglis objected that this plan would subject the comparatively undamaged *Reno* to injury, that it was important to keep one cruiser in fighting trim, and that since his ship was already damaged he should undertake the dangerous task.

The *Birmingham*, after three attempts to approach, had just succeeded in making fast a spring line and pointing her starboard bow in to the *Princeton*'s port side forward of amidships. The two vessels lay in the trough of the sea at an angle of thirty degrees, separated by about fifty feet at the closest point. An unusual number of the *Birmingham*'s officers and men were topside—engineers manning hoses, two divisions preparing tow lines, and many hands standing by along the sides to handle lines. Suddenly, at 1523, a terrific explosion tore off a major part of the *Princeton*'s stern and the after section of her flight deck, throwing pieces of the ship the size of a house into the air. The decks of the *Birmingham* were swept by a blast of debris ranging from tiny shrapnel to large sections of plating and including 40-mm gun barrels, steel helmets, gas masks, tool chests, and beams from the flight deck.

Although her captain reported that scarcely "a single officer or man on the *Princeton* escaped injury of some nature in this tremendous blast," it was the *Birmingham* which suffered by far the worst casualties. "From the main deck up," said Capt. Inglis, "the ship was a veritable charnel house of dead, dying, and wounded." Two hundred and twenty-nine were killed almost instantly and 420 were wounded, more than half of them seriously. The first lieutenant and his assistant were killed instantly, the navigator and officer of the deck were seriously injured and unconscious, and the captain and executive officer were painfully wounded. Blood ran freely in the water ways and made the decks unsafe under the feet of the corpsmen. Above the main deck the ship was "perforated to an almost unbelievable extent." There was no panic and no outcry, and officers reported numerous unselfish actions. "Men with legs off, with arms off, with gaping wounds in their sides, with the tops of their heads furrowed by fragments, would insist, 'I'm all right. Take care of Joe over there,' or 'Don't waste morphine on me, Commander, just hit me over the head.' "

A search for survivors in the after section of the *Princeton* revealed nothing but mangled bodies. The ship still appeared seaworthy, but she had lost all steering and motive power; moreover, since her fires had flamed up anew and her main magazines might explode, the captain did not feel justified in asking other ships to run the risk of repeating the *Birmingham's* tragedy. Instead, he asked destroyers to send boats alongside to remove all hands. Capt. Inglis recommended to Admiral Sherman by voice radio that the *Princeton* be sunk, but his message did not get through.

Admiral Sherman was at the moment engaged in fighting off another air attack upon the main body of the task group about thirty-five miles to the northeast of the *Princeton* group. Five Judys succeeded in evading the combat air patrol and dived through the clouds on the carriers, which were recovering planes and were therefore unable to make evasive maneuvers. The attack concentrated on the *Essex*, at which all planes aimed their bomb loads, though without obtaining any hits.

The *Essex* batteries shot down one Judy, and the commander of the *Lexington* air group, returning from a strike in the Sibuyan Sea and awaiting opportunity to land, dived in and splashed another Judy. A few minutes later a single plane slipped in from astern, dropped a bomb which landed near the *Lexington*, and escaped apparently without damage.

For the rest of the day enemy air activity was comparatively quiet. It had been a glorious day for the defensive, as well as for offensive, air power. According to Sherman's report, 120 Japanese planes had been shot down by fighters and antiaircraft fire while attacking his task group, and in addition fighter planes had destroyed forty-seven aircraft near Luzon—a total of 167 for the day. The task group's own losses were ten planes, five pilots, and four crewmen; yet this group had borne the brunt of the enemy's air offensive, both land and carrier-based.

Admiral Mitscher's staff aboard the *Lexington*, while keeping close check on the progress of air strikes on the Japanese Central Force in the Sibuyan Sea, was eagerly awaiting reports from the search planes which had been sent north. More than an hour and a half had passed since they had been launched. At 1640 arrived the first of several contact reports which presented initially a somewhat confused and alarming picture. Lt. (jg) H. N. Walters sighted a large enemy force which he reported in latitude 18° 10′ N., longitude 124° 30′ E., about 130 miles east of the northern coast of Luzon, on course 210°, speed fifteen knots. He circled the force trying to estimate its composition, clouds and flak obstructing his view all the while, and finally reported the composition as *four* battleships, one with a flight deck aft, five to six cruisers, and six destroyers.

This was a discovery of vital importance (if inaccurately estimated), yet it still left the Japanese carrier force unaccounted for. A few minutes later the search plane farthest to the west sighted two *Terutsuki*-class destroyers some ninety miles north and a degree and a half to the west of the first contact, and reported scoring a near miss on one of the ships. In a day of unprecedented contact reports, however, the one sent in at 1640 was perhaps the most exciting and gratifying. The eyes of the fleet in this case were those of Lt. (jg) S. E. Crapser, who sighted the Japanese carriers through a gap in the clouds, circled them for some time, then sent in his estimate of the force: two large 1941 *Shokaku*-class carriers, one light carrier, three light cruisers, possibly one heavy cruiser, and three or more destroyers. He reported them in a position about fifteen miles to the north of the battleship force previously sighted and nearly sixty miles to the east, latitude 18° 25' N., longitude 125° 28' E., on a westerly course, speed fifteen knots. After making sure that his important contact had reached other planes and would eventually get to the ship, Crapser climbed to 7,500 feet and pushed over for a one-plane attack on the carrier task force. His bomb failed to release, and he was immediately jumped by five enemy fighters, one of which his crewman shot down as Crapser pulled into the clouds to escape.

Aboard the *Lexington* Mitscher's staff was having difficulties and arguments in attempting to evaluate these contact reports. Transmission had been very bad, and there were obviously errors on the part of pilots, both of identification and position. Some intelligence officers believed that both planes were reporting the same force. A bit of arithmetic indicated that there was very probably an error in the number of battleships reported. Seven battleships had already been sighted and attacked during the day, and unless our intelligence was badly at fault, the Japanese had only two remaining battleships in operation. The one reported to have a flight deck aft would be the *Ise* or the *Hyuga*, both of which were known to have been converted in this manner, although our forces had never before made contact with them since their conversion. Each ship was known to have retained eight of her 14-inch guns. Our intelligence regarding available enemy carriers was limited, but the accuracy of the report of those sighted was rightly suspect.

As soon as the search plane pilots landed they were put through a close grilling in a corner or Flag Plot by Admiral Mitscher and Commodore Burke. It was finally concluded that in addition to two picket destroyers, two groups had actually been sighted, though they were probably in about the same longitude, with the carrier group some fifteen miles north of the battleship group, the latter in latitude 18° 10′ N., longitude 125° 30′ E., and the former as originally reported. This placed the enemy about 190 miles to the north, bearing 020° from the northernmost of our three task groups. That conclusion was sent to Admiral Halsey by Admiral Mitscher, who estimated that one group was made up of four battleships *or* heavy cruisers, five cruisers, and six destroyers, and the other of two *Shokaku* carriers, one light carrier, three light cruisers, and three destroyers. Both groups were moving at a deliberate speed, fifteen knots, on a westerly course.

The numerous inaccuracies in the estimates and reports of the search planes were especially unfortunate in view of the important decisions that were to be based upon them. Particularly was this true of the estimates of heavy gunnery in the enemy force. Actually, Admiral Ozawa's Northern Force contained only two converted battleships, the armament of which was inferior to any two of Halsey's heavy ships, three light cruisers, and ten destroyers in addition to the one large and three light carriers. Nevertheless, the possible presence of four battleships and twelve cruisers had been suggested and was thereafter taken into account. On the basis of the reports Admiral Halsey said that he "concluded that the Northern Force was disposed in two groups, estimated to contain a total of at least seventeen ships and possibly as many as twenty-four ships."

At 1645 Admiral Mitscher suggested to Sherman by voice radio that "in view of contact to north" the *Princeton* be sunk. This marked the decision of a question long held in abeyance. The necessity for guarding the crippled carrier had restricted the movements of Sherman's task group and prevented it from concentrating with the two other groups to the south. Admiral Sherman concurred and instructed the *Reno* to carry out the grim mission. After all survivors were removed, the cruiser fired two torpedoes, one of which apparently exploded the forward magazines of the *Princeton,* which disintegrated in a few seconds. Her casualties during the day were 108 killed or missing, and 190 wounded. The *Princeton* was the first major ship of the fleet lost to enemy air attack since the heavy cruiser *Chicago* was sunk off Rennell Island in January 1943.

By the time the reports of the contact to the north were received it was too late for Sherman's group to launch a strike against the Japanese Northern Force with the hope of getting the planes back aboard before dark. Admiral Mitscher's first plan, urged by Commodore Burke, was to conduct a night attack upon the enemy's carriers with the surface force attached to Sherman's group. It was Mitscher's belief that this small surface force, without assistance from surface units of the other task groups, would be capable of dealing with the enemy's Northern Force in a night action. At 1712 he directed Sherman to be prepared after dark to detail the battleships *Massachusetts* and *South Dakota,* two light cruisers, and a squadron of destroyers to proceed north and attack with gunfire. This enterprise had to be abandoned in view of radically revised plans later originated by Admiral Halsey.

Earlier in the afternoon, shortly after 1500 and more than two hours before word of the contact with the Northern Force reached him, Halsey had transmitted a battle plan to Mitscher and all his task group commanders. His dispatch announced that Task Force 34 would be formed, consisting of the battleships *Iowa, New Jersey, Washington,* and *Alabama,* two heavy cruisers, three light cruisers, and two squadrons of destroyers, all from the task groups of Bogan and Davison. Halsey, in the *New Jersey,* would be officer in tactical command, with Vice Admiral Willis A. Lee, Jr., in the *Washington,* commander of the battle line. Instructions for the task groups of Sherman and McCain would follow later. This gunnery force was to engage the enemy Central Force decisively if it sortied from the Strait, while the carriers kept clear. A dispatch two hours later further explained that Task Force 34 would be formed when directed by Halsey and if the enemy sortied. At the time Mitscher conceived his plan of sending his small surface force to engage the Japanese Northern Force and for some time thereafter, he assumed that Halsey's plan for guarding the strait with a heavy gunnery force would be carried out. It was not until later that Admiral Halsey changed his plan.

The commander of the Third Fleet now had nearly all the pieces of the puzzle assembled on his battle chart, for by dusk of the 24th he knew the approximate location and composition of all the enemy surface forces in the vast theater. These forces—virtually all that the Japanese had—were scattered over an expanse of six hundred miles, from the Sulu Sea to the Philippine Sea off the northern tip of Luzon. The battle plan of the enemy could not be known, but the target of the three Japanese task forces could hardly be doubted: the "soft" shipping in Leyte Gulf.

Admiral Halsey's plans for countering the triple threat of the Japanese Navy would be fundamentally influenced by his information concerning the capabilities and intentions of the enemy's Central Force, potentially the most powerful of the three. For this vital information he was, of course, dependent upon reports made by the pilots of the strike groups and upon the intelligence officers who evaluated and assessed their accuracy.

It would be well to recall here some of the difficulties of evaluating this type of information. While the pilot is trained in identification and drilled in careful observation, his closest look at a target is often at the end of a dive where flak is thickest and danger greatest, and where he has many things to think about in addition to the bridge structure and the precise number of gun turrets of the ship under attack. Rain, gun smoke, and clouds often interfere with vision, and photographs do not always settle disputes. Errors in identification and position of targets were notoriously frequent. Only the most experienced A.C.I. and staff officers, who had repeatedly seen "capsized cruisers" and ships recently reported "down at the bow" or "dead in the water" disconcertingly turn up in the enemy's battle line, could feel their way through endless duplication and unintentional error to arrive at accurate evaluations.

News of the strikes against the Central Force delivered in the mid-afternoon was reaching Halsey by dispatch, flash report, and voice radio about the same time that the important reports of contact with the Northern Force were coming in. There had been three of these afternoon strikes in the Sibuyan Sea, one by the planes of each of the three task groups.

Bombers and fighters from the *Essex* and *Lexington*, Admiral Sherman's task group, made the first of these last three attacks, the second of the day from that task group. Pilots reported that they had scored seven 1,000-pound and two 500-pound bomb hits on the *Musashi*, which they "observed to stop dead in the water," with four near misses on a *Kongo*-class battleship, and had strafed a cruiser and several destroyers. These reports were sifted and the pilots quizzed by the experienced staff officers of Admiral Mitscher, who after the evaluation reported to Admiral Halsey that two heavy cruisers and one battleship, none of them identified, were damaged. The report added cautiously that because of clouds the estimate of damage was considered poor.

Normally the reports of the strikes of the other two task groups would have been passed up to the fleet commander by way of the task force commander, as were the results of the strike from Sherman's task group, and would probably have received the same conservative evaluation. Admiral Mitscher, however, with Sherman's task group was still about 150 miles to the north of the task groups of Bogan and Davison. The two latter groups were closer together, approaching a rendezvous after dark off San Bernardino Straits, where Davison at Halsey's direction would assume tactical command. Communication with Mitscher was necessarily slow, and since Halsey was with Bogan's group, the reports of the two last strikes were made directly to him.

The results of the last two strikes were reported more optimistically than any other of the day. One of these was the first and only strike that Davison's task group, the southernmost, which had already attacked the enemy's Southern Force, was able to launch against the Central Force. It is evident from the determination with which the squadrons from the *Enterprise* and *Franklin* pressed home their attack that the pilots were bent on making the most of their single opportunity. They claimed, among other things, eight torpedo hits and eleven bomb hits on a *Yamato*-class battleship and thought it and a destroyer were "probably sunk." This claim was toned down before it reached the Third Fleet Commander, although the task group commander did report to Halsey that one *Yamato* battleship had been bombed and torpedoed and left on fire and down at the bow, that a *Kongo* was left smoking and apparently badly damaged, that another battleship was bombed and torpedoed, and that one light cruiser was seen to roll over. He also said that the enemy force was on a westerly, or retirement, course when last sighted.

The last air group over the targets was from Bogan's task group. It was the third strike of the day from the *Intrepid* and *Cabot*, and it can hardly be doubted that fatigue had begun to dull perceptions and sensibilities. Only six torpedo planes were able to join the bombers and fighters. Pilots made no great claims for their own attack and were unable to take any photographs. As a result of their observation, however, the task group commander reported to Halsey that two battleships of the *Kongo* class were damaged and circling, apparently uncontrolled, some distance from the other ships, and that one was on fire and listing. Only four battleships were sighted, two with each enemy group, and one group lacked a heavy cruiser and the other two destroyers that were present that morning. The first force was said to be composed of two battleships, three heavy cruisers, one light cruiser, and five destroyers; the second, of two damaged battleships, three heavy cruisers, one light cruiser, and six destroyers—23 ships in all. When last seen, about 1600, they were estimated to be in latitude 12° 42' N., longitude 122° 39' E., which was, as Bogan pointed out, some fourteen miles *west* of a position previously given, and they were still on a westerly course, perhaps retiring.

Admiral Halsey's flag was in a battleship, where he could not readily question returning pilots. The admiral and his staff officers had not been with the fast carriers as long as had Mitscher and his staff. Information regarding the last strikes had come in the form of flash reports, which were subject to revision and evaluation. That they were not taken at full face value is evident, although in his dispatch to Admiral Nimitz and General MacArthur (with Admiral King and Admiral Kinkaid as information addressees), Admiral Halsey said that one *Yamato*-class ship was left afire and down at the bow, a *Kongo* was smoking and badly damaged, both remaining battleships had been heavily hit, a light cruiser had capsized, and that torpedo hits had been scored on two heavy cruisers and bomb hits on a third. It was evident that at this point the Central Force was no longer believed to be capable of any very serious threat.

As darkness fell off San Bernardino Strait, dimming the blacked-out ships to shadowy profiles, one of the most momentous tactical decisions of the naval war was being made in Flag Plot aboard the battleship *New Jersey*. It was entirely Halsey's decision, and in the nature of things had to be. It was arrived at with incomplete and faulty information—and, again, in the nature of things had to be. There was no time to wait for further information and no means of obtaining some that was needed, nor was there time for more exhaustive study of reports and photographs.

Three separate Japanese forces were known to be approaching our beachhead in the Philippines, each moving at a deliberate speed which indicated to Halsey's mind "a predetermined focus" and "a carefully worked-out coordinated Japanese plan . . . with 25 October as the earliest date of planned concerted action." A message from Kinkaid had been intercepted which indicated that steps were being taken to repel the Southern Force, and Halsey assumed that he need not concern himself with that threat.

The Central Force, on the other hand, was admittedly the responsibility of the Third Fleet. This force, however, had been under heavy attack by the planes of the Third Fleet all day. The last three strikes apparently did not sight one of the *Yamatos* at all, and the second one was reported to have taken terrific punishment. The reported results of these strikes "indicated beyond doubt," to Admiral Halsey, "that the Central Force had been badly mauled, with all of its battleships and most of its heavy cruisers tremendously reduced in fighting power and life." The first report of a night plane from the *Independence,* sent out to shadow this force after dark, reached Admiral Halsey a few minutes before he arrived at his decision. This indicated that the Central Force was still in about the position where it was last attacked and that a battleship and three destroyers were fifteen miles to the west of the main force.

The Japanese Northern Force of carriers and battleships, unlike the Central Force, had not yet been brought under attack. Its exact composition was not known, but at the maximum strength estimated—some twenty-four ships—it constituted, Admiral Halsey believed, "a fresh and powerful threat. It was decided," he continued, "that [the] earliest possible attack on the powerful Northern [carrier] Force was essential for breaking up the enemy plan and retaining the initiative." He saw open to him three alternative courses of action. They are quoted word for word:

"(a) Divide the forces, leaving Task Force 34 to block San Bernardino Straits while the carriers with light screens attacked the Northern Force;

"(b) Maintain [the] integrity of our own entire striking strength, concentrated off San Bernardino Straits;

"(c) Strike the Northern Force with all of our own striking strength concentrated, and leave San Bernardino Strait unguarded."

Each of the three alternatives was considered in the light of the tactical and strategical situation, and the following conclusions were reached. They are given in the words of Admiral Halsey's own report:

(a) was rejected; the potential strength of the undamaged Northern Force was too great to leave unmolested, and requiring Task Force 34 to engage the Center

Force while at the same time exposed to attack by land-based and possibly carrier-based air attack was not sound. This alternative spread our strength and risked unprofitable damage in detail.

(b) was rejected because it permitted the Northern Force to function as planned unmolested, and because destruction of Japan's carrier force would mean much to future operations.

(c) was adopted; it maintained the integrity of the Blue [U. S.] striking fleet; it offered [the] best possibility of surprise and destruction of [the] enemy carrier force. It was particularly sound and necessary if the strength of the Northern Force proved to be the maximum reported. It was recognized that the Center Force might sortie and inflict some damage, but its fighting power was considered too seriously impaired to win a decision. Finally, it was calculated that the Third Fleet forces could return in time to reverse any advantage that the Center Force might gain, and Commander Third Fleet was firmly convinced that (c) would contribute most to the overall Philippines campaign even if a temporarily tight situation existed at Leyte.

"It was a hard decision to make," said Halsey, and having made it he admitted that for some time thereafter he was "gravely concerned" over the possible fate of our forces to the south.

At about 2020 the commander of the Third Fleet sent off the message which put the new plan into action. The task groups of Bogan and Davison were ordered to proceed northward at twenty-five knots to a point of rendezvous with Sherman's group, which was closing from the northwest. When the three groups joined up about an hour before midnight, the commander of Task Force 38, Admiral Mitscher, was to take charge of all three and proceed northward to deliver a dawn attack against the Northern Force. The entire weight of the Third Fleet carrier force, more than ninety warships, instead of the small attack force Mitscher had originally proposed for the mission, was to be hurled at Ozawa's force—which proved later to contain only nineteen ships. Everything was pulling out from San Bernardino Strait. Not so much as a picket destroyer was left. Task Force 34 was not formed until early the next morning, and the ships which were to compose it were still part of the three task groups. At about the same time Halsey directed McCain's task group, now hurrying back from the direction of Ulithi, to proceed to a point in the vicinity of latitude 14° N., longitude 129° E., and to be prepared to launch search planes to locate the enemy Northern Force the following morning.

Immediately after these orders were dispatched, Halsey sent another message informing the commander of the Seventh Fleet of his decision and plans. He gave Kinkaid the latest known position of the Central Force, which was about where it was last attacked, and said that reports indicated that it was badly damaged. He then said that he was going north *with three groups* to strike the enemy carrier force at daybreak.

The decision was made. The orders had been sent. Hundreds of subordinate commands and their subordinates set in motion the wheels. Bearings had to be taken, speed built up, distances, formations, fuel, ammunition calculated, the whole vast organization, down to the preparation of battle lunches in the galleys, had to be geared to the new orders.

Sixteen minutes after sending his measure to Kinkaid, Admiral Halsey received word by voice radio from the *Independence* that one of her night "snoopers" had just sighted the enemy Central Force between Burias and Masbate Islands! Incredible! For when this new contact was plotted it showed that the Central Force had made good a speed of twenty-four knots or better. It was difficult to believe that the battered ships which had crept across the Sibuyan Sea, averaging from ten to eleven knots between the original contact in the morning and the last reported position, could have put on this miraculous burst of speed. If it were reliable, the contact indicated that the enemy was probably going to attempt the passage of the strait.

Of course, it might be only some of the undamaged units that had been sighted. Details were lacking in the report, and the time of the sighting was not given, though the contact must have been made after dark. At any rate an urgent message was sent off to Kinkaid saying that *part* of the enemy force had been seen in the position indicated.

Nothing more was heard from the *Independence* snooper for nearly two hours. No change of plan or course was ordered as a result of the contact report. Halsey proceeded northward at twenty-five knots with two task groups while Mitscher at a slower pace was coming southeast to join him. The rendezvous was made as scheduled before midnight, and the Third Fleet, which had fought the trying day's action separated into three groups, was at last concentrated for the dawn strike against the enemy carriers. Halsey directed Mitscher by voice radio to slow down the fleet to sixteen knots, hold the northward course until midnight, then proceed northeastward toward latitude 16° N., longitude 127° E.

The group of light ships that had been crippled in their effort to save the *Princeton* was detached about this time to proceed to Ulithi for repairs. At 2317 the *Birmingham, Gatling, Irwin,* and *Morrison* ordered left rudder and dropped out of the task group formation. Capt. Inglis, who had recovered sufficiently to take the conn, called to Admiral Sherman by voice radio: "Will try to return soon as possible. Goodby. Good luck. And hit them hard for us."

At 2304 the *Independence* called in another report from her snooper. The enemy, she said, had been sighted off *Bukal* Island on a northwesterly course. No time of the contact was given and no particulars. Moreover, a search of the charts revealed no Bukal Island. Obviously a garbled transmission. It was notorious that night planes worked under difficult conditions. This was the last report of the plane, since the *Independence,* steaming north out of the area, had to recall her aircraft. The report could hardly be trusted sufficiently to warrant any drastic change of plans. Fifteen minutes later, however, the *Independence* gave the longitude and latitude of the contact, which placed it between Burias and Ticao Islands. Then eleven minutes after midnight some amplification of details came through: battleships, number unspecified, were sighted in column, one of them believed to be of the *Yamato* class, the formation trailing an oil slick that stretched the length of Burias Island. The course was given northeast, but the transmission could have intended southeast. Still no time of the sighting given.

The position placed the enemy within less than forty miles from San Bernardino Strait! There were many hurried calculations on the battle charts in Flag Plot of the *New Jersey* and the *Lexington* at that late hour. Task Force 38 by that time was in the neighborhood of latitude 14° 54', longitude 125° 50', some 165 miles northeast of the entrance to San Bernardino Strait, and about 220 miles from Leyte Gulf. Should a sudden change of plans at this late date, involving such a vast number of ships and men, be risked?

The chances were calculated. Admiral Halsey admitted the "doggedness" of the Japanese. He had seen it displayed often in the Solomons. He said that he "recognized the possibility that the Central Force might plod through San Bernardino Strait and go on to attack Leyte forces, à la Guadalcanal." He decided, however, that "this enemy force must be blindly obeying an Imperial command to do or die, but with battle efficiency greatly impaired by torpedo hits, bomb hits, topside damage, fires, and casualties. From long experience with the Japs," declared the admiral, "their blind adherence to plan, and their inability to readjust disturbed plans, the Commander Third Feet had long ago adopted a policy of attacking first."

The commander of the Third Fleet did not readjust his own disturbed plans—did not even admit they were disturbed. He adhered to his strategy of attacking the Northern Force with everything he had, leaving San Bernardino Strait unguarded in spite of the reported progress of the Central Force. For some unknown reason, the final contact report of the *Independence* night plane was not forwarded to Kinkaid.

Neither Halsey nor any officer in his fleet knew that the Japanese Central Force was by that time steaming through San Bernardino Strait with spectacular navigating prowess at a speed which permitted the fleet to make good above twenty knots average during the night. The explanation was fairly simple, but it was not revealed until a United States naval mission unearthed the facts in Tokyo after the war. The facts were that the damage inflicted by our air strikes of the 24th had been greatly overestimated.

Admiral Kurita's fleet actually lost only one vessel as a result of our air attacks. That one, to be sure, was a prize such as had never gone down under attack of any sort—air, surface, or subsurface. She was the *Musashi*, sister ship of the *Yamato*, the two of which were by far the largest and in many ways the most powerful warships in the world. One of them displaced a tonnage more than that of five heavy cruisers. According to official Japanese reports, the *Musashi* took a total of twenty-one torpedoes in addition to many bombs. Careful interrogation of survivors and study of reports by American officers, however, lead to the conclusion that there were only ten certain and four possible torpedo hits and sixteen bomb hits. Although the bombs made a shambles of some of her topside areas, it was the torpedoes, about equally divided between her sides, which caused the flooding that eventually sank her. The *Musashi*'s death throes continued for four hours after the last attack. At 1935 the great ship gave a sharp lurch to port, capsized, and plunged by the bow. More than half of her 2,400 officers and men were reported lost. The *Musashi* was the third Japanese battleship definitely known to have been sunk by our Navy, the first in nearly two years, and the only one up to that time sunk entirely by air attack.

The heavy cruiser *Myoko* received damage to her shafts from a torpedo hit which compelled her to retire, though she was able to reach Singapore under her own steam. No other ship in the force was damaged enough to impair her fighting capacity seriously.

It is evident that our pilots concentrated on the battleships, and on one in particular. The only torpedo hits scored were the ten or more on the *Musashi* and one on the *Myoko*. All four remaining battleships took a few bombs, but apparently none of the cruisers. The *Yamato* took four bomb hits, although according to Admiral Koyanagi "the damage was not so great as to interfere with fighting or navigation." He saw one bomb explode instantaneously on her foredeck and do little damage. The other three penetrated before exploding and made her heavy by the bow, though she remained capable of a speed of twenty-six knots, and her 18-inch guns could still deliver a greater tonnage of explosive steel than any ship in the world. The *Nagato* received some damage to her communication system, but her batteries were still in fighting trim. As for the rest, Kurita reported "nothing important on other ships." According to him and others they were in good fighting condition. The destroyers received none but minor damage from strafing and near misses, and the disappearance of three or four of them was accounted for by their detachment to escort the *Takao* (damaged by our submarines on the 23rd), and to stand by to recover survivors of the *Musashi*.

At about 1000 that morning Kurita received word from Nishimura that he was under air attack and that his operation was not going well in the Sulu Sea. Kurita assumed that the damage was more serious than was actually the case, but he ordered no change in plans. Both he and his Chief of Staff complained of the poor information they had regarding American naval forces and of lack of air reconnaissance. All the fleet's seaplanes, save one or two spotting planes of the battleships, had been flown off one or two days before the fleet moved in and sent to San Jose, Mindoro. From that base they were sent to search east of the Philippines for our ships. No information ever came back from them. Nor, incredibly enough, did Kurita receive any reports from the Japanese land-based planes which had been attacking our landing forces in the Leyte area for a week. He believed there were between one hundred and two hundred transport vessels in the gulf, along with seven battleships and the appropriate number of cruisers and destroyers. He apparently knew nothing of the CVE groups off Samar, and knew the location of only one of the three Third Fleet carrier groups, the one under attack.

After fighting off six air strikes from our carrier planes, Kurita ordered his fleet to reverse course to the westward before the last planes of the sixth strike withdrew. At 1630 he sent the following message to Admiral Toyoda: "On account of the enemy air attack situation we will withdraw temporarily to await results of the attack by friendly forces." He was evidently hoping that the attacks of Japanese land-based planes would put a halt to the air strikes by their attacks on our carriers. Since no further attack came Kurita once more turned eastward to resume his mission.

At 1925 an order came through from Admiral Toyoda: "Trusting in Divine aid, the entire force will attack." Explaining his order after the war, Toyoda said, "The meaning of that order was, while it does not appear in the wording . . ., that damage could not be limited or reduced by turning back, so advance even though the fleet should be completely lost. That was my feeling when sending the order."

Kurita proceeded toward San Bernardino Strait at twenty knots. At 2224 he sent the following order from the *Yamato*: "The First Diversion Attack Force will proceed south along the east coast of Samar and penetrate Tacloban." Tacloban was our northernmost landing beach in Leyte Gulf. "It is strongly desired," urged the admiral, "that the whole force throw its entire power into the fray so as to attain its aims."

The schedule of operations called for the passage of San Bernardino Strait at 1800 on the 24th in order to coordinate properly with the movements of Nishimura, who was scheduled to arrive in Leyte Gulf by way of Surigao Strait at about 0500 the following morning. Kurita was to arrive about an hour later. Because of our air attacks and his temporary reversal of course, Kurita fell behind his schedule some six hours, and now planned to break into Leyte Gulf at about 1100. The admiral took his large force through the shoals and narrow channels of San Bernardino Strait at midnight at a speed of twenty knots, a feat which commands respect. "We navigated in single column through the narrow places," he said, "and as it was very clear, I could determine the position visually."

"Fatigue was evident at this time," replied Admiral Koyanagi when asked about the condition of personnel of the Japanese fleet, "but their fighting spirit was very high; still they were very fatigued."

The Japanese were aware that as they emerged from the narrow waters of the strait in single column they would present a vulnerable target to a battle line, to submarines, or even carrier planes. They were expecting to have to fight their way out of the strait. The ships were at battle stations as they emerged. Nothing happened. Kurita set course for Leyte Gulf.

III

THE BATTLE OF SURIGAO STRAIT

While Admiral Halsey was steaming north to strike the Japanese carrier force, Admiral Kinkaid was proceeding with his arrangements for a night battle to the south under the assumption that the fast battleships and cruisers of the Third Fleet were still lying off San Bernardino Strait ready to fall upon any part of the enemy Central Force which ventured a sortie. The Seventh Fleet therefore made preparations to meet one Japanese force of greatly inferior power instead of two forces which, if combined at full strength, would outclass our gunnery available in Leyte Gulf.

Kinkaid's assumption that San Bernardino Strait was still guarded resulted from his interpretation of two messages of the commander of the Third Fleet. The first of these, designated Battle Plan, was sent to all Third Fleet task force and task group commanders shortly after 1500 and was intercepted by the Seventh Fleet commander, who was not an addressee. The message merely announced that Task Force 34, consisting of certain ships, would be formed. It did not state when nor for what purpose. The Seventh Fleet staff interpreted the verb "will be" as a command to be executed, and believed, as Kinkaid said, that the task force "was being formed" at that time.*

Halsey's message to Kinkaid at about 2025 announcing his decision to proceed to the north simply stated that he was going *with three groups*. Because of his interpretation of the dispatch intercepted earlier, Kinkaid misunderstood the later

---

* It might be observed here that in common usage "will be" is capable of being interpreted as imperative mood, present tense as well as indicative mood, future tense. Apparently the Seventh Fleet command did not intercept Halsey's dispatch of two hours later saying that Task Force 34 would be formed by the Third Fleet's commander if the enemy made a sortie.

dispatch. "As the fast battleships had been removed from the carrier groups and organized as Task Force 34," he explained, "it was assumed that Task Force 34 was still guarding San Bernardino Strait." Halsey's message had not stated that Task Force 34 was or was not being left behind, nor that the composition of the three task groups had been changed. As a matter of fact, the task force was "organized" by that time, but it was not formed and detached until early the following morning.

The ambiguity of Halsey's messages, however, left the disposition of Task Force 34 unclear, not only to Kinkaid, but also to Admiral Nimitz's staff at Pearl Harbor. The misapprehension at the Seventh Fleet command was not cleared up until the following morning—under the most trying circumstances.

Early in the afternoon of the 24th Admiral Kinkaid had decided to deploy his entire gunnery and torpedo force across Surigao Strait to block that approach to the enemy. The forces of the Seventh Fleet were more than an adequate match for the Japanese Southern Force, then estimated to consist at most of the two old, though modernized, battleships *Fuso* and *Yamashiro* with twelve 14-inch guns, four heavy cruisers, four light cruisers, and ten destroyers. Since it was the intention to destroy rather than merely to repulse this force, however, it was logical to use all the gunnery and torpedo strength of the Seventh Fleet, rather than a part. In a phrase more remarkable for pungence than for gallantry, Admiral Oldendorf expressed the tactical principle involved: "Never give a sucker a chance."

Admiral Kinkaid laid his plans accordingly, keeping Admiral Halsey informed as to the disposition of his forces. He ordered Rear Admiral Jesse B. Oldendorf, commander of the Bombardment and Support Group, made up of the heavy gunnery of the fleet, to make all preparations for a night engagement. The Close Covering Group of cruiser and destroyers commanded by Rear Admiral Russell S. Berkey was assigned to Admiral Oldendorf's command as reinforcement. In addition, the commander of the motor torpedo boats of the Seventh Fleet, Comdr. Selman S. Bowling, was ordered to station the maximum number of PT's in lower Surigao Strait. As a precaution against surprise by the enemy's Central Force, "Black Cats" (Catalina flying boats) were ordered to make a night search north of Leyte Gulf and east of Samar Island, and the commander of the CVE's was ordered to make a dawn search to the north. The sixteen CVE's and their screening vessels were to remain in their usual stations to the east of Leyte Gulf. This was to be a night action, strictly a "Gun Club" affair, without assistance from the air. Even the scout planes of the heavy ships were flown off to safety.

There had been even more difficulty in following the movements and in estimating the strength of the Japanese Southern Force than in the case of the Central Force. Contact with the Southern Force had been lost during the morning and had not been regained. A plane search in Mindanao Sea about dusk had failed to locate it. While it could be expected to coordinate its movements with those of the Central Force, there seems to have been no doubt in the Seventh Fleet command that it would persist in an effort to reach Leyte Gulf through Surigao Strait.

The composition and nature of the Japanese Southern Force was never known with any accuracy during the battle that followed, nor was it cleared up until after the end of the war. It is now apparent that we were incorrect in assuming that one force was involved, for there were really two Japanese forces in the strait that night under quite independent commands—an incredibly inept arrangement in view of the tactical situation.

The force sighted and attacked in the Sulu Sea by Third Fleet planes on the morning of the 24th consisted of the battleships *Fuso* and *Yamashiro*, the heavy cruiser *Mogami*, and four destroyers, all under the command of Vice Admiral Nishimura, who was subordinate to Vice Admiral Kurita. His mission was to enter Leyte Gulf through Surigao Strait at about 0500 and fall upon our amphibious forces and fleet in support of Kurita's force, scheduled to arrive in the Gulf through its eastern entrance at about 0600.

The Japanese strategy and battle plan were known only to Admiral Nishimura and his flag captain until about three days before the battle, when the force was refueling at Brunei Bay. There a conference of the commanding officers of ships which were to compose the force was called, and for the first time the plan was revealed to them. Until then they had assumed that the entire No. 1 Diversion Attack Force would proceed to the objective together under immediate command of Admiral Kurita. The two battleships of Nishimura, which had only recently arrived at Singapore, had never fought together with the *Mogami* and the four destroyers in any action and apparently had never trained with them. Some of the commanding officers had not met prior to the conference in Brunei Bay. According to Cmdr. Shigeru Nishino, captain of the *Shigure*, the only vessel which survived the battle, "Nishimura's tactical conceptions were quite different from those of the other ships under his command." There was considerable discussion of the prospects of success in the operation at the conference, in which the admiral took no part. Some commanders considered the operation suicidal and did not expect to survive, while others believed there was a fair chance of success.

"We determined to do our best," said the skipper of the *Shigure.* "Then we had a few drinks."

Entirely independent of the command of Nishimura or Kurita was the Japanese Fifth Fleet, then composed of the two heavy cruisers *Nachi* and *Ashigara,** the light cruiser *Abukuma*, and four destroyers, under the command of Vice Admiral Shima. It had been the original plan for Shima to cooperate with Vice Admiral Ozawa and his Northern Force, but this plan was abandoned at the last minute. Shima sortied from Bako with orders merely to cooperate with Kurita in an attack upon Leyte from the south. There seems to have been no time for even the most elementary planning, for Shima apparently did not learn until he had left Bako—and then only through an intercepted message—that Nishimura's force had been detached and was to precede him through

---

* Erroneously reported by Army Air Forces to have been sunk by Capt. Colin P. Kelly, Jr., in December, 1941. The *Ashigara* was one of several cruisers in the Leyte action previously reported sunk by the Air Forces.

Surigao Strait. Until that time he had expected to make the southern approach alone. He was not even in direct communication with Nishimura, since the two fleets were maintaining radio silence, and he had not been informed of the route of Nishimura's approach. He only knew that the admiral was expected to enter the Strait from the south at about 0200 on the 25th. Shima accordingly planned to make his entrance at about 0600 in order, explained one of his staff officers, "to attack the remainder [of the United States Fleet in Leyte Gulf] after the confusion of Kurita's attack." Admiral Shima's force arrived at Coron Bay, in the Calamian Group across the Strait from Mindoro Island, before dusk on the 23rd. They were disappointed at not finding tankers in Coron Bay ("We did not know the movement of the tankers," admitted the staff officer), and after fueling the destroyers from the cruisers, departed southward through the Sulu Sea at 0200 on the morning of the 24th. Shima had no communication with Nishimura throughout the day and did not even know that his force was brought under air attack on the morning of the 24th, although he was only some fifty miles away at the time.

The two groups composing the "Southern Force" were organized as follows:

"C" FORCE OF NO. 1 DIVERSION ATTACK FORCE (Vice Admiral Nishimura)	FIFTH FLEET (Vice Admiral Shima)
Battleships	*Heavy Cruisers*
Fuso	Nachi (F)
Yamashiro (F)	Ashigara
Heavy Cruiser	*Light Cruiser*
Mogami	Abukuma
Destroyers	*Destroyers*
Michishio	Shiranuhi
Asagumo	Kasumi
Yamagumo	Ushio
Shigure	Akebono

In spite of the fact that these two forces were assigned a mission where tactical cooperation was so close that two of their units actually collided during the battle, they had no common superior short of Admiral Toyoda in Tokyo.*

The disposition and movements of the opposing forces would be limited by the narrow waters of Surigao Strait, which connects Mindanao Sea with Leyte Gulf and is bounded by Leyte and Panaon Islands on the west, and by Dinagat and Mindanao on the east. The strait is about thirty miles in length and broadens from a width of about twelve miles at its southern entrance to about twenty-five miles where it merges with Leyte Gulf. Allowance had to be made for strong currents within the strait as well as for the rugged coasts, which would interfere with radar search on the flanks.

It was not for the Japanese and American admirals converging upon the strait to introduce it into the pages of history. There was no more historical name in the area than Surigao, for it was through this narrow gateway that the Portuguese discoverer Ferdinand Magellan first sailed into the archipelago, and it was a few miles west of the strait that he met his death. Between 1521 and 1955 history had pretty much neglected Surigao.

Since he was well informed of developments during the 23rd and 24th, Admiral Oldendorf had anticipated Admiral Kinkaid's order to prepare for a night action and had already formulated his battle plan. In the late afternoon of the 24th he held a conference aboard his flagship *Louisville* with Rear Admiral Berkey, who was to command the right flank, and Rear Admiral George L. Weyler, commander of the battle

---

* The failure of Nishimura and Shima to join forces before the battle and enter the strait together is attributed by one Japanese officer to a personal antipathy. It seems that while Nishimura was older and had more battle experience than Shima, the latter was his senior in rank. "Nishimura did not want to be under the command of Shima," declared the officer. This explanation, however, overlooks the fact that Nishimura's force was part of Kurita's and subject to his command, whereas Shima's was an independent command responsible to the Japanese Southwest Area Command. This does not excuse the inept organization of the forces at the higher level.

line. Oldendorf, in addition to assuming overall tactical command for the battle, would command the left flank.

The forces assembled to fight this important engagement had been employed almost exclusively in bombardment work, which gave them little opportunity to train for surface firing and torpedo attacks. A serious handicap discussed at the conference was the shortage of heavy armor-piercing ammunition in all the battleships and a scarcity of ammunition of all types throughout the force. Because of the bombardment mission of the battleships, they were cut to between 20 and 30 percent of their normal allowance of armor-piercing shells, their only effective ammunition against heavy ships, and some of this small allowance had been expended against the tougher targets ashore. Five days of bombardment work had exhausted all but about 10 percent of the regular bombardment projectiles of the heavy ships and all but approximately 20 percent of the 5-inch shells of the destroyers. The fuel supply of all ships was also low. The 25th had been the scheduled day for replenishment of fuel and ammunition, but obviously this schedule could not be carried out in the emergency, nor was there any adequate supply of heavy armor-piercing projectiles available in the area. The only torpedoes available were those with which the destroyers were loaded.

"Loading a ship for a joint bombardment and surface action," observed one of the cruiser captains, "might be compared to harnessing a horse for a plowing job with the expectation that at any second he would be expected to stop plowing and with the same trappings enter the Kentucky Derby."

At his conference aboard the *Louisville* Admiral Oldendorf explained that in view of the shortage of ammunition his force could fight a sharp decisive engagement, but not a long and extended one. Allowance would also have to be made for a possible encounter with the Central Force in case it eluded the Third Fleet and attacked from the east. He considered it essential, therefore, that "the battleships fire at ranges where their percentage of hits and their fire effect would both be high," somewhere between 17,000 and 20,000 yards. This would neccessarily bring the battle line within range of the Japanese major guns and long-range torpedoes, which would have to be carefully guarded against. Since only half of the six old battleships were at that time equipped with the latest radar fire control devices, the advantage they enjoyed over the enemy's battle line in effective fire power was not nearly so great as their numerical superiority might suggest.

To Admiral Oldendorf the tactical situation suggested a "wonderful opportunity" for the offensive use of torpedoes, and he emphasized that every such opportunity should be immediately acted upon. The PT boats would doubtless make the most of their opportunity in the southern end of the strait, after which the three destroyer squadrons (twenty-six destroyers in all) would attack in succession, retiring up the sides of the strait in order to keep a land background against the enemy's radar, as well as to avoid the fire of our own ships.

The force was to be deployed in a familiar battle disposition, with the guide in the center of the battle line, the left flank at a distance of 14,000 yards, and the right flank between 10,000 and 14,000 yards. Destroyer Squadron 54 would constitute a picket line patrolling across the strait to the south. The order of these forces was, from east to west:

Left Flank	Center	Right Flank
(Rear Adm.	(Rear Adm.	(Rear Adm.
Oldendorf)	Weyler)	Berkey)
Cruisers	*Battleships*	*Cruisers*
Louisville	West Virginia	Phoenix (CL) (F)
(CA) (FF)	Maryland	Boise (CL)
Portland (CA)	Mississippi (F)	HMAS Shropshire
Minneapolis (CA)	Tennessee	(CL)
Denver (CL)	California	*Screen: Destroyers*
Columbia (CL)	Pennsylvania	(Division 47 of
Screen: Destroyers	*Screen: Destroyers*	Squadron 24)
(Squadron 56)	(Division "X-Ray")	Hutchins
Newcomb	Claxton	Daly

R. P. Leary	Thorn	Bache
A. W. Grant	Welles	HMAS Arunta
Robinson	Aulick	Killen
Halford	Cony	Beale
Bryant	Sigourney	PICKET LINE
H. L. Edwards	PT BOATS	(Squadron 54)
Leutze	(Lower part	Remey
Bennion	of the strait)	McGowan
	13 PT sections	Melvin
	3 boats each	McDermut
		Monssen

In his deployment of forces Admiral Oldendorf strengthened the left flank at the expense of the right. The commander of the latter was permitted to station his destroyers about four miles down the channel from the cruisers because of crowded conditions. The strong currents of the strait and the slow speed necessitated by the limited area made it difficult to maintain stations. The battle line was to take its position above the extreme northern end of the strait, across the lower end of the gulf, and steam east and west in ten-mile legs at a speed of five knots.

After dark the PT boats took up their stations at the extreme southern end of the strait and out in Mindanao Sea, and the picket line formed by Destroyer Squadron 54 began patrolling across the strait five or six miles below the battle line. The other forces, left, right, and center, took up their positions as ordered, forming one vast arc of deadly fire power. Since Oldendorf had no means of learning the position and speed of the enemy force, its approach would have to be awaited.

The moon went down a few minutes after midnight, leaving the waters of the strait in pitch darkness and limiting visibility to less than three miles while against the land masses it was almost zero. Occasional flashes of lightning, which illuminated the strait momentarily, promised rain squalls later. The night was clear in the upper part of the strait and there was no wind. The sea was a flat calm without swells.

The six elderly veterans in the battle line had seen many unexpected adventures since disaster overtook them in Pearl Harbor, some of them as many as ten amphibious operations. The limitations of their age and gait, however, had confined them to the roles of bombardment, support, and the fueling of smaller vessels. They had long since seen themselves superseded in the battle line by powerful young giants of the *Iowa* and *North Carolina* classes. For the moment, however, the old battleships found themselves in a position which only the *Washington* and *South Dakota* of their trim successors had ever enjoyed and which the remaining ones were to await in vain. It promised to be the classic situation of battle line against battle line, all but forgotten in this new type of fast air warfare, and there was the additional possibility of realizing the midshipman's dream of crossing the enemy's "T." As they steamed back and forth at the stately pace of five knots, the ancient vessels seemed for the moment about to vindicate the wisdom of their generation at a late and improbable age.

The fighting began far out in Mindanao Sea, sixty miles southwest of the lower entrance to the strait and about one hundred miles from the battle line, where the outermost patrol of PT boats was stationed. Thirty-nine of these fast, small craft in thirteen sections of three boats each were patrolling all possible approaches to the strait in addition to the waters of the strait itself, keeping below latitude 10° 10′ in order to stay clear of the fire of our heavier ships. Three sections were stationed out in Mindanao Sea, five in and around the narrow entrance to the strait, and five to the north within the strait. They were under orders to report the enemy when sighted and then attack independently. The only real defense of these small boats, which are trained to attack anything afloat, is their speed and the skill and daring of their crews.

At 2215, Ens. Peter R. Gadd, skipper of PT Boat 131, picked up two targets by radar six miles south of Bohol Island at ten miles distance. The three boats of the section, under the command of Lt. W. C. Pullen, swung around on a collision course to intercept the enemy and prepared for a torpedo attack. When they had closed to within three miles the light haze lifted and they made out in the darkness ahead what they believed to be two battleships, two cruisers, and a destroyer. Before the PT boats could gain position for an attack, however, the enemy opened fire with everything from 20-mm. to 8-inch gun salvos, straddling one boat with accurate fire in the first salvo, then repeatedly lifting its bow out of the water with later ones. The battleships illuminated with star shells from astern while a destroyer caught the boats with her searchlight, then flanked and chased them, firing accurately and keeping up the pursuit for about twenty-five minutes. The PT's retired behind smoke, firing their automatic weapons at the searchlight. All three boats were hit and damaged, one by shrapnel, another by a direct 8-inch shell hit, and the third by a shell of medium caliber which demolished her bow and forward deck, killed one man, and wounded three.

None of the boats were able to get through a report of the contact during the action because of damage to their radios and interference of land masses. One of them finally located a boat of another section which sent off a report that was relayed to Admiral Oldendorf at 0026. In the meanwhile the area in which the boats were operating had become cloudy and frequent rain squalls increased the difficulty of locating and identifying the targets as they continued toward our main force.

The next PT boat section to report a contact was one commanded by Lt. (jg) D. H. Owen, stationed about fifteen miles off the entrance to the strait. Owen's boats managed to fire two torpedoes at 0035, with unobserved results, before they were caught by the searchlight of the battleship that had been their target. They were brought under heavy fire and straddled many times but escaped under a smoke screen without damage.

The torpedo boats made their heaviest attack of the night in the lower end of Surigao Strait about 0200, shortly after the leading group of heavy ships passed through the narrow entrance. Three sections closed boldly to short ranges and in rapid succession launched a total of twenty-one torpedoes at battleship, cruiser, and destroyer targets. A section of three boats under Lt. Comdr. R. Leeson, stationed off the tip of Panaon Island, opened the attack from the west. Maneuvering to gain a good position for firing on a battleship, Leeson's boat was illuminated and brought under concentrated fire. He nevertheless continued to close the target until he had fired three torpedoes, then turned sharply at full speed and dodged out of the searchlight beam. After three or four minutes his boat was jolted by three underwater explosions, though there were no visible signs of these explosions near his target. The two other boats of this section also fired torpedoes, but scored no hits.

The illumination of Leeson's boats to the west silhouetted two Japanese battleships and three smaller vessels against their own star-shells and searchlight and revealed them clearly to Lt. Comdr. F. D. Tappaan, whose section was stationed on the eastern side of the strait. Each of the PT's fired two torpedoes at a target identified as a heavy cruiser but they were unable to observe the results while retiring through a smoke screen under intense fire.

The PT section commanded by Lt. (jg) J. M. McElfresh, stationed ten miles to the north, had already started an attack on a cruiser and three destroyers about two miles ahead of the group attacked by Leeson and Tappaan when they saw Leeson's boats illuminated. McElfresh fired four torpedoes at the van destroyer of the leading group, two of them from the suicidal range of between 300 and 400 yards while his boat was in the beam of the destroyer's searchlight and receiving broadside fire. He knocked out one searchlight with gunfire, whereupon a second was turned on him by the same destroyer. There followed a flash and an explosion in the hull below the searchlight, which led McElfresh to believe one of his torpedoes had found its mark. Ens. H. A. Thronson took the second destroyer in column as his target and launched two torpedoes. As he retired he heard several large explosions in the direction of the enemy, and twenty minutes later a fire broke out on the target. The third boat was caught by a searchlight beam and smothered by broadsides before it could launch an attack. Three 4.7 shells struck the craft, killing two men, wounding three, and smashing the little craft up so badly that it had to be beached.

Although they launched several attacks on retiring ships later, this was the last of the PT attacks during the approach of Nishimura's force. All but nine of the thirty-nine boats were under fire during the course of the night action; three officers and three men were killed, and one boat was lost. While no hits claimed by the PT's in the approach phase of the battle have been confirmed, the boats had some effect in throwing the enemy off balance. "The skill, determination, and courage displayed by the personnel of these small boats," in the opinion of Admiral Nimitz, "is worthy of the highest praise."

There could no longer be any doubt that the Japanese were committed to running the gauntlet that Admiral Oldendorf had prepared for them. Contact reports from the patrol boats were now flowing in to indicate the enemy's progress northward, and at 0215 the flagship's radar picked up his advance force at a distance of more than twenty-five miles. The Japanese continued to plow doggedly up the strait. "Their strategy and intelligence," remarked one officer as he tracked their progress, "seemed to be inversely proportional to their courage." Our ships went to general quarters, while three squadrons of destroyers prepared to continue the torpedo attack begun by the PT boats.

Five ships of Destroyer Squadron 54, stationed three miles apart across the strait some five miles below the battle line, were omitted from the battle plan, but upon the special request of their commanding officer, Capt. J. G. Coward, they were given the honor of opening the destroyer attack, provided they clear the area immediately thereafter. They formed up in two groups, to attack from both sides of the enemy column, the *Remey*, *McGowan*, and *Melvin* from the east and the *McDermut* and *Monssen* from the west. At 0226

Capt. Coward, in the *Remey,* called Admiral Oldendorf by radio, "I'm going to start down in a few minutes," and three minutes later both groups were headed south to attack. They did not know the nature of their targets, but the situation as far as it was understood was explained to all hands by the destroyer skippers. "I have never been in a quieter, more tense atmosphere," wrote one of them, "than existed from the moment we started down."

The targets gradually separated on the radar until some seven were indicated on the screens, estimated to be two battleships, one cruiser, and four screening vessels. Capt. Coward increased speed to twenty-five knots as the opposing forces closed rapidly on almost head-on courses. Suddenly, at 0258, the eastern attack group found itself caught in the brilliant beam of an enemy searchlight, which went out after about ten seconds. Coward immediately assigned targets, swung left to 90° briefly, then back to 120°, and increased speed to thirty knots. He then ordered the ships to make smoke and at the same time instructed the eastern group to "fire when ready."

Beginning about 0300 the three ships fired twenty-seven torpedoes set at intermediate speed, range about 11,500 yards. As soon as torpedoes were away the destroyers swung around to the left to retire up the coast of Dinagat Island behind a smoke screen. They took a northeasterly course, zigzagging independently and making all possible speed, a maximum of about thirty-three knots.

Immediately after a powder flash in one of the *Remey's* torpedo tubes the Japanese again illuminated the group by searchlight, then with brilliant, well-placed star shells, after which they opened gunfire. The first salvos fell short, but range rapidly improved until splashes were drenching the decks of some of the destroyers. At 0309, about the time the torpedoes should have completed their runs, two explosions were reported in the vicinity of the targets and three to five were heard. Although the retiring destroyers were kept under fire until 0313 they suffered no hits.

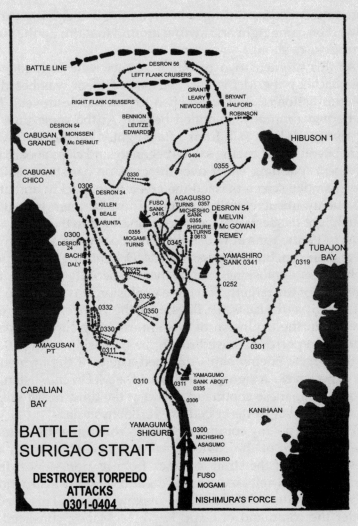

CHART 2.

While the enemy's attention was thus diverted to the east, the *McDermut* and *Monssen* were making their approach on the west, hugging the coast of Leyte. They were taken under fire but not illuminated at 0308. Three minutes later the destroyers commenced firing two full salvos, a total of twenty torpedoes, at ranges between 8,750 and 9,100 yards. They then came right and swung around to retire up the coast very close to shore.

At this moment two of our PT boats were sighted near the beach by the *McDermut*, and one of them was heard to ask permission of another to open fire on the destroyers. The *McDermut* promptly identified herself. At the same time an intense green light as if from a flare lighted up the destroyers from beyond, and enemy salvos began to land close aboard the *Monssen*, splashing water over the guns on her stern. Skillful use of smoke screen masked the green flare quickly, and after the enemy unsuccessfully attempted to pick them up with a searchlight the destroyers escaped unharmed to the north.

At 0319, the time at which the torpedoes were due to complete their run, both *Monssen* and *McDermut* saw two, or possibly three, explosions, one of them especially large, in the direction of the targets. The large explosion was sighted from as far away as the *Louisville*, flagship of the main force. This may have been the explosion of Nishimura's flagship *Yamashiro*, which is reported to have broken the battleship in two. Both of the largest enemy ships dropped astern of the formation after the attack. A signalman aboard the *McDermut*, listening in on the Japanese command circuit at the time, heard voices break into what he described as "verbal hysteria."

While the enemy column was staggering under this attack, the destroyers of the right flank were sweeping down the western side of the strait to attack from its port side. Admiral Berkey had released his screen at 0300 with instructions to proceed down the shore line making smoke. This group, under the command of Capt. K. M. McManes, consisted of one division of Destroyer Squadron 24 plus the Australian ship *Arunta*. It was divided into two sections, one led by Capt. McManes in the *Hutchins* with the *Daly* and *Bache*, and the other led by Comdr. A. E. Buchanan, of the Royal Australian Navy, in HMAS *Arunta* with the *Killen* and *Beale*.

Like many commanders of the modern navy, Capt. McManes fought his squadron from a corner of the combat information center of his flagship, bent over the pale light of a twelve-inch radar scope, an ear phone clamped over his head, and looking more like a physicist in his laboratory than the captain of a fighting ship in the heat of battle. The advantages were obvious, for the radar enabled him to pass the western group of Squadron 54 twice in pitch dark at a distance of a few yards in narrow waters and to distinguish enemy from friendly vessels throughout the complicated action. At 0310 he directed Buchanan's section to break off and deliver its attack while McManes continued to the south.

Comdr. Buchanan brought his column of three ships to course 152° and closed with the enemy at twenty-five knots. The targets by this time appeared to have divided into two groups, with one very large ship and three smaller ones leading three or four others. They were on a northerly course at an average speed of eighteen knots when Buchanan gave the order to fire torpedoes. An instant before firing, the *Killen* identified her target in a flash of light as a battleship of the *Yamashiro* class and quickly changed the setting of her torpedoes to a depth of twenty-two feet. After firing a half salvo each, at a range of between 7,000 and 8,000 yards, the three destroyers swung around to retire on a northwesterly course at 0326. The *Killen* fired two more torpedoes at the same target three minutes later but checked fire when she saw the enemy was changing course. At the expected time a large flash and explosion occurred in the enemy column. Comdr. Buchanan believed this to be a hit by the *Killen,* or perhaps the *Beale.* Shortly after the section turned to retire toward the shore, a Japanese salvo fell between the *Killen* and *Beale* but did no damage.

Finding himself in an excellent position to attack, Capt. McManes swung his section left to a northerly firing course, parallel to that of the enemy at 0326. Just as the ships turned a bright greenish star shell burst broad on the starboard bow, illuminating the column. The ships got off a half salvo of torpedoes at 0329 to the starboard, range about 7,000 yards, and immediately thereafter opened fire with their 5-inch guns. The

Japanese replied vigorously with 5-inch and 8-inch salvos and continued to illuminate with star shells. Most of the fire was poor, though one salvo narrowly missed the *Hutchins*, which evaded it by a quick change of course. The enemy command had apparently lost grasp of the tactical picture, for his first reaction to our gunfire was to flash what seemed to be recognition signals in our direction by searchlight and red flares. When we replied to the signal with redoubled gunfire, enemy ships opened with all batteries in several directions, "frantically showering steel through 360°."

Japanese torpedomen were apparently better informed. Lookouts on the *Daly* held their breath while they watched two torpedo tracks, too close to permit evasive maneuver, approach their bow, and saw the water sizzle with their bubbles at the stem and bridge as the *Daly* crossed the tracks. "The enemy torpedo deficiency lies in his religion, not in his ballistics," concluded the skipper of the *Hutchins*.

McManes brought his ships around in a turn to the south, retracing their approach course for about ten minutes, when some of the lagging targets appeared to reverse course. He kept them under fire while he circled back south. At 0344 three round balls of dull orange flames lit up the night to the westward, and three explosions, "unmistakable torpedo hits" according to the captain of the *Daly*, were heard by all bridge personnel and repair parties of that ship. The column checked fire momentarily, turned northeast to close the enemy, resumed fire, and began hitting on the third salvo. In the light from explosions, the *Bache* and *Daly* identified their target as a heavy cruiser. The vessel was aflame all along her deck, and pieces of her superstructure were blasted into the air as each salvo landed. McManes discovered a large target to the south of the flaming cruiser, almost dead in the water, and directed the *Hutchins* to let fly her last half salvo of torpedoes, which she did.

Comdr. Buchanan in the meantime brought the *Arunta* section around to the south to support McManes, and both sections remained in the shooting match until our heavy ships to the north opened fire and they had to clear out. Torpedo hits seemed to have been scored by both sections.

Because of the severe Japanese losses in ships and men, the picture of the battle from the enemy side remains fragmentary and obscure. According to the captain of the *Shigure* the first torpedo hits were made at about 0335, although other evidence indicates earlier hits. It was while the enemy ships were assuming their battle disposition, with the four destroyers (*Shigure* last) falling in ahead, followed by the *Yamashiro, Fuso,* and *Mogami,* in that order. Hits were made on all three destroyers in the van by attacks from both sides. The *Yamagumo,* third in column immediately ahead of the *Shigure,* was struck on her port side at about 0330, reeled out of the formation, at once, and sank soon afterward. The *Michishio* and *Asagumo* staggered out of column, badly damaged by torpedoes, but continued northward, the *Michishio* until about 0355 when she sank, and the *Asagumo* until she turned back about 0357.

Nishimura's flagship *Yamashiro* received one or more torpedo hits which are believed to have exploded her magazines, since the 30,000-ton ship exploded violently and broke in half under attack. By voice radio Nishimura announced: "We have received a torpedo attack. You are to proceed and attack all ships." That was the last heard from the admiral. The *Fuso,* whose captain then assumed command, but apparently issued no orders, continued north with the *Mogami* and two damaged destroyers. The *Shigure,* which managed to evade all torpedoes, increased speed to twenty-six knots and continued to advance a little longer without locating any targets. Her commander was not sure of his position and turned back south to look for the flagship. When a lookout reported he thought he saw the *Yamashiro* sinking, the captain gave up the search and turned north again about 0355, still unable to establish contact with the *Fuso* or to get any orders. He seems to have been a rather badly confused man.

The heavy ships of our battle line and flanks were still holding their fire, waiting for the range to close, while the largest of the three destroyer attacks was still to be delivered—that of the left flank screen. This was made up of nine ships of Destroyer Squadron 56, under the command of Capt. Roland N. Smoot, whose flag was in the *Newcomb*. At 0337 Admiral Oldendorf issued the order, "Launch attack—get the big boys!" Smoot immediately ordered, "Sections, column right," maximum speed, and the three sections of the squadron maneuvered to clear the cruiser column and take a southerly course. One section was ordered to attack from each flank of the enemy column and one from the starboard bow.

Before this attack was launched the left flank cruisers opened salvo fire and the whole main body of our force soon joined in. The spectacular climax of the Battle of Surigao Strait had been reached.

Exactly what targets the torpedo attack had left for the heavy ships, and in what state of repair they had left them will probably never be known. It is evident, however, that this was "a field day for the cans," as one of their skippers declared. Whether it represented "the largest combined and concentrated torpedo attack in our navy's history" or not, it is true that if those launched by the PT boats are included, a total of more than 130 torpedoes was fired by our forces in the course of the battle. "The waters through which the enemy passed," observed the commander of Destroyer Squadron 24, "were so full of torpedoes it is difficult to see how any enemy ship could have failed to sustain damage." He was apparently referring to Nishimura's group of seven ships, which was the only one brought under torpedo attack by the destroyers. Of these it is believed that the battleship *Yamashiro* and the destroyers *Michishio* and *Yamagumo* had been sunk and the battleship *Fuso* had received damage from torpedo hits before our battle line and other heavy ships had fired a shot. These ships, incidentally, were the only ones sunk before dawn, when our cruisers took up pursuit of retiring vessels and aircraft closed for their kills. The heavy casualties among enemy personnel, especially at the command level, and the destruction of records during the battle leave many questions unanswered.

On the flag bridge of the *Louisville* Admiral Oldendorf was receiving a steady flow of contact reports, many of which indicated that the enemy force was led by its heaviest ships. Another peculiarity of the tactics of the enemy was that he kept to the middle of the strait in column, occasionally zig-zagging under destroyer attack, but not taking advantage of the protection of either shore.

The important and almost incredible thing was that the Japanese continued to plod up the strait into the jaws of the trap prepared for them. The nearer they approached, the nearer was the realization of the gunnery admiral's dream—"T-ing" the enemy's column and enfilading it with broadsides from all ships. "We were in the ideal position," exclaimed the flag captain, "a position dreamed of, studied and plotted in War College maneuvers and never hoped to be obtained." It was old-line, textbook tactics, perfect in conception, but very nearly impossible of realization. Only under conditions of extremely low visibility or marked disparity in speed of opposing forces was an opportunity for such tactics likely to occur.

In the gathering dusk at Jutland, Admiral Scheer had twice unknowingly taken his column end-on into the center of the British Battle Fleet, a fatal position for the Germans had the British been able to take advantage of it. Admirals and ensigns have discussed the lost opportunity ever since. The only modern naval commander to employ these famous tactics successfully and conclusively was Admiral Togo, who by taking advantage of the slowness and ineptness of the Russian Imperial Fleet at the Battle of Tsushima had turned the enemy's column into the Japanese line and destroyed it. In Surigao Strait, forty years later, Admiral Nishimura, a product of Togo's school, steamed into the same plight unawares. Admiral Oldendorf's opportunity, if more limited, promised gratifying results—provided his own destroyers did not deprive him of targets or the Japanese did not retire too early. The agitation on the flag bridge of the cruiser *Louisville* was understandable.

At one anxious moment, when it appeared that the enemy was going to reverse course and retire, Oldendorf ordered

Weyler to "close the battle line," but followed this with an immediate cancellation, "Do not close the battle line." Weyler then informed his superior that he had instructed the battle line to open fire when the range had closed to 26,000 yards (thirteen miles) instead of waiting for a range of 20,000 yards as originally planned. No order of execution followed, however, and the big guns remained silent, while fire controlmen held the directors on their targets—some of them with the best radar equipment—for more than a half an hour. Since he did not know whether his first targets would be heavy or light vessels, Admiral Weyler had directed the battleships to load their projectile hoists with armor-piercing shells and be prepared to shift to bombardment shells after the first five salvos.

The battle line and the cruisers of both flanks were nearing the end of their easterly runs at 0350, with their main batteries trained to the starboard. The targets were changing course and speed irregularly, and some of them lagged behind the leading group of one large vessel, later identified as the *Fuso,* and two or three smaller ships. Considerable anxiety was expressed by some captains lest our retiring destroyers be confused with the enemy. A new group of enemy ships, five small and one larger, had appeared to be southward on the flagship radar, but it was beyond range, following the others by several thousand yards, and more than twenty miles from our cruisers. The foremost target was at a range of 15,600 yards from the flagship, in the left flank, and about 21,000 yards from the battle line flagship when Oldendorf gave the order for all ships to "open fire."

First the left flank cruisers, three heavy and two light, opened up at 0351 with their 8-inch and 6-inch guns, then the three light cruisers of the right flank about one minute later, followed by first one then other battleships firing over the cruisers.

Blinded temporarily by the flash of the first salvo of the *Louisville,* for lack of a buzzer warning from his over-eager gunners, Admiral Oldendorf quit the bridge for Flag Plot. Capt. Smoot, steaming south down the center of the strait with Destroyer Squadron 56, was in an excellent, if precarious, position to see the spectacle, for both cruiser and battleship fire passed over his destroyers on the way to the target. It was "the most beautiful sight I have ever witnessed," he wrote. "The arched line of tracers in the darkness looked like a continual stream of lighted railroad cars going over a hill. No target

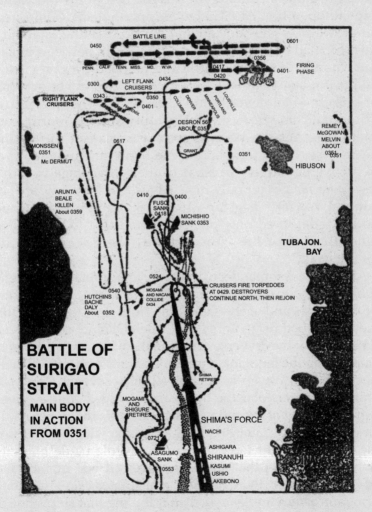

CHART 3.

could be observed at first, then shortly there would be fires and explosions, and another enemy ship would be accounted for." The captain of the *Columbia* counted ten large explosions among the targets, six of them after our heavy guns opened fire.

The *West Virginia*, with her 16-inch guns and her superior radar fire control equipment, was the first of the old battleships to open fire. At 0353 her skipper noted, "Could hear gunnery officer chuckle and announced that first salvo hit." This ship had been extensively refitted with new equipment three months before the battle and manned by a new crew, the great majority of which—including two of her gun turret officers—had never been to sea before. The third turret officer had come from submarine duty and the fourth from small craft. Yet the *West Virginia* with sixteen salvos and the *Tennessee* with thirteen led the battle line in amount of fire delivered, largely because of their advantage in radar. The *California* got off only nine salvos and the *Maryland* six. Admiral Weyler's flagship *Mississippi*, equipped with outmoded radar, fired only one salvo, and that to unload her guns after "cease fire" was ordered. The *Pennsylvania* did not fire at all.

At 0356 the commander of the battle line ordered ships right, from 90° to course 120°, in order to get a better target bearing for the turrets and at the same time close the targets slightly. They continued firing until 0401, when Oldendorf suggested to Weyler that they reverse course to the west, since they were overlapping the left flank cruisers. The turn was immediately executed upon Weyler's order by all ships save the *California*, which misunderstood the order and changed course fifteen degrees instead of executing "Turn 15." This threw her badly out of position and almost caused a collision with the *Tennessee*. The incident might have thrown the whole battle line into confusion had not the latter ship reversed her engines and narrowly avoided the *California*, which later came back into formation astern the *Tennessee*, after fouling that ship's line of fire for about five minutes.

A great many hits and straddles were claimed, but several ships complained that they were unable to spot their salvos because of the concentration of fire on their targets, and it was obviously impossible to distinguish shots with any accuracy. Distribution of fire had been left up to individual ships and captains, with the result that a majority of them opened on the leading heavy targets. It was evident that these ships were being hit, but how many times and by whose guns it is impossible to say. The *Fuso* appears to have turned west at about the same time our battle line reversed course. Both she and the *Mogami,* which had already turned south, were flaming brilliantly.

While return fire was seen by several ships, it was never great in volume and always ineffective. The two light cruisers *Denver* and *Columbia,* probably silhouetted against the gun flashes of the battle line, were straddled several times, apparently by 8-inch or larger caliber salvos. Some of the splashes were very close to both ships and a few fragments were found on their decks later, but neither ship sustained any damage. The *Boise* saw several splashes to the rear of the right flank and heard shells passing overhead.

The captain of the *Shigure* continued to see "vague flashes of fire in Leyte Gulf," but was still unable to locate any targets or to establish contact with the officer in tactical command aboard the *Fuso.* His radar was so poor that he could not distinguish ships from land masses and could make out neither friend nor foe. He fired his gun but no torpedoes in the general direction of the flashes. All the while his ship was "receiving a terrific bombardment," he said; "there were so many near misses that the gyro compass was out. The ship was constantly trembling from the force of near misses, and the wireless was out."

The *Shigure* seemed to steer a charmed, if somewhat aimless course, however, for she took only one direct hit, an 8-inch shell which did not explode. The captain finally sighted the *Fuso* and *Mogami,* both of them afire, both receiving and returning gunfire. There was a "big explosion" on the *Fuso* following shell hits, after which she appeared to be out of control. "At 0413 or 0415, being unsuccessful in finding the enemy, and determining that the rest of our force had been annihilated, I decided to withdraw without receiving orders from anyone," said the *Shigure's* captain. He began his retirement at thirty knots, but soon lost steering control and had to stop to repair his rudder.

In spite of our use of deliberate radar-controlled salvo fire, we were soon embarrassed by our shortage of ammunition. After ten minutes of firing the *West Virginia* discovered that she had only 110 rounds of AP ammunition left. The *Denver* and *Columbia* found that they had expended a high percentage of their 6-inch AP shells in the first few minutes of firing, and thereafter deliberately slowed their fire in the midst of the action in order to conserve ammunition.

All captains of the heavy ships were haunted throughout the action by the horror of confusing our own destroyers with the enemy and firing upon them. It can readily be understood that the destroyer captains were not without their own apprehensions concerning the same danger.

Comdr. Buchanan, in H.M.A.S. *Arunta*, was steaming down the channel with his three destroyers—"rather like Mr. Micawber, hoping for something to turn up," the Australian said. "It did!" he added. He was startled to hear one of the heavy ships to the north describe his column as "three enemy ships." "With a vivid recollection of what the gunfire of our cruisers and battleships had done to the enemy fresh in our minds," he said, "we retired at twenty-five knots." Admiral Berkey corrected the mistake, thus saving Buchanan "from an engagement with the battle fleet."

Other destroyers were not so fortunate.

It will be recalled that shortly before our heavy ships opened fire, Admiral Oldendorf had ordered Destroyer Squadron 56 to launch a torpedo attack. The firing courses of all three sections of this squadron lay down the middle of the strait between the battle line and left flank cruisers to the north and the enemy column to the south.

Capt. Thomas F. Conley, Jr., in the *Robinson*, with the *Halford* and *Bryant*, constituting Section II, led off with an attack from the east. Seeing the cruisers open fire, Conley called to his ships by radio, "This has to be quick. Stand by your fish!" He took his column in under fire by enemy guns against the protective background of Hibuson Island. A large target was smothered with smoke and shell splashes which prevented identification. At 0356 the three ships fired fifteen torpedoes to the starboard and turned left, retiring close to the shore of the island, still under erratic gunfire.

Section III attacked next from the west, led by Comdr. Joe W. Boulware in the *Heyward L. Edwards* with the *Leutze* and *Bennion*. At the very moment of "torpedoes away," at 0358, this section was taken under fire, shells falling close aboard and wetting down the decks with splashes. Since the targets turned west shortly after torpedoes were launched, Boulware did not believe his section made any hits. He turned right, making smoke, and retired toward the western shore of the strait, while Section II was hugging the opposite side.

Capt. Smoot took Section I, consisting of the *Newcomb*, *Richard P. Leary*, and *Albert W. Grant*, down the center of the channel under the arching tracers of our battleships and cruisers to attack on the starboard bow of the enemy column. His intention was to turn left and fire to the starboard. When the enemy unexpectedly turned to a westerly course, however, it became necessary to alter the plan suddenly, turn right to parallel the enemy course, and fire to port instead of starboard. Since all three destroyers were receiving heavy fire from the enemy when they launched torpedoes at 0404, the column immediately turned right to a northerly course. This was done in order to present the smallest possible target angle, to open range faster, and to make the most effective use of smoke screen. The new course took them up the middle of the strait toward the cruiser line instead of to the west and up the shore line as they were instructed.

At the turning point the destroyers were about midway between the blazing battle lines—some 6,800 yards from the enemy and about 8,000 yards from our left flank cruisers. Both our own and the Japanese ships showed up brilliantly in occasional gun flashes or explosions, and the destroyers were evidently silhouetted against both lines.

The last in the column and the longest to be exposed as a broadside target, the *Grant* was smothered under a cross fire of shells from both the Japanese line and our own cruisers. She took several bad hits abaft the bridge which knocked the forward fireroom and engine room out of commission. Scalding steam, pouring through two shell holes from the forward engine room, made it necessary to abandon the after engine room also. All power forward was lost almost immediately, and all the ship's lighting except emergency circuits went out.

Realizing that his ship might be sunk at any moment, Comdr. Terrell A. Nisewaner ordered her last half salvo of torpedoes fired at the enemy. This was accomplished by a wounded torpedoman's mate who, in the midst of flying shrapnel and fires which menaced the war heads of the projectiles, swung his mount clear of the danger and, when the automatic devices from the bridge failed, fired the salvo by percussion.

Shells from both directions continued to riddle the *Grant*. One hit forward at the waterline and flooded a storeroom and the forward berthing compartment of the crew; another shell hit a 40-mm gun, exploding its ammunition and starting a fire, and others struck the galley, the scullery room, the after berthing compartment of the crew, and the forward stack. In all the *Grant* took some twenty shells, eleven of them from our own cruisers, one near miss from a large caliber shell, and the remaining hits from the enemy. The ship rapidly lost speed, and steering control had to be shifted aft.

Admiral Oldendorf, who from the start had feared such an accident, learned at 0410 that the three destroyers were retiring up the middle of the strait and that they were under fire by our own guns. He immediately ordered all ships to cease fire and waited for the endangered destroyers to clear the channel or be identified. All guns at once became silent, except a few with "hot" shells which were unloaded toward the enemy.

Surigao Strait, until that moment blazing and thundering with gunfire, suddenly became dark and silent. As if in obedience to the same command, the Japanese also ceased fire.

The *Richard P. Leary*, retiring northward with the *Newcomb*, sighted two torpedo wakes passing up her starboard side and two on her port side, all of them very close aboard and on a course parallel with her own. She reported at once, "Passing through torpedo water." Assuming that the enemy had fired torpedoes to the northward, Admiral Weyler executed ships right to a northerly course with the *West Virginia*, *Maryland*, and *Mississippi*, seeking not only to avoid torpedoes, but also to clear the three remaining ships of the battle line, which were re-forming after the confusion caused by the *California*'s turn.

The crew of the *Grant*, in the meantime, was struggling desperately to keep the ship afloat. She was low in the water, flooding rapidly, and listing badly. Damage control parties groped in the darkness through live steam and hot oil to close valves, shore up gaps, put out fires, and stop flooding. One repair party, specially trained to assist in medical emergencies, had been almost completely wiped out by a shell. The *Grant* had 129 casualties—thirty-four dead one missing, and ninety-four wounded. To make the situation even more grim, the only medical officer aboard and one of the two pharmacist mates were killed by the first shell hits. Many of the wounded were in danger of being burned to death. Officers and men, including Comdr. Nisewaner, felt their way into the flooded, oil-soaked and burning engine rooms and rescued many. With his bare hands, D. W. Barnes, MM2c, beat out flames which were "making living torches out of the wounded." In spite of shortage of hands and suitable pumping facilities, heroic efforts brought the flooding under control and kept the *Grant* afloat until help arrived and she could be towed to safety.

As soon as he learned that all of his destroyers were clear of the channel except the *Grant*, which was now dead in the water, Admiral Oldendorf gave the order at 0419 for the right flank cruisers and the battle line to resume fire. None of these ships, however, could find any targets. Our battleships were still steaming north, opening range, and took no further part in the action after the "cease fire" order at 0410. Nor, for more than an hour, could the cruisers discover a suitable target within range.

Several ships which had been tracking the large leading Japanese vessel, on which most of the fire of our main force had been concentrated, saw the ship disappear from their radar screens at about 0418. That marked the sinking of the battleship *Fuso.* Down the strait two fires were burning, one to the east and one to the west of where the *Fuso* sank. All surviving ships of the force under attack were retreating southward at ranges between fourteen and seventeen miles.

PT boats and destroyers, however, had reported contact on another group of five or more enemy ships, which had also been located by the radar of our heavier vessels.

The new contacts to the south were the ships of Admiral Shima's Fifth Fleet, the movements and mission of which were to remain a mystery until after the war. Shima had learned by radio that Kurita's Central Force had been delayed by our air attacks in the Sibuyan Sea and would therefore probably not reach Leyte Gulf at the scheduled time. Since Nishimura's force would be without Kurita's support when he reached the Gulf, "his position would be even worse than before," as one of Shima's staff officers observed. Shima had planned to enter Surigao Strait at about 0600, but in order to give more effective support to Nishimura he advanced the time of entry to 0300. Observing radio silence, he did not inform Nishimura of the change, nor did he communicate with him at any time during the day. He believed that the other force was about forty miles ahead of him, but was never in sight of it.

About midnight the flagship *Nachi* overheard Nishimura's voice radio command circuit announce that his force was under attack by torpedo boats, and about three hours later he overheard an order to reverse course to avoid torpedoes.

This was the only information received of Nishimura, who probably went down with the *Yamashiro* unaware that the Japanese Fifth Fleet was rushing to his support a few thousand yards astern.

Shima's force, with two destroyers screening ahead of the two heavy cruisers and one light cruiser, entered the strait at 0305, a little more than an hour later than Nishimura had made his entrance. The ships turned east at 0313 and then to a northerly course six minutes later, while the two van destroyers fell in astern and the heavy cruisers took the lead with the flagship *Nachi* in the van.

At 0321 the light cruiser *Abukuma*, flagship of the screening force, was hit by a torpedo on her port side and dropped out of the formation. She was badly damaged, down at the bow, and reduced to a speed of about ten knots. The explosion had knocked out the *Abukuma*'s radio room, flooded it, killed all of its crew, and suffocated personnel on her bridge. Some thirty men were killed.

The torpedo attack was made by PT boat 137, commanded by Ens. M. Kovar, who was stationed off the southern tip of Panaon Island. Kovar had fired at one of the destroyers, then steaming south to fall in astern, but his torpedo passed under the stern of the destroyer and struck the cruiser, which he never saw and did not know that he had hit. He felt a jar but saw no explosion and could not see the ship because of the smoke screen laid by the destroyers. The destroyers fired star shells at once and a cruiser opened fire, but Kovar escaped without damage.

Leaving the *Abukuma* behind without escort, the rest of Admiral Shima's force continued northward, building up a speed of twenty-eight knots. At 0345 the flagship sighted burning vessels to the northward and on both sides of them a very dense smoke screen. As they steamed toward the smoke screen the Japanese could see gun flashes and tracers beyond the smoke but were unable to make out any ships, American or Japanese, aside from those on fire. They passed the burning ships and continued into the smoke.

The destroyer *Shigure*, retiring with damage, sighted Shima's force a few minutes later and challenged by flashlight. "I am the *Nachi*," was the answer. The destroyer replied, "I am the *Shigure*. I have rudder difficulties." That and nothing more! Her commander explained that the reason he gave no further information to Admiral Shima was that he "had no connection with him and was not under his command." He also assumed that the admiral would draw his own conclusions from the sight of burning vessels to the northward. Shima continued northward, drawing whatever conclusions he could from the smoke screen.

Admiral Shima's torpedo officer complained that his radar was not working effectively and that it revealed no targets. At about 0420, however, he picked up one group of American ships, and a moment later the cruisers turned and fired their her port side and began laying a smoke screen. The second cruiser in line, the *Ashigara*, turned safely and fell in astern of torpedoes on course 20°, range to the target about 13,000 yards. These were evidently the torpedoes which the destroyer *Leary* saw passing her sides on a parallel course and which she reported to the commander of the battle line.

Just as she reached her firing point, the *Nachi* sighted a large burning ship ahead which she assumed to be dead in the water. This was the *Mogami*, badly damaged and without steering control, although she was not dead in the water but retiring at low speed. "We were all concentrating on the attack," testified an officer who was on the *Nachi's* bridge at the time, "so did not know the course of the *Mogami*." The *Nachi* turned full right rudder and stopped both engines, but in spite of this collided with the *Mogami* on a converging course of about ten degrees. The flagship pulled free of the burning cruiser with a hole in the *Nachi*, which was shipping considerable water and steaming southward slowly, investigating her damage.

Admiral Shima's destroyers continued northward at high speed to make a torpedo attack but were unable to find any targets and therefore fired no torpedoes. After an investigation revealed that the *Nachi* could not make sufficient speed to continue the attack and no more American ships could be located behind the smoke screen, Admiral Shima recalled his destroyers and at 0443 took a southerly course to retire from the battle. The *Mogami,* after maneuvering for several minutes, got under way at low speed and headed south.

That the Japanese were routed and in confused retreat was obvious to Admiral Oldendorf. The natural temptation was to order an all-out pursuit to overtake and finish off the cripples. The tactical situation at the moment, however, made this extremely hazardous. Our own destroyers and PT boats down the strait were looking for opportunities to unload their few remaining torpedoes, and it could not be known how many Japanese destroyers, crippled or not, were lurking against the dark cover of the shore line awaiting the same opportunity. One of the PT boats, moreover, had reported that her screws had struck a heavy submerged object in deep water, which might mean that a submarine was in the strait.

Oldendorf waited until 0431 before ordering any pursuit started. It was well that he did, for it was in that interval that Shima's destroyers were ranging northward in search of targets. The admiral finally ordered Destroyer Division "X-Ray," the battle line screen of six vessels under Comdr. Miles H. Hubbard, to head south, attack with torpedoes, and retire northward hugging the coast. A moment later Oldendorf brought the left flank around by column movement and headed south cautiously at fifteen knots with the five cruisers, which were joined later by the left flank destroyers. The three right flank cruisers started down the west side of the channel at 0451.

The *Louisville,* leading the left flank cruisers down the strait, soon regained radar contact with remnants of Nishimura's force and gave chase on course 180°. Contact was also made with Shima's ships at a distance of 25,500 yards, but they headed south out of range. The scattered targets nearer at hand, two of them burning fiercely, increased speed in spite of their condition, and Oldendorf likewise speeded up in order to close them. One of the burning ships, probably the *Mogami*, was selected as a target. At 0524 the cruiser column turned right to course 250° and five minutes later commenced firing on this ship from a range of about ten miles. Arching tracers converged on the burning target and explosions followed. "This ship was completely ablaze and burning worse than the *Arizona* burned at Pearl Harbor," according to the captain of the *Columbia*. In spite of this, she continued to the southward, making seventeen knots. If this was the *Mogami*, she survived an almost unbelievable pounding that night.

In the meantime another target, identified as a destroyer, became silhouetted against the flames, was taken under fire by several cruisers, and also burst into flame. Although three burning ships remained in sight, Oldendorf decided to abandon the chase and at 0539 gave the order to cease fire. The right flank cruisers had already reversed course and the left flank soon followed northward.

Destroyer Division X-Ray had taken up pursuit of one of the Japanese ships, but since the enemy had a lead of more than fifteen miles and was making good time, it became evident that it would be a long chase and that daylight would come before a torpedo attack could be made. They were ordered to abandon the chase and join the cruisers.

Toward the lower end of the strait some of the PT boats were having their second shot at the enemy. McElfresh's section sighted the *Mogami* about 0600 limping southward at low speed, but missed with two torpedoes. Another PT section fired four torpedoes at a destroyer and felt a terrific jar. Other boats picked up the enemy and reported their contacts, but as daylight approached they were compelled to keep at a distance.

There was sufficient light by 0600 to make visible the scene of the night battle for a considerable distance. Debris and wreckage, some of it afire, littered the area for miles, and great oil slicks stretched up the strait. Several small boats were sighted. The destroyers were ordered to pick up survivors from the great patches of Japanese in the water. The survivors were in poor shape, most of them thickly coated with fuel oil and without life preservers.

The stoical reaction of the Japanese to their plight and to the efforts of our destroyers to rescue them was typical of their conduct on previous occasions of this sort. "The survivors in the water seemed bent on ignoring us completely," said Capt. Conley, "and few of them would glance directly at the ship." The *Claxton* saw an enemy officer exhorting his men not to surrender, but they showed little inclination to take our lines even when officers were not present. When one small boat loaded with survivors was approached and offered assistance by the *Halford*, the Japanese rose without a word and leaped overboard. Of the hundreds of men sighted in the water only a handful could be persuaded to accept rescue.

Oldendorf reversed course with the left flank at 0617 and steamed back down the strait for another look as daylight brightened. The sun rose about 0630. A few minutes afterward, the admiral ordered the *Denver* and *Columbia* with the three destroyers *Claxton*, *Cony*, and *Thorn* to break off from the column and proceed southward to polish off cripples, whose smoke could now be seen.

By 0700 the *Denver* group had two targets in sight, although the more distant one was so thickly smothered by flame and smoke that the ship could not be identified. The other was a destroyer with her whole bow blown off and heavy oil smoke billowing from her stern, dead in the water. This ship was taken under fire by the cruisers and destroyers at 0707, range about six miles. The target went down at 0721. She was the *Asagumo*, one of the two destroyers of Nishimura's force which had survived the ordeal up the strait. Nothing more could be seen of the enemy save five or six columns of smoke rising over the horizon to the south.

Admiral Oldendorf had suggested to Admiral Kinkaid earlier that an air attack be launched by the escort carriers off Samar to finish off cripples which might escape. Only four minutes after the *Asagumo* sank, planes from the CVE's sighted the Japanese ships below the entrance to Surigao Strait and west of the northern tip of Mindanao. Admiral Shima's group, fighting off attacks by our PT boats, had retired through the entrance and joined up with the *Mogami* and *Abukuma*.

The first strike by the CVE planes failed to finish off the cripples, but while the enemy was still trying to assemble his ships about an hour later a second strike was delivered. This time the much battered *Mogami* received her fatal blow. The destroyer *Akebono* was left behind with the stricken *Mogami* and the *Ushio* with the *Abukuma*, while the *Nachi* and *Ashigara* retired westward with two destroyers. The *Mogami* sank about an hour later off the southern tip of Leyte Island, after her survivors had been transferred to the *Abukuma*. The *Abukuma* finally went down the following day about noon under attack by B-24's of the Army Air Force. Although army bombers flew several missions and attacked many ships during the battle, the crippled cruiser was their only victim.

Steaming back up Surigao Strait and surveying the wreckage of enemy ships, Admiral Oldendorf and his whole command had ample cause for satisfaction with their night's work. Of the ships which entered the strait under Admiral Nishimura's command only the damaged *Shigure* made good an escape. Two 30,000-ton battleships and three destroyers were sunk within the strait and the *Mogami* and *Abukuma*, the latter of Shima's force, were so badly crippled that they fell easy marks to our planes. No ship of our force was lost and the only damage and casualties were those suffered by the *Grant* and six PT boats. Japanese casualties were undoubtedly very high, probably more than 5,000.

At 0728 Oldendorf received from the commander of the Seventh Fleet a cordial dispatch of congratulations and a hearty "Well done." Seventh Fleet morale was—for the moment—about at peak.

Ten minutes later there arrived a second dispatch from Admiral Kinkaid which drastically altered the outlook and took the edge of elation off the victory. Japanese battleships and cruisers, reported Kinkaid, were firing on our CVE's off Samar Island and approaching the eastern entrance to Leyte Gulf. The sequel to the Seventh Fleet victory threatened to be an unprecedented military disaster.

With his fuel dangerously low, his torpedoes almost exhausted, and his ammunition near the vanishing point, Admiral Oldendorf set course for Leyte Gulf.

IV

THE BATTLE OFF CAPE ENGAÑO

Vice Admiral Ozawa, commander of the Japanese Northern Force of carriers, entered the Battle for Leyte Gulf expecting, he said, the "complete destruction" of his fleet. In that expectation he was not to be disappointed, at least in so far as his carriers were concerned. His attitude, however, was dictated neither by the Shinto Code nor by Oriental fatalism, but by a deliberate plan. Under interrogation in Tokyo after the war, Ozawa fully confirmed the purpose of his mission as it was indicated in the plans for the *Sho* Operation. When asked to characterize the primary purpose of his mission, the admiral replied without hesitation:

"A decoy, that was our first primary mission, to act as a decoy. My fleet could not very well give direct protection to Kurita's force because we were very weak, so I tried to attack as many American carriers as possible, and to be the decoy or target for your attack. I tried to let Kurita's fleet have little attack from you. The main mission was all sacrifice. An attack with a very weak force of planes comes under the heading of sacrifice of planes and ships." Ozawa gave Admiral Toyoda credit for originating this plan.

Deliberate sacrifice of the remaining Japanese naval air power, while undoubtedly a desperate measure, was not so desperate and revolutionary as it might at first appear. The sacrifice had, in effect, already been made by Toyoda when he stripped Ozawa's carriers of more than half their planes for the defense of Formosa. Already seriously depleted and unable to rebuild their strength in time for the defense of the Philippines, the Japanese carrier air groups were ordered to give up 150 of their planes. For the *Sho* Operation the plan was to rely mainly upon land-based air power. Ozawa entered the action with only 110 planes (only twenty more planes than the normal complement of one of our CV's), none at all for the flight decks of the converted battleships and less than thirty apiece for the carriers; about eighty of the 110 planes were fighters, the remaining ones bombers and torpedo planes. The Japanese pilots are reported to have had only eighty hours of flight experience. Since it had been decided to commit the remaining carriers in this action anyway, it is difficult to see how they could have been employed more effectively than they were.

The fleet under the command of Admiral Ozawa, identi-fied by the Japanese as the "Main Body" and referred to here as the Northern Force, was composed of one large and three light carriers, two converted battleship-carriers, three light cruisers, and ten destroyers, six of them of the heavy *Terutsuki* class. These units were organized as follows:

CARRIERS	SCREENING FORCE
	Light Cruisers	*Destroyers*
Carrier Division 3	Oyodo	Shimotsuki
Zuikaku (CV) (F)	Tama	Fuyutsuki
Chitose (CVL)	Isuzu	Suzutsuki
Chiyoda (CVL)		Hatsutsuki
Zuiho (CVL)		Wakatsuki
Carrier Division 4		Akitsuki
(Battleship-carriers)		Kuwa
Ise		Maki
Hyuga		Sugi
		Kiri

Toyoda had provided his lure with bait that would have a fascinating appeal for a carrier admiral. The prestige of the car-rier was at its peak in the fall of '44, when even conservative tacticians were calling it a "carrier war." It would have been a rash man indeed who would have deprecated the importance or scorned the opportunity of wiping out the enemy's carrier forces. Our intelligence officers at that time, of course, did not know how empty were the hangar decks of the Japanese carriers, nor how hopeless was the Japanese high command of rebuilding the deteriorated air groups and training the necessary pilots. It would have seemed improbable to the point of absurdity to suggest in October 1944 that a modern naval

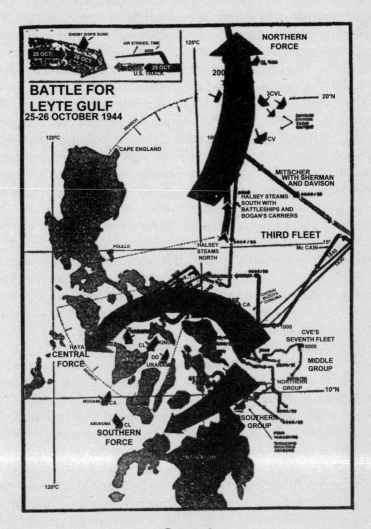

CHART 4.

power would stake the existence of its fleet on the gunnery of its surface ships and throw away its last carriers as an expendable diversion force.

Ozawa confessed that he was skeptical of the success of his mission from the start. "I had not much confidence in being a lure," he said, "but there was no other way than to try." The *Sho* Operation was excessively complicated and its component parts were scattered over a vast theater. "I knew that the decoy operation," he continued, "even using regular surface carriers for decoy would be more difficult." He gave the mission "a 50-50 chance" of succeeding.

The Northern Force maintained radio silence during its approach until the 23rd, then broke the silence "for the purpose of luring." Throughout the daylight hours of the 24th, while Admiral Halsey's Third Fleet was launching a succession of air strikes at Kurita's Central Force in the Sibuyan Sea, Ozawa's carriers were operating east of northern Luzon, sometimes within little more than a hundred miles of Sherman's task group. During the morning Ozawa received a contact report from Japanese land-based planes, giving the position of Sherman's group, but sent out his own search planes to verify the report before launching his attack. The carrier-based strike, which spent itself against our task group about mid-day, was made up of about eighty planes, all the Japanese had except for a small and inadequate air cover of twenty fighters which were kept over the fleet.

For some unaccountable reason Ozawa was convinced that his force had been sighted by our search planes during the morning before his strike was launched and could not be shaken in his conviction, under questioning, that he had seen and identified our planes himself. Expecting an attack from our carriers to follow soon after launching his own strike, he ordered his carriers to take a northwesterly course.

Of the results of his strike on our task group Ozawa said that he heard nothing throughout the day. The only planes that returned to their bases were those which were turned back by bad weather and were unable to attack our carriers. As for the remaining planes, those which survived counterattack by our fighters, from thirty to forty landed on Luzon. They were ordered to do so, according to Ozawa's Chief of Staff, since "our ships would be sunk, because we went too near [the third fleet] on purpose to lure your ships to the north. Surely we would be sunk; that was our mission." Communications from land were so poor that no reports on results of the strike reached the fleet from Luzon. "Generally speaking," testified Ozawa "naval shore communications were very poor from the standpoint of equipment, technical ability, and so on." He might well have made a similar generalization about Japanese communications afloat and in the air.

The only information the Northern Force commander received concerning the progress of Kurita's Central Force during the day was the message sent by Kurita about 1630, saying he was reversing course. By that time Ozawa had about despaired of diverting the Third Fleet air power to the northward, since the only attention his fleet had received had been the dare-devil one-man attack by one of our search planes, which was quickly driven off without releasing its bombs. The admiral concluded that his luring mission had been a failure and that Kurita had abandoned his mission under attack from our carriers. Then at about 1930 came Toyoda's order from Tokyo instructing the fleet to proceed with its mission: "Trusting in Divine aid, the entire force will attack." The carrier force again came about and headed southeast.

From some source Ozawa heard that two carriers in Sherman's task group were damaged and that only two battleships were present. Toward evening he ordered Rear Admiral Matsuda to form a detachment consisting of the two converted battleships *Ise* and *Hyuga* and four *Terutsuki*-class destroyers and steam southward to attack our carrier group in a night battle. Matsuda continued southward until about the middle of the night. Once he saw flashes in the distance that he took for a Japanese air attack on the American carriers, although "it might have been an electrical storm," he added. He did not inform Ozawa of the supposed contact, and before he could satisfy himself about it he was ordered to rejoin the carriers, which he did before sunrise.

Early in the morning Ozawa again headed northward, though he denied that his purpose was to save his carriers. "The chief concern was to lure your force further north," he said; "we expected complete destruction." Since he heard little from Kurita and Nishimura during the night he "took it for granted that they were progressing smoothly."

"The carrier forces to the north were our meat," said Admiral Sherman; "they were close enough so that they could not get away."

Since midnight the carriers and battleships of the Third Fleet had been steaming northeast at a speed of sixteen knots to gain position for a dawn strike on the Japanese Northern Force. While opinion as to the strategy was not unanimous in the Third Fleet, once the decision had been made and the fleet committed there was a universal determination to carry it through and among some commanders a whole-hearted enthusiasm for the plan. "The situation was entirely to my liking," continued Admiral Sherman, "and I felt that we had a chance to completely wipe out a major group of the enemy fleet, including the precious carriers which he could ill afford to lose."

There was also considerable enthusiasm for the tactics of Admiral Halsey's plan. He proposed to withdraw the fast battleships and a screen of cruisers and destroyers from all three carrier task groups to form Task Force 34, advance this powerful gunnery force ahead of the carriers, launch his air strikes over the heads of the battleships like long-ranged artillery, then send in the surface force like infantry to mop up cripples and stragglers and slug it out with the enemy's heavy ships. If nothing interfered with the plan, there seemed to be no reason why, with their vastly superior air and gun power, the battleship and carrier task forces could not wipe the Northern Force out of existence.

Shortly before 0100 the *Independence* launched night planes to search ten sectors to the north and northeast. No contact with the enemy force had been made since the search planes had returned the previous afternoon after making the original contact. Every care was to be taken not to overrun the "daylight circle"* of the Northern Force and thus permit it to come between our force and Leyte Gulf. It was not believed that the enemy was tracking our force, although an enemy snooper appeared on the radar screen about 0140 and approached within twenty miles of the task force. The *Enterprise* launched two night fighters which soon reported that they had "splashed one *Mavis*."[†]

At 0208 one of the *Independence* search planes reported contact with an enemy force of three large and three small ships about eighty miles north of Task Force 38 heading southeast, course 110°, speed fifteen knots. This was undoubtedly the *Ise* and *Hyuga* and destroyers, though they were not so identified. Half an hour later another report was received indicating a large group of enemy ships about forty miles astern of the first one reported.

Admiral Mitscher at once recommended to Admiral Halsey that the fleet course be changed from northeast to north and that Task Force 34 now be formed. Halsey approved both recommendations, and at 0253 Mitscher directed Admiral Lee, commander of Task Force 34, to form his force and proceed ahead of the carriers. The three task groups under Sherman, Bogan, and Davison, prior to the removal of the units of Task Force 34, were lined up approximately as they had been on the morning of the 24th,[‡] except that Sherman's group had been reduced by the sinking of the *Princeton* and the detachment of the cruiser *Birmingham* and the destroyers *Morrison*, *Gatling*, and *Irwin*, which were steaming toward Ulithi for repairs. Altogether there were five large carriers and five light carriers plus supporting ships.

---

* The maximum distance in any direction which the force could steam from a given point by daylight.

† A Japanese four-engined flying boat.

‡ See page 42.

The Heavy Surface Striking Force, or Task Force 34, under Admiral Lee, was constituted as follows:

BATTLE LINE
(Vice Adm. Willis A. Lee, Jr.)
Battleships
Iowa
New Jersey (FIF)
Massachusetts
Washington (FF)
South Dakota
Alabama

RIGHT FLANK
(Rear Adm. F. E. M. Whiting)
Light Cruisers
Vincennes (F)
Miami
Biloxi
8 Destroyers

CENTER
(Rear Adm. C. T. Joy)
Heavy Cruisers
Wichita (F)
New OrleansMobile
4 Destroyers

LEFT FLANK
(Rear Adm. L. T. DuBose)
Light Cruisers
Santa Fe (F)

6 Destroyers

Any two of the six fast battleships would have jumped at the chance of taking on the two converted battleships of the Northern Force, and any two would have been capable of handling them. Of the six only the *Washington,* Lee's flagship, and the *South Dakota* had ever exchanged salvos with Japanese capital ships. The long-awaited opportunity seemed about to materialize.

There was some urgency in the formation and advance of the battleship force, which was rather slow in forming, since it was evident that a surface battle might develop at about 0430 should the Japanese Northern Force maintain the southerly course it was pursuing when last heard from. To facilitate the new formation, the fleet guide was slowed to fifteen knots at 0330, and at 0419 Task Force 38 changed to a westerly course in order to open distance on Task Force 34. But the night surface battle failed to develop.

One of those accidents which seemed to plague our night search planes throughout the operation was responsible for losing contact with the enemy at this point. Because of engine trouble the *Independence* plane which had made the original contact was forced to return to its base. The relief tracking plane that was sent out to regain contact was unable to do so because of difficulties with radar equipment. In fact the pilot began reporting his own fleet as an enemy contact. Another plane reported two enemy destroyers about 200 miles to the northward of the original contact, but radar contact with the main enemy forces was never regained during the night. Dawn searchers would have to be relied upon to relocate the enemy fleet, and search sectors were assigned between due north and twenty degrees south of west.

In the meantime the two task forces continued to steam northward at reduced speed. Word was received from Admiral Kinkaid that surface forces of the Seventh Fleet were engaging an enemy fleet in Surigao Strait and southern Leyte Gulf. At about 0300 Admiral Halsey informed Kinkaid, as well as Admirals King and Nimitz, of the position of the Northern Force when last reported and added that his own force of "three groups" was concentrated.

In answer to Kinkaid's urgent dispatch inquiring whether Task Force 34 was still guarding San Bernardino Strait, sent at about 0410 and not received for two and a half hours, Halsey replied that the fast battleships were with the carriers engaging the Japanese Northern Force.

Mitscher had ordered all his task group commanders to have their first deck-load strike armed and ready to launch at daybreak. At earliest dawn, shortly before 0600, planes began to roar off the flight decks in all three task groups— first the combat air patrol, then the dawn search planes, and finally the first strike group. Altogether the latter consisted of approximately sixty fighters, sixty-five bombers, and fifty-five torpedo planes. Although the enemy was not yet located, the strike groups were launched with the search planes and vectored fifty miles northward where they were directed to orbit until contact was made and they could be vectored to the target. This scheme would prove an advantage only if the enemy were located in a reasonable length of time.

The sun rose about 0630 and another hour passed without a contact report from the search planes. The strike groups had been in the air an hour and a half. It had been estimated before dawn that at 0400 the enemy force was between thirty-five and eighty-five miles from the position of Task Force 38. Obviously a bad guess, or it would have been located by this time. Would it prove another lost opportunity, such as the morning of the Battle of the Philippine Sea, when Mitscher's search planes had been unable to locate the Japanese task force? But the enemy could not have steamed out of range of the search planes this time.

Two young intelligence officers on Mitscher's staff, Lieutenants E. Calvert Cheston and Byron R. White, had been insisting on their belief that the Japanese carriers could be to the east of the scheduled search sectors, which did not extend east of due north. They were finally given permission to try out their theory. Instead of launching more search planes, they vectored out a division of four fighters from the combat air patrol.

At 0735 one of the fighters reported the enemy force 140 miles to the northeast, bearing 015° from Task Force 38. The contact was not with part, but with the whole force concentrated—the large carrier *Zuikaku*, three light carriers, two converted battleships, three light cruisers, and eight destroyers—seventeen ships in all. Two picket destroyers were not with Ozawa at the time. The carriers were on a southerly course, steaming at twenty knots when sighted.

The weather was excellent for the work at hand, clear with only a few clouds on the horizon, and a wind from the northeast at sixteen knots. The strike group, which was vectored northeast as soon as the contact was reported, sighted the wakes of the vessels at 0810, more than thirty miles to the north. Comdr. David McCampbell, the record-breaking commander of Air Group 15 from the *Essex*, was selected by Mitscher to be target coordinator for the strike. Squadrons from all the task groups were present, including some from the *Enterprise* and *Franklin* of Davison's task group—the only airmen who attacked all three enemy forces, those in the Sulu Sea and Sibuyan Sea on the 24th and now the Northern Force in the Philippine Sea.

The most remarkable thing about the enemy carriers was the absence of planes on their flight decks and the small number in the air. That they were caught this way was attributed at the time to a "tactical surprise." Concerning this report, Admiral Halsey said that he was "puzzled by the fact that there were scarcely any planes on the decks of, or in the air near, the enemy force, and no signs of bogies around our own force." It was not a matter of "surprise," of course, but simply a lack of planes.

Fifteen or twenty enemy fighters rose to intercept our strike group and attacked aggressively at first, shooting down one Avenger and damaging other planes. The interception was broken up quickly by our fighters, however, and after several Japanese planes were shot down the remaining ones withdrew, leaving our strikes with no air opposition whatever for the rest of the day.

The carrier force had changed to a northwesterly course by the time our strike arrived, then swung to the north. The ships were in tight formation with battleships in close support, but under attack they maneuvered individually. Antiaircraft fire was similar to that met in the Sulu and Sibuyan Seas. Again the battleships opened with their main batteries at extreme ranges, and all ships sent up accurate and intense fire, their tracers and bursts colored to identify the shooting of individual ships. So thick were the bursts that they made a formation like cumulus clouds. During the day ten of our aircraft were destroyed by enemy gunfire.

Selecting the carriers as his principal targets, McCampbell assigned the *Essex* planes to a light carrier of the *Chitose* class. Bombing Squadron 15 circled the formation and opened the day's attacks by diving out of the sun and dropping twelve half-ton bombs on the carrier. Eight direct hits were claimed.

Since they left the carrier burning and exploding, McCampbell attempted to divert Torpedo 15, which had been assigned the same target, to a near-by battleship. Several of the Avengers had already started their runs on the carrier, however, and two of them scored torpedo hits. The *Lexington* bombers apparently attacked the same ship and scored more hits. The carrier soon developed a heavy list to port and slowed to fourteen knots. After the strike, McCampbell watched her explode and sink.*

Reviewing the results of the strike, Admiral Carney, Third Fleet Chief of Staff, complained of "an inherent mammalian tendency to jump on cripples." It was true that damaged ships were sometimes repeatedly attacked, when they might have been left to the surface force to finish off later. Nevertheless, severe damage was inflicted on several ships. Another light carrier of the *Chitose* class was left dead in the water as a result of several direct bomb hits; a violent explosion was seen on a light cruiser after a torpedo hit, and some damage was believed to have been done to one of the converted battleships and two destroyers. While one torpedo and many bomb hits were claimed upon the large carrier *Zuikaku*, flagship of the force, it was not learned until after the war that the damage inflicted on her communication system had compelled Admiral Ozawa to transfer his flag to the light cruiser *Oyodo*.

Aboard the flagship of the American force to the southward a crisis of quite a different, though scarcely less harassing, nature, was shaping up about the same time. The *New Jersey*, with the battle line, was now well in advance of the carrier force. Shortly after contact with the Northern Force was reported to him, Admiral Halsey directed Admiral Lee, Commander Task Force 34, to stand toward the enemy at twenty knots. Then, about 0800 he sent a message to Admiral McCain, giving him the location of the Northern Force and directing him to join the attack upon it as soon as practicable. McCain's task group, which had so far remained out of

---

* Chart 5 presents the progress of the battle as our pilots reported it and as they identified the ships. It is of value in spite of errors.

the action, was then about 260 miles to the southeast fueling from tankers. McCain had also sent out search planes which located the Northern Force later.

At about 0825 Admiral Halsey was handed a dispatch from the Seventh Fleet marked "Urgent." Its contents and the fact that it was sent in plain language instead of cryptogram was even more eloquent of its urgency. Japanese battleships and cruisers, it said, were firing on our CVE's northeast of Leyte Gulf! On the heels of this arrived a second one from Kinkaid eight minutes later saying that the Third Fleet battleship force was desperately needed off Samar Island immediately. Kinkaid assumed that Halsey's battleships had remained on guard at San Bernardino Strait.

If the need was immediate there was little the fast battleships could do, since at that moment they were more than 350 miles from Leyte Gulf, steaming north. Kinkaid's appeal had been sent before he received Halsey's reply indicating that Task Force 34 was not guarding San Bernardino Strait. Neither of the messages from the Seventh Fleet had revealed the strength of the enemy force menacing Leyte Gulf, and it had been the conviction of the Third Fleet commander that even if part of the Japanese Central Force did succeed in carrying through with its mission, "à la Guadalcanal," it would not, after the mauling administered in the Sibuyan Sea, be able to cause serious damage. But how the admiral could have convinced himself on the previous night that, as he said, he would be able to "return in time to reverse any advantage that the Center Force might gain" at Leyte, and relieve any "temporarily tight situation," is not at present clear.

At 0830 Mitscher's first strike group was still in the air and his second strike was just being launched. Flash reports from the first strike were beginning to arrive, indicating severe damage to the Japanese carrier force and mentioning several cripples—meat for the hungry gunners of the new battleships.

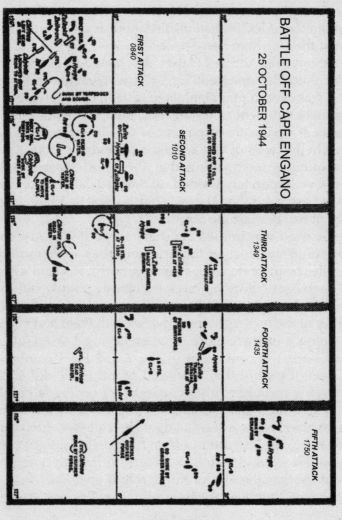

CHART 5.

The first order issued by the Third Fleet commander after receiving the startling messages from the Seventh Fleet was directed to the commander of Task Force 34 by voice radio: "Close enemy at twenty-five knots." The enemy to the *north*, not to the south. He then canceled his order directing McCain to join in the strikes on the Northern Force and instructed him instead to proceed southwest at the best speed and launch strikes at the earliest possible time against the Central Force off Samar Island.

McCain's task group was still in the fueling rendezvous, with one of its carries and one cruiser taking fuel. Upon receiving Halsey's message, McCain immediately ordered them to cast off from the tankers and turned to the southwesterly course, building up speed to thirty knots. With three large carriers and two light carriers, this task group had the most powerful air force of any in the Third Fleet. McCain was farther from the beleaguered CVE's at that time, however, than he was from Halsey, and it would be more than an hour before he could come within extreme striking range, even at top speed. Two and a half hours more would be required for the planes to reach the target after launching.

Halsey's only response to Kinkaid's appeals at this time was a dispatch saying that he had ordered McCain to launch a strike as soon as possible. But these were only the first of a series of nine urgent messages which continued to jam the air of the Pacific with frantic calls for aid. Messages between the fleets were requiring from an hour and a half to two hours for transmission and delivery at the time.

Five minutes after sending his reply to Kinkaid, the Third Fleet commander received a third appeal from the Seventh Fleet commander at 0900 and a few minutes later a fourth. They had been sent within two minutes of each other. Both requested immediate assistance from air strikes and fast battleships. But this time Kinkaid gave the composition of the enemy force—four battleships and eight cruisers, plus other vessels—and added the ominous information that the ammunition supply of his battleships was low.

No more comfort was to be derived from the assumption that a crippled remnant of Kurita's Central Force had managed to limp through San Bernardino Strait to create a diversion. If Kinkaid's figures were correct, it was not a remnant but virtually the entire force—minus one battleship—which on the previous day had been blasted by six air strikes! It was difficult to believe. Some officers could not believe it, at first. Perhaps it was the estimate of excited men under a surprise attack.

Admiral Halsey replied immediately, giving his position, stating that he was then engaging the Japanese carrier force, and repeated that he had ordered McCain, with five carriers and four heavy cruisers, to come to the assistance of the Seventh Fleet at once. The fast battleships continued to steam northward at high speed. So did the carrier groups astern.

Then about 1000 came a dispatch from Pearl Harbor . . . Admiral Nimitz also wanted to know what had become of the fast battleships of the Third Fleet! This had hardly been read when Kinkaid's fifth dispatch came up from the radio room—another appeal for assistance in a tone more desperate, if possible, than the previous appeals.

Flag Plot in the *New Jersey* had weathered other crises during the brief career of the battleship as the Third Fleet flagship, but never one like this. The cries of the Seventh Fleet were being heard, literally, halfway around the world. Yet to reverse course at this late hour and break off an action that promised certain and spectacular success appeared to some to be a futile gesture. A high speed run half the length of the Philippines would necessitate the refueling of the smaller vessels of the screen, a time-consuming ordeal that would delay the task force for hours. The battleships would not reach the scene of action until the following morning and would probably not be able to intercept the enemy's central force before it could escape. They might well be caught between two actions and therefore participate in neither. They would have to take air cover with them, thus cutting to less than half the air power Halsey had planned to bring to bear upon the Northern Force. Hundreds of miles astern was a situation about which little was actually known. A few miles ahead were believed to lie rewards for which risks appeared to be worth taking—and for which several had already been taken. Task Force 34 continued northward.

Mitscher's second air strike was now approaching the targets. At 1006, by voice radio, Halsey ordered all task group commanders to instruct their pilots to confine attacks to undamaged ships and to leave the cripples to be finished off later.

The second strike, a small one only about one-fifth the size of the first, consisted of twelve Hellcats, six Helldivers, and eighteen Avengers organized from planes available at 0830 aboard the *Lexington, Franklin,* and *Langley.* Since two groups failed to make the appointed rendezvous, the strike was ill coordinated, and bomber and torpedo planes lacked adequate fighter cover during their approaches. No air opposition was encountered, but two planes were severely damaged by gunfire. Because of damage apparently resulting from catapult launching, none of the five *Langley* Avengers was able to make an effective torpedo attack. The *Lexington* torpedo squadron claimed hits on the large carrier, one on a battleship, and one on a light cruiser, and the *Franklin* pilots reported half-ton bomb hits on two light carriers, both of which were left smoking.

By the end of the second strike it appears that the enemy formation had split into two groups, the one astern consisting of cripples and several covering vessels circling them for protection. One light carrier was said to be dead in the water covered by a battleship and a destroyer; one light cruiser was also dead in the water and being circled by two destroyers, and a second light cruiser was thought to have been badly damaged, or possibly sunk. The group of cripples was not far from the waters in which the force was first reported.

Since 0735, when the original contact of the morning was reported, Task Force 34 had been standing toward the enemy, for the first hour at twenty knots and thereafter at still better speed. Since the Northern Force had been maneuvering radically under attack and part of the time, at least, had been on a converging course, southward, the distance between the two forces had closed rapidly in three and a half hours. Mitscher's carrier groups had been left far astern, strung out from twenty to thirty miles to the rear. At 1108 Admiral Bogan reported that one of his planes had just sighted three carriers dead in the water. By that time Lee's battleships were within forty-five miles of the enemy cripples.

"We were all but standing on our toes on the Flag Bridge," recalled one officer of Halsey's staff, "expecting Japanese masts to appear over the horizon any minute." It had been nearly three hours since Kinkaid's first appeal was received.

The six fast battleships were in column, each with a "bone in her teeth" from high speed and a head wind, when at exactly 1115 the big gray bows came about slowly, then continued, hard over, all the way through a 180° turn. Left Flank, Right Flank, and Center came about likewise. Reverse course, southward . . .

"The 'Old Man,'" reports one of the officers present at the occasion, "was fit to be tied."

"My golden opportunity," the admiral called it in retrospect. What anguish of spirit the decision to turn back must have cost a man of Halsey's temperament may only be surmised.

The pursuit had to be broken off, however. It was the only thing to do. Messages of distress continued to pour in from the Seventh Fleet. The enemy, it was reported, was attempting to force his way into the gulf; again, he was returning to attack the jeep carriers. Later the situation looked better; the enemy force appeared to be retiring, but assistance was still needed. A few minutes later, however, at about 1320, a message was received saying that the situation again had become quite grave, that transport shipping was threatened, that air support had been broken up by attacks on the CVE's, which were being forced into the gulf, and that combatant ships were too low on fuel and ammunition to be relied upon for defense.

When Task Force 34 reversed course the cruisers *Wichita*, *New Orleans*, *Santa Fe* and *Mobile* and the ten destroyers of Squadron 50 were detached and proceeded to rejoin their original groups in Task Force 38. Bogan's task group, including the

Intrepid, Cabot, and *Independence,* was detached from Mitscher's force and ordered to steam south with the battleships to furnish air cover as well as striking power. Mitscher was left with two groups of Task Force 38, those of Sherman and Davison, and ordered to continue the attack upon the Japanese carrier force. The Japanese force, incidentally, had two battleships, Mitscher none. Halsey took all the heavy ships south with him.

The moment the pursuit was broken off Halsey got off a reply to Nimitz's question, reporting that the fast battleships were with him, but that he was now headed south with them and Bogan's task group to go to the rescue of the Seventh Fleet. He also informed Kinkaid about the same time that he was coming to his assistance but that he could not be expected earlier than 0800 the following morning.

At 1034 the air search radar of the flagship *New Jersey* had picked up a contact with a "bogey" estimated at the time to consist of eight to ten planes at a distance of forty-nine miles to the northeast in the direction of the enemy force. These enemy planes orbited briefly in the vicinity of the Japanese carriers, then disappeared in the direction of Luzon. Since our airmen had been puzzled at catching the enemy carriers with their flight decks virtually bare, it was concluded that the enemy must be expecting his planes to rendezvous with the carriers after returning from Luzon, where they had spent the night. The "bogey" picked up in the neighborhood of the carrier force, therefore, was believed to have been the Japanese air group which had arrived too late and had been forced to return to land. Halsey so reported in his message to Nimitz. In newspaper accounts of the battle this incident was later elaborated into a story of a great group of enemy planes which flew out to a rendezvous within ammunition, only to find their carriers in flames or in a sinking condition and to be compelled to turn about and head back for land with empty gas tanks. A great many planes were said to have fallen into the sea.

As a matter of fact the Japanese were expecting no rendezvous with their air groups. There were no enemy carrier groups left. Ozawa sent his small group of remaining planes, not more than twenty, to Luzon during the morning. This may account for the radar contact with planes over the enemy carriers. Another radar contact was made at almost the same time on planes approaching from the southwest, but they were not intercepted and appeared to have turned back at a distance of about eighty miles from our carriers. Otherwise there is no basis for the story of the Japanese air group that arrived too late.

An immediate high-speed dash southward to the rescue of the distressed Seventh Fleet would have afforded some release of feeling to the frustrated Gun Club, but the battleships were denied even this satisfaction. Instead they were compelled to sweat out a long, grueling delay while task groups re-formed, scattered units rejoined, carriers recovered planes, and refueling was accomplished. About noon Task Force 34 was dissolved as a separate command and its remaining units formed a screen about the carrier task group of Admiral Bogan, who assumed tactical command. The entire force then slowed to sixteen knots while the battleships, milch cows of the fleet, topped off the destroyers.

At 1600, the fueling finally completed, Admiral Halsey organized a new task group composed of the fastest of the fast battleships, the *Iowa* and the *New Jersey*, three light cruisers, and eight destroyers, and departed at high speed to the southward to attempt the interception of the Japanese Central Force. Messages from Kinkaid had continued in an alarming vein, but one indicated that there were a number of enemy cripples off Samar Island and that others were retiring toward San Bernardino Strait. Rather than accommodate his pursuit to the speed of the slower battleships of the *North Carolina* and *South Dakota* classes, Halsey left four of his heavy ships with Bogan's carriers and headed for San Bernardino Strait, at a speed of twenty-eight knots, with two.

In the meantime Admiral Mitscher continued to launch strikes from his reduced carrier force against the enemy carriers, which at the time Halsey turned back had lost only one light carrier and suffered damage to other units. The detachment of Bogan's carriers and the diversion of McCain's reduced the air force to less than half that originally intended to be hurled at the Japanese carriers, while the withdrawal of Task Force 34 left Mitscher without the support of heavy ships.

Although there was need for haste, since the larger part of the enemy force was known to be retiring northward at high speed, more than three hours elapsed between the second and third strikes. Made up largely of planes that had returned from the dawn strike and had been refueled and rearmed, the third strike group consisted of some 160 planes about evenly distributed as to type. They took off shortly before noon and reached their targets about 1330.

Comdr. T. H. Winters, target coordinator for the strike, led the group northward, passed over the crippled ships without pausing, then pushed ahead with his wingman to locate the main body of undamaged ships. Winters found the *Zuikaku*, the light carrier *Zuiho*, one of the battleships, a cruiser, and three destroyers, all apparently undamaged, steaming northward at twenty knots. He reported his discovery to Mitscher, who ordered him to "sink the carriers," the undamaged ones.

After checking the speed and course of the targets, Winters ordered the *Lexington* and *Langley* groups to combine on the two carriers. This time there was a light film of cumulus clouds over the targets, of which the bombers took advantage in making their approach. Gaudily colored antiaircraft fire rose from the ships, together with white bursts of phosphorus with long tentacles, and a new shell that sent whirling spring-like brass wires into the air. One of the *Essex* planes flamed and went down under the barrage, while several others took hits.

Twelve *Lexington* bombers armed with half-ton armor-piercing bombs dived on the *Zuikaku* and planted several hits along her flight deck. These were followed shortly by nine *Essex* Helldivers similarly armed, which claimed additional hits on the large carrier. The results of the torpedo plane attack on the same ship were variously reported, though it seems probable that a few hits were scored. Large fires were started on the light carrier *Zuiho* by bombing attacks.

Winters directed the planes from Davison's carriers to delay their dives until he went down to investigate the results of the first attacks. Once under the cloud cover he found the *Zuikaku* burning, smoking heavily, almost dead in the water, and listing twenty degrees to port. While she seemed about done for, the light carrier *Zuiho* had extinguished her fires and was floating normally. Winters climbed back "upstairs," with shrapnel damage to his plane, and directed the *Franklin*, *Enterprise*, and *San Jacinto* planes, which had been awaiting their turn aloft, to attack the light carrier. The attack of these groups started up the fires on the *Zuiho* again, but as the planes left for their base she was still headed north under her own steam.

Waiting for a new strike group to arrive over the targets, Winters made a ten mile circle around the new cripples, during which he sighted a battleship and two cruisers between ten and twenty miles south of the main body headed north. He informed Mitscher of the contact and returned to the scene of the last air strike.

Winters arrived over the main enemy group just in time to witness the death throes of the *Zuikaku*. Mitscher's pilots had settled some long-standing scores with their strikes of the 25th, for the *Zuikaku* had earned an impressive name in the Pacific. She was the last survivor of the six Japanese carriers which attacked Pearl Harbor on the morning of December 7, 1941. During the three years that followed she drew blood from our airmen at Coral Sea, in two Solomons actions, Stewart Island and Santa Cruz, and again in the Battle of the Philippine Sea. She had a hand in the sinking of two of our finest carriers. The last of Japan's prewar first-line carriers and the last ship of CarDiv One, pride of the Imperial Fleet, the *Zuikaku* had run through her luck. At about 1430 Winters watched her roll over slowly to starboard and sink without any explosion. She was flying "a battle flag of tremendous size, perhaps fifty feet square," he said.

Thirty minutes later the first elements of the fourth strike of the day, a small one this time consisting of a series of minor attacks, arrived under the coordinating direction of Comdr. Malcolm T. Wordell. At about 1500 several half-ton bombs and two torpedoes finished off the crippled *Zuiho*, thus evening the score for the old *Hornet*, which the *Zuiho* had assisted in sinking in the Battle of Santa Cruz. Japanese destroyers maneuvered to recover survivors of the two carriers. There were now three carriers down and one to go—the cripple left far to the south and deserted by her screening vessels.

Believing the crippled carrier to have been abandoned, Admiral Sherman suggested that she be taken in tow as a "souvenir." Admiral Mitscher reluctantly rejected the suggestion in favor of his plan to send Rear Admiral Laurence T. DuBose north with a force of cruisers and destroyers to engage and sink the Japanese stragglers. By 1330 Mitscher believed the carrier groups had approached as close as they dared to the enemy, about sixty miles from the nearest targets, and ordered that the carriers proceed no farther. In a discussion over voice radio, DuBose said that he doubted that the cruisers "could handle the situation" to the north, for if the enemy "should be able to get those two battleships together, it is going to be tough on the cruisers. However," he added, "if you think it possible, we will do it."

A bit later Mitscher received word from Winters that the battleship and destroyer guarding the southernmost stragglers appeared to be retiring northward and deserting the cripples. He promptly ordered DuBose to proceed with his mission.

At 1429 the cruiser force, consisting of two light cruisers, two heavy cruisers, and twelve destroyers, stood toward the enemy at twenty-five knots on course 010°. DuBose's flag was in the *Santa Fe* (CL) and with him were the *Mobile* (CL), *Wichita* (CA), *New Orleans* (CA) and twelve destroyers of Squadron 50, of which Capt. Carlton R. Todd, in the *Porterfield*, was commander. DuBose was instructed to be prepared to make night torpedo attacks on any worthwhile targets and was assured of a combat air patrol of four planes during the daylight and two night fighters from the *Essex* to do his snooping. The cruisers launched six Kingfisher float planes to look for downed aviators, and Mitscher, who was always solicitous of his pilots "in the drink," specially ordered that the destroyers make sweeps in search of them.

In less than an hour the cruiser force was passing through heavy oil slicks, which indicated that they were in combat areas. The destroyer *Cotten*, with the aid of the planes, located two aviators on rafts and picked them up in good condition. The *Callaghan* and the *C. K. Bronson* later recovered two more pilots.

The ubiquitous Comdr. Winters, returning to base about 1600 after an eventful mission, sighted the friendly cruisers coming over the horizon about twenty miles to the south. He turned and circled above the Japanese light carrier lying dead in the water, called to the cruisers giving them a bearing, and assured them that no battleships were nosing about. The cruisers turned to an approach course and at 1625 the heavy cruisers *Wichita* and *New Orleans* opened fire with their 8-inch guns, range 20,000 yards. The *Santa Fe* and *Mobile* also opened when the range had closed to 15,000 yards. The carrier *Chitose*, which had been firing at Winters, turned her guns on the cruisers. Her shot fell far short.

By 1640 the *Chitose* was a mass of flames above which towered a dense column of black smoke. DuBose then ordered all ships except the *New Orleans* to cease firing and directed his starboard destroyer column to go in and finish off the target with a few torpedoes. The destroyers headed in for the kill. At 1647, however, the *Chitose* commenced to roll over to port, lay momentarily on her side, and then sank before the destroyers could execute their attack. Numbers of survivors were seen to swarm over her sides before she went down, but the destroyers were refused permission to pick them up. The force formed up and headed northward for what promised to be good hunting.

Comdr. Winters returned at last to his base with the satisfaction of being the only American airman to witness the sinking of three Japanese carriers within two hours. The *Chitose* was the last of Ozawa's flat-tops.

There was time left for one more air strike before sundown, provided it was a fast one. Of the ships originally sighted in Ozawa's Northern Force there now remained afloat the two 30,000-ton battleships, *Ise* and *Hyuga*, both apparently in an excellent state of repair; three light cruisers, the *Oyodo* (flying Ozawa's flag), the *Isuzu* and the *Tama*, one or both of which were probably damaged; and some eight destroyers. Pilots consistently reported heavy cruisers attacked, but this was one of their many errors of identification.*

The fifth and final air strike of the battle overlapped and merged with the light fourth strike, and both were coordinated by Comdr. Wordell, who remained over the targets from 1500 until after 1800. Of the ninety-six planes launched a little after 1600 from the *Essex, Lexington, Langley* and *Enterprise*, fifty-two were fighters armed with half-ton and quarter-ton bombs. Ten of the thirteen Avengers carried one-ton general purpose bombs instead of torpedoes. For most of the pilots this was the fag end of two days of unprecedented air battles, during which some of them had participated in strikes on three Japanese fleets in as many different seas. They were bent on making a kill this time, but many of them were taking the experience on their nerves' ends.

Wordell was out to get the battleships and directed the great bulk of the strike against those two targets now in different groups separated by about ten miles. Our airmen attacked with their usual spirit, diving repeatedly into intense antiaircraft fire and sustaining several casualties, some of them fatal. But in the light of sober after-knowledge of what was actually accomplished it seems pointless to detail the "confirmed hits" and claims of the pilots. The air group of one carrier alone claimed thirteen direct hits on one battleship. A careful

---

* Apparently pilots mistook the light cruisers for heavy cruisers and large *Terutsuki*-class destroyers for the light cruisers.

tabulation of hits scored on the two heavy ships during all the strikes of the day, which attempted to eliminate duplication of claims, arrived at the figure of twenty-two direct hits on one battleship, fifteen on the other. Ten of these were torpedo hits. Near misses were not counted. The conclusion reached by one air group commander would be familiar to anyone who followed the naval air war: "Japanese war ships," he said, "can absorb an incredible amount of punishment before sinking."

From the best Japanese sources available after the war it is learned that only one direct hit was made on the *Hyuza* and none on her sister ship. Near misses damaged the blisters of the *Ise*, but no direct hits were made on her. Captain Ohmae, Chief of Staff to Ozawa, inspected both ships after their return from the battle and reported "very slight" damage which "did not hamper navigation." "I was witnessing the bombing," said Ohmae. "I thought that the bombing of the afternoon wasn't so efficient." The case of the *Ise* and *Hyuga* probably explains a good deal about the alleged "toughness" of Japanese warships.

Other targets were attacked, apparently with some effect. Eight fighters from the *Enterprise* armed with half-ton armor-piercing bombs claimed hits on a light cruiser, but probably left her less "hopelessly damaged" than was reported. *Langley* fighters strafed several destroyers, one of which was said to have "disappeared" after the attack and possibly sank as a result of the strafing, although it was not actually seen to sink. When Wordell left the area about 1800 the surviving enemy ships were strung out in scattered groups along a line stretching forty-five miles in a northeasterly direction.

After watching the *Chitose* go down about 1700, Admiral DuBose recovered his float planes, sent two "Black Chickens" (night planes) northward to scout for further targets, and took a northerly course with his cruiser force. Wordell reported the bearings of his next likely targets, one bearing 330° at twenty-five miles and a group of three bearing 325° at thirty-five miles. DuBose decided to pass up the single and head for the group. These ships were reported by the night planes to be two destroyers and a light cruiser, the latter stopped and the former circling. They were probably recovering survivors.

Half an hour after sunset the flagship *Santa Fe* picked up the targets on her radar at a distance of seventeen miles. One of the "pips" on the screen was soon observed to be pulling away to the northward. At 1851 DuBose gave the order "commence firing," light cruisers on the nearer targets, heavy cruisers on the farthest one. It had grown dark by this time and nothing could be seen in the direction of the enemy until one of the nearer vessels began to return our fire. The farthest target, on which the *Wichita* was firing, worked up a speed of thirty knots in about ten minutes after fire was opened and by 1906 had pulled out of the range. DuBose decided not to give chase and disperse his force, but to concentrate on the two remaining targets.

Two direct hits were seen on the largest of the enemy ships at 1911, after which fires broke out, flamed a few minutes, then died down. By this time our advanced ships were within six miles of their target and firing steadily. The third ship was pulling away to the northward—out of range. Working up rapidly to a speed of twenty-six knots, the ship under fire maneuvered to dodge salvos. The *Mobile* heard shells passing overhead and saw splashes near by. Twice the target maneuvered to gain position for a torpedo attack, and each time DuBose ordered changes of course, evasive maneuvers which slowed up the pursuit. An explosion was seen on the enemy ship and another fire flamed up briefly a few minutes, but she continued northward at high speed. The action settled down to a long chase. It was taking an unconscionable amount of time to sink one destroyer.

At 1929 three destroyers, the *Cogswell, Ingersoll,* and *Caperton,* started to close for a torpedo attack while the cruisers took the target under slow fire to cover their approach. At 2012, after the enemy had slowed down, the three destroyers fired a half salvo of torpedoes each at a range of about 7,000 yards and opened fire with their 5-inch guns. The enemy returned fire. At the time when the torpedoes were expected to reach the target flashes were seen, and later a dull explosion was heard. While this may have indicated hits, the evidence is not conclusive. Swathed in smoke and slowed to seventeen, then to ten knots, the enemy nevertheless continued to fire for about twenty minutes. The cruisers soon had him under fire at short range, and the *Santa Fe* illuminated him brilliantly with star shells. Identification was doubtful at the time, but later evidence indicates that the ship was a 2,400-ton *Terutsuki*-class destroyer.

"Request you put a fish in him," said DuBose to Capt. Todd. The *Porterfield* headed in for the target at 2057.

"He has gone down. We were cheated," reported the destroyer two minutes later.

"It breaks our heart," replied the admiral.

During the latter part of this action DuBose's two Black Chickens had been conducting a search for further targets in the immediate vicinity, and to the northward. They reported that the nearest Japanese ships were forty-six miles north of DuBose, steaming northward at twenty-two knots. Beyond them was another enemy group, also retiring, at twenty knots. The two ships originally with the sunken destroyer could not be located. After estimating the time required to intercept the nearest targets at a speed of thirty knots, DuBose decided that in view of the rendezvous with Mitscher, now well to the south, and the necessity of refueling all of his destroyers on the following day, he had best not attempt the long chase. A further consideration *may* have been the presence of Japanese battleships to the northward. At 2150 the destroyers and cruisers formed up and headed southeast for a rendez-vous with the carriers the following morning.

This closed the surface phase of the Battle off Cape Engaño. The air phase had ended with the approach of darkness. There remained only the subsurface phase—the opportunity for which the "Wolf Packs" were waiting.

Since the brilliant action in Palawan Passage on the 23rd, which cost the Japanese two heavy cruisers and a third one crippled and put out of action, our submarines had kept well clear of the combat areas, impatiently awaiting their turn to strike the enemy during his retirement. Early on the morning of the 25th Vice Admiral Charles A. Lockwood, Jr., Commander Submarines Pacific, had ordered seventeen submarines to take up patrol positions which would cover all probable escape routes. Seven pigboats were instructed to patrol Luzon Strait, three were off the northeast tip of Formosa, one off the northwest tip, and two fresh wolf packs, "Roach's Raiders" and "Clarey's Crushers," each with three submarines, were ordered to proceed westward at best speed to take up stations northeast of Luzon in the probable retirement track of the Japanese Northern Force. Lockwood assured them that theirs was "the chance of a lifetime," and told them to "Go get 'em."

Comdr. John P. Roach's Raiders, the *Haddock, Tuna,* and *Halibut,* heard distant explosions early in the afternoon and by 1700 were near enough to the enemy to listen in over high-frequency radio to the excited conversation between our pilots during the final air strike. They were tantalized by hearing Comdr. Wordell's description of the targets, "one battleship, two cruisers," and heard one pilot say, "Let's get going and get this over with." There followed the sound of a plane going into a power dive, then, "Yippee! I got a battleship!" "Forget the battleship. Get the cruiser."

Lt. Comdr. Ignatius J. Galantin of the *Halibut* began to be concerned lest the airmen deprive him of all targets. His concern was dispelled at 1742 by the appearance of the pagoda mast of a Japanese battleship on the horizon at a range of about fifteen miles. At least he thought it was a battleship. He waited until he sighted two escorting vessels, then dived for his approach. At 1843 he fired six torpedoes from his forward tubes at a range of 3,400 yards. The battleship made a last minute zig. Four minutes after firing came the first explosion, then in succession four more. From below the surface the crew listened intently to many lesser explosions, "similar to a ship breaking up." Only two sets of screws could be heard topside, and these alternately stopped and started as if ships were picking up survivors. The expected depth charges were not heard.

At 1950 the *Halibut* surfaced. A brilliant half moon made visibility excellent. Galantin and a lookout sighted "a very large mound" in the direction from which the explosions had come, presumably the hull of a capsized ship, since there was no superstructure. As the *Halibut* cautiously approached, the hull disappeared from view and faded from the radar screen. The submarine commander's inclination was to imitate the cry of the pilot, "Yippee, I got a battleship." Official sources, however, credited him with no kills.

A few miles away Comdr. Roach in the *Haddock* watched gun flashes and star shells from the surface action of DuBose's cruisers. He "decided not to go into this melee until our forces quit, then try to catch them on the way home." At 2135 he watched helplessly while two small vessels, probably the ones which escaped from DuBose, pulled out of his range. "Disappointment was a foot thick on this ship," he reported.

Some sixty miles farther to the northeast Comdr. Bernard A. Clarey, with the *Jalleo*, *Atule*, and *Pintado*, received the contact report from Roach's group and worked into position for an interception. The *Jalleo*, Lt. Comdr. Joseph B. Icenhower, picked up two targets by radar and, calling the *Pintado* to join her, dived to periscope depth at 2242. After a good look at close range in the moonlight, Icenhower identified his target as a light cruiser. When the range closed to 1,200 yards he fired three torpedoes from his bow tubes. All three missed. He then swung left for a stern shot and at 2305 let go with four torpedoes at a range of 700 yards. He watched the results through his periscope. The first hit was about amidships, the second about at the aftermast, and the third between the bow and the bridge. All were accompanied by brilliant flashes and smoke which enveloped the ship in a black pall. The *Jalleo* went down to 150 feet to reload. When she surfaced thirty minutes later there was nothing in sight.

The *Pintado* arrived on the scene in time to witness the explosions and closed to be in position to attack if the ship escaped the *Jalleo*. No further torpedoes were required, however, for the cruiser sank in plain sight of the *Pintado* at 2310. The ship was the light cruiser *Tama*.

In the meantime at about 1930 Admiral Ozawa received word aboard the *Oyoda* from the destroyer under attack by DuBose that an American force consisting of two battleships with cruisers and destroyers were headed north. Believing that he had adequate strength left to cope with such a force, Ozawa immediately ordered his surviving ships to reverse course and close the pursuing force for a torpedo attack. At that time he still had two battleships, at least one light cruiser in good shape, and six or more destroyers, a force that would probably have been capable of dealing with DuBose's cruisers and destroyers.

Considering the overwhelming superiority of gun power with which the Third Fleet steamed north the previous night to annihilate Ozawa's force, the battle had suddenly taken an ironic turn in its closing phase. The pursuer had now become the pursued, the decoy the aggressor, and though they did not make the assumption, it was the Japanese and not the Americans who had the superior gun power in the end. Ozawa continued to steam south for about two hours after reversing course. DuBose had not begun his retirement to the southeast until 2150. The probable track of the two forces suggests that the Japanese did not miss an interception by much although neither they nor the Americans were aware of the fact. The Battle off Cape Engaño might have had a less fortunate ending. Failing to make contact, Ozawa finally turned north and continued his retirement.

Radar search, air reconnaissance, and radio communication have not eliminated from naval warfare two of its oldest characteristics—confusion and misapprehension. Both were present on each side of the Battle off Cape Engaño. Our overestimation of the enemy force, both its gun power and air power, was matched by the enemy's underestimation of our strength. A few of the numerous ironies of the Third Fleet strategy have been suggested. The most ironical plight, however, was that in which Admiral Ozawa found himself. For while his luring mission had succeeded beyond his expectation, the wholesale sacrifice of ships which it entailed proved in the end to have been futile for the simple reason that he was completely unable to put through to Kurita the report that he had succeeded in diverting the Third Fleet northward.

It is not known why a sixteenth-century Spaniard should have named as he did the obscure point of land from which this battle took its name. *Engaño* is a Spanish word translated variously as "mistake, deception, lure, hoax, misunderstanding, misapprehension, misconception"—in about that order of preference.

V

THE BATTLE OFF SAMAR

Dawn of the 25th found the three escort carrier groups of the Seventh Fleet moving slowly westward at fourteen knots from their assigned night stations seaward into positions closer to Leyte Gulf. The day's missions, which they started launching at earliest dawn, included not only the routine combat and antisubmarine patrols for their own ships and those in the gulf, but air support and spotting missions for the troops ashore as well as strikes against enemy ships retiring from the battle of Surigao Strait. It promised to be an active day, with several long-distance flights scheduled, and perhaps for that reason the northernmost of the three CVE groups moved in closer to land than usual.

Admiral Kinkaid had ordered two searches of the sea area between San Bernardino Strait and the escort carriers, one by night and one at dawn. By a fateful miscarriage in operations, however, both searches proved ineffective. Nothing was heard from the Black Cats sent up to the Strait at night, and the dawn search assigned the CVE *Ommaney Bay* of the southernmost group was not launched until the sun was more than half an hour high and the usefulness of the search was already lost.

The fact was that attention was naturally focused on exciting events to the southward in Surigao Strait. By interception of messages some of the CVE's had been able to follow the course of the battle. Anticipating an opportunity for air strikes on cripples the following morning, Kinkaid had ordered all carriers of the Middle Group to be prepared at dawn to launch strike groups armed with torpedoes and semi-armor-piercing bombs on short notice. Officers and men had worked hard during the night to have everything in readiness.

153

As for the Japanese Central Force, it was known to have been engaged by Third Fleet planes during the daylight hours of the 24th. The commander of the escort carrier groups, Rear Admiral Thomas L. Sprague, like Kinkaid, assumed that the strait was still guarded. Halsey's reply to Kinkaid's message asking if the strait were guarded arrived after that question had been answered by evidence of a more concrete nature. This was the chain of circumstance, delay, and misapprehension that led to the situation of the escort carriers at dawn of the 25th. At that time Admiral Thomas Sprague and the other group commanders assumed that not only the battle line of the Third Fleet, but the Philippine Islands as well lay between them and the Japanese fleet.

The Northern CVE Group, with six carriers, three destroyers, and four destroyer escorts, had reached a position some fifty miles east of Samar and about halfway up the coast of the island. The ships were in a circular formation, zigzagging on a northerly course at fourteen knots. A combat air patrol of twelve fighters had been launched at 0530 and within the next half hour a support group of four torpedo planes and in addition the local combat and antisubmarine patrols were dispatched to their target areas. These routine tasks squared away, ships' companies had no reason to look forward to anything more exciting than a possible air raid. By 0630 most of the ships had ended their morning alert and secured from general quarters.

At sunrise the sea off Samar was calm under a gentle wind of six to ten knots blowing from a northeasterly direction. The sky was about three-tenths overcast with cumulus clouds and visibility was generally good, but spotty because of considerable haziness and scattered rain squalls in the vicinity.

At 0637 a radioman on the flagship *Fanshaw Bay* intercepted Japanese conversation on the interfighter director net, but this was attributed to a renewed enemy attempt to "jam" our circuit and little was thought of it. Eight minutes later, however, lookouts sighted antiaircraft bursts above the horizon to the northwest at a distance of about twenty miles, and almost simultaneously Combat Information Center of the flagship made radar contact with an unidentified surface craft bearing 292°, distance eighteen and one-half miles. A change of course to the southwest, 220°, was at once ordered.

Then at 0647 came an excited and "almost unintelligible" transmission from an antisubmarine plane of the *Kadashan Bay* of the Middle Group, which was then about twenty miles southeast of the Northern Group, reporting to his base that he had sighted the Japanese fleet and was under fire. A local plane from the *St. Lo* reported that the force consisted of battleships, cruisers, and destroyers bearing 340°, distance about twenty miles from the Northern Group. Then through a long glass a signalman aboard the *Kitkun Bay* watched in dismay as the pagoda masts of Japanese battleships and cruisers loomed slowly above the horizon.

As the men ran to their battle stations a series of orders came over voice radio in quick succession from Admiral Sprague.* First was a change of course to 90°, due east, then, "Launch all planes as soon as possible," next, "Speed 16," then everything possible. The new course brought the carriers neither full into the wind nor into a full retirement course away from the enemy, but it was intended to bring them close enough to the northeasterly wind to permit the slow vessels to launch planes and at the same time avoid any further closing of the enemy line than was necessary. Planes were soon roaring off the flight decks armed with whatever they had aboard at the time.

At 0658, about five minutes after the enemy ships came into sight and while they were still hull-down on the horizon, lookouts saw the expected flashes from their direction and waited for the first splashes. The spotting salvo of heavy-caliber shells, which marked the beginning of the Battle off Samar, fell near the center of our formation. Admiral Kurita had opened fire from the *Yamato* at a range of more than fifteen miles. It was

---

* Rear Admiral C. A. F. Sprague in command of the Northern Group. To avoid confusion with the commander of the three CVE groups, Rear Admiral Thomas Sprague, the latter's full name will be given when he is referred to hereafter.

the first time in naval history that American ships had been brought under fire by 18-inch guns.

The opening salvo was followed immediately by another which fell about 300 yards off the starboard bow of the *White Plains* just as that carrier was beginning to launch aircraft. She was then straddled repeatedly by yellow, red, green, and blue splashes, dye-marked shells of heavy caliber. At 0704 splash water whipped across the bridge of the *White Plains* from another straddle. "This salvo measured the carriers as calipers," reported Capt. Sullivan, "diagonally from the port quarter to the starboard bow, four shells dropping microscopically close forward and two aft." This sample of shooting was as excellent as any gunnery officer could demand. Exploding below the surface, one shell shook and twisted the vessel violently, throwing men from their feet, damaging the starboard engine room, and knocking out all electrical power and steering control for several minutes. One fighter on the flight deck jumped its chock and chewed about three feet out of the wing of another fighter with its propeller. Planes continued to take off under fire, however, and the ship began making thick, black funnel smoke immediately after the last salvo bracketed the vessel.

Apparently writing the *White Plains* off after she started making smoke, the Japanese shifted fire to the *St. Lo*, which was also on the northern and more exposed side of our formation. One near miss on her port side splashed water on the catwalk and flight deck. Several bursts of shrapnel scattered fragments over the ship and caused some casualties. The enemy was closing rapidly and increasing his accuracy of fire.

"At this point," wrote Admiral Sprague, "it did not appear that any of our ships could survive another five minutes of the heavy-caliber fire being received, and some counteraction was urgently and immediately required. The task unit was surrounded by the ultimate of desperate circumstances." He first ordered the seven screening vessels to lay a smoke screen, and soon the destroyers and the DE's were running long curtains of black funnel and white chemical smoke astern of the formation. The carriers contributed their own heavy funnel smoke to the screen, making a very effective concealment.

The position in which the escort carriers found themselves was entirely unique in the Pacific War. Never before, even in the early days of unequal struggle, had American naval forces been surprised and brought to action by a major enemy fleet capable of greatly superior speed and fire power. Unwarned, the CVE's were caught within range of enemy guns, steaming on an almost head-on course toward a fleet that was apparently capable of destroying them in a few minutes. No comfort was derived from the assumption that units of the Japanese force were able to make a speed of thirty knots, while the jeep carriers were not able at that time to push much beyond seventeen knots.

Of all the types of fighting ships in the huge Pacific fleet the CVE's or "jeep carriers" would doubtless have been the last deliberately chosen to fight the heaviest surface battle of the war. They were thin-skinned merchantmen with flight decks, those of the Kaiser class, produced in great numbers in an emergency and never intended to stand off battleships. They were limited in fire power, lacking in the protective features of larger ships, and they did not even have the speed that is the last defense of the weak. Their complement of planes, the only effective defense they had, was definitely limited, and they could not launch and recover them with the ease of the big CV's.

Ground support work was the specialty of the air squadrons of the CVE's, and many of their pilots had never before engaged a surface fighting ship or an enemy plane. The bomb and torpedo allowances of the escort carriers were tailored to fit the special requirements of ground support missions in which they were engaged. Attack upon major Japanese warships was definitely not among the missions contemplated. The carriers were limited to an allowance of nine to twelve torpedoes to the ship and a bomb supply that had been greatly reduced by intensive operations.

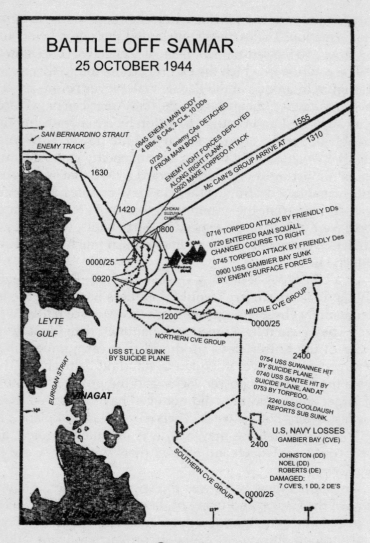

CHART 6.

Seven days of close support flying had brought on symptoms of nervous fatigue among the pilots that were familiar to flight surgeons—sleeplessness, loss of appetite, and bungled landings. Personnel in the ships' air departments, who had been putting in an average of seventeen hours a day for the past week, were also feeling the strain.

Two of the jeep carriers, one of them damaged by a bomb, were detached on the 24th. The remaining sixteen were organized in a Southern Group, a Middle Group, and a Northern Group, all three under the command of Rear Admiral Thomas L. Sprague, whose flag was in the *Sangamon* and who also commanded Carrier Division 22 and the Southern Group of which it was a part. This group was composed of the *Sangamon, Suwannee, Santee,* and *Petrof Bay,* the first three of which were converted tankers, much larger than the Kaiser-class CVE's. They were screened by three destroyers and three destroyer escorts. The Middle Group under the command of Rear Admiral Felix B. Stump was made up of his own Carrier Division 24, *Natoma Bay* (F) and *Manila Bay,* and Carrier Division 27, Rear Admiral William D. Sample in the *Marcus Island* with the *Kadashan Bay, Savo Island,* and *Ommaney Bay,* with three destroyers and four destroyer escorts. The organization of the Northern Group, which was fated to play a more prominent role than the other two, is given in detail:

NORTHERN GROUP, REAR ADMIRAL C. A. F. SPRAGUE

CARRIER DIVISION 25, ADMIRAL SPRAGUE

Fanshaw Bay (F), Capt. Douglass P. Johnson
Saint Lo, Capt. Francis J. McKenna
White Plains, Capt. Dennis J. Sullivan
Kalinin Bay, Capt. Thomas B. Williamson

CARRIER DIVISION 26, REAR ADMIRAL RALPH A. OFSTIE

Kitkun Bay (F), Capt. John P. Whitney
Gambier Bay, Capt. W. V. R. Vieweg

SCREEN COMDR. WILLIAM D. THOMAS

Hoel (DD) (F), Comdr. Leon S. Kintberger
Heermann (DD), Lt. Comdr. Amos T. Hathaway
Johnston (DD), Comdr. Ernest E. Evans
Dennis (DE), Lieut. Samuel Hansen
John C. Butler (DE), Lt. Comdr. John E. Pace
Raymond (DE), Lt. Comdr. A. F. Beyer, Jr.
Samuel B. Roberts (DE), Lt. Comdr. Robert W. Copeland

On the morning of the 25th, the three groups were spread out over an area of 120 miles off the gulf with the Southern

Group ninety miles southeast of Suluan Island at the entrance to the gulf, the Middle Group fifty miles northeast, and the Northern Group sixty miles north-northeast of Suluan.

Shortly after the Japanese opened fire on the Northern Group, Sprague broadcast an urgent appeal for help, giving in plain language his position and the bearing and distance of the enemy. This message reached Admiral Kinkaid's flagship *Wasatch* in Leyte Gulf at about 0724 and constituted his first information of the presence of the Japanese fleet on the eastern side of the Philippines. Assuming from his interpretation of Halsey's dispatches that a battleship force was being left to guard San Bernardino Strait, but lacking specific information on that all-important question, Kinkaid sent a dispatch at about 0410 asking Halsey where his heavy ships were. It was not received until 0648. Some time later Kinkaid received Halsey's reply saying that Task Force 34 was not guarding the strait. Within fifteen minutes after he received Sprague's alarming news, Kinkaid sent three dispatches to Halsey requesting immediate aid.

Kinkaid's anxiety was not only for his CVE's under fire but for the entire Seventh Fleet, the transports, the Allied beachhead, and the land forces on Leyte. While part of the amphibious shipping had been pulled out, many vulnerable targets remained. From the position reported by Sprague, the Japanese fleet was within three hours' steaming of the entrance to Leyte Gulf. In spite of the large fleet under his command, Admiral Kinkaid was not prepared at the time to move to the support of the carriers, and it was doubtful that he could put up an effective defense of the Gulf. His cruisers and the majority of his destroyers were deep in Surigao Strait finishing off cripples after the night battle and pursuing enemy ships. The night gunnery battle on top of five days of bombardment had left the ammunition supply of all ships dangerously low and all but exhausted the torpedoes of the destroyers. Many ships were in desperate need of fuel. Even if the old battleships could be rushed into position, they were at a disadvantage of five to six knots in an engagement with the battleships of the Japanese Central Force. The heavier enemy ships could probably keep at long range, outmaneuver our old battleships, and quickly exhaust their limited supply of ammunition.

Regardless of these numerous disadvantages Kinkaid ordered Oldendorf to organize a striking force of three battleships, the *Tennessee, California,* and *Pennsylvania,* the cruisers *Louisville* (F), *Portland, Minneapolis, Nashville,* and the Australian *Shropshire* and Destroyer Squadrons 21 and 56. Ordered to make rendezvous at the eastern entrance to the gulf, these ships began a desperate scramble for fuel and ammunition.

At about the same time, the commander of the support aircraft of the Seventh Fleet ordered a rendezvous over the Leyte area of all aircraft from the CVE's that were not at that time moving against enemy ships escaping from the Battle of Surigao Strait. Also the strikes which had been launched from the carriers and were headed for Leyte were ordered back to their groups to lend support to the CVE's under attack. The Middle and Southern Groups were instructed to launch all available aircraft and send them north.

In the meanwhile the enemy was pursuing his attack on the carriers vigorously and with heavy volume of fire. As long as the CVE's maintained their easterly course, which was necessitated by wind conditions in launching planes, they were on a gradually converging course with the enemy. By 0721 the enemy battle line had closed to less than 25,000 yards. It was at about that time that the carriers plunged gratefully into the cover of a heavy rain squall that reduced visibility to half a mile or less and the ceiling to 500 feet. As soon as they were under cover of the squall the formation turned right to a southerly course, still zigzagging to avoid enemy fire. As visibility decreased Japanese salvos fell off markedly and there were only a few splashes near the ships during the ten or fifteen minutes that the squall lasted. That rain was an important piece of luck.

It is said that radar and air reconnaissance have made surprise at sea a thing of the past. But apparently the Japanese were as surprised by the sight of our masts as we were at the sight of theirs. While the CVE groups had been operating east of Leyte and Samar for a week and had been under attack by enemy planes, it seems that the attacks were made by land-based planes and that Kurita had not been informed about the escort carriers. "We had no information of the presence of your task force east of Samar," said Kurita's Chief of Staff, Admiral Koyanagi. "We were quite taken aback when we met your force off Samar on the morning of the 25th, and some people even said they were Japanese carriers." Although scouting planes were launched from the ships, they seem to have returned no valuable information, and the Japanese greatly overestimated the strength of the force under attack. They took the force for a fast carrier group of the Third Fleet. Koyanagi thought that it was "composed of five or six carriers, a few battleships, and a few cruisers." He himself saw no battleships, but "there were those who said they saw battleships." "We could not see from the *Yamato* to the carriers. The smoke was very effective."

At the time contact was made Kurita's force was on a southwesterly course (200°) with the battleships *Yamato, Nagato, Haruna,* and *Kongo* in column in the middle of the formation, a column of four heavy cruisers at a distance of about two miles on the left flank, and on the right flank at about the same distance another column of two heavy cruisers. A screen of six or eight destroyers led by the light cruiser *Noshiro* was deployed about 15,000 yards off the starboard bow of the right flank and another of four destroyers and the light cruiser *Yahagi* was in a similar position off the port bow of the left flank. It was a formidable force of twenty-two warships. "We planned to first cripple the carriers . . . and then to mow down the entire task force," wrote Kurita in his action report. He quoted a Japanese slogan: "A sighted enemy is the equivalent of a dead enemy."

Kurita's first maneuver was a change of course to an easterly direction. "I altered course to 110°," he said, "in order to come up-wind of your formation. The resultant formation

was in line ahead, all units. . . . The intention was to reduce
the range, keeping to the windward of the American forces."
The maneuver would also prevent our force from escaping
seaward, hamper the launching of attack planes by preventing the carriers from heading into the northeasterly wind, and
enable the Japanese line to turn our flank and force Sprague's
formation to head in the direction of Leyte, for which Kurita
was bound. "Our first intention was to fight to the last with
the ships; then if we won to go on into the Bay [Leyte Gulf],"
said Koyanagi. There they intended to destroy our transports
and retire through Surigao Strait.

When our ships began to emerge from the rain squall they
could see through rifts in the smoke screen that the main
enemy force had closed to less than 25,000 yards. The carriers were now fleeing southward at about seventeen knots,
their best speed. As the enemy gained upon them he began to
advance heavy cruisers of the *Tone* class at high speed toward
their left flank and to deploy a column of destroyers to the
right flank, while the battleships and other cruisers closed
on an intermediate course astern at a lower speed. With
their superior speed, the flanking movements would soon be
able to pull abeam and, if they desired, encircle the carriers
and turn them back into the jaws of the Japanese battle line.
While no serious damage had yet been done by enemy gunfire, salvo splashes from the cruisers were again creeping up
on the carriers to the rear and some of the screening vessels
had been hit.

At this point, about 0740, Admiral Sprague ordered the
seven vessels of his screen to deliver a torpedo attack. The three
new flush-deck destroyers, *Hoel*, *Heermann*, and *Johnston*, and
the four smaller destroyer escorts, *Dennis*, *Butler*, *Raymond*,
and *Roberts*, were scattered astern and abeam the carrier formation laying smoke between it and the enemy. The torpedo
action that followed, fought in and out of thick black and
white smoke and through blinding rain squalls, had many of
the aspects of a night battle. Although the low visibility was a
welcome protection from enemy fire, it made the coordination

of attacks very difficult and left tactical control largely in the hands of individual skippers, who often had all they could do to avoid collision with each other. The engagement soon turned into a melee in which our vessels steamed in and out of the enemy's formation and between his columns, dealing out and taking blows on all sides. Loss of the records of the ships that were sunk adds to the difficulty of picturing the action.

Comdr. Thomas, commander of, the screening group, in the *Hoel,* ordered the destroyers to go in for the first torpedo attack and the slower destroyer escorts to follow in their smoke for the second. Heading north toward the Japanese line, Lt. Comdr. Copeland of the *Roberts* told all hands over the bull horn that this would be "a fight against overwhelming odds from which survival could not be expected." That was a substantially accurate estimate of the prospects of the seven attacking ships. None of their skippers could have been unaware of this.

The destroyer *Johnston* anticipated by several minutes the order for a torpedo attack. Finding himself within 18,000 yards of a heavy cruiser, probably the *Chikuma,* which was firing on our ships, Comdr. Evans opened fire with his 5-inch guns and was immediately straddled by a salvo from the enemy. Running in alone under fire, her guns blazing, the *Johnston* fired more than 200 rounds in rapid salvos and believed that she scored many hits on the heavy cruiser. At a range of about 10,000 yards the destroyer launched a salvo of ten torpedoes, then wheeled to retire into a heavy smoke screen. The smoke obscured the target, but underwater explosions were heard that indicated probable hits, and when next seen the cruiser was ablaze in her after part.

As she emerged from the smoke at about 0730, the *Johnston* took her first hits, three projectiles of a major caliber, followed quickly by three 6-inch shells. One of the heavy shells exploded in the after engine room, knocking it out. At the same time the three 5-inch guns aft, the steering engine, and the gyro compass were all put out of commission, and the ship's speed was reduced by about half. Fortunately a rain squall provided ten minutes of respite immediately after she was hit and enabled her to make the most needed repairs and start the rescue of wounded. While she was still under the squall her radar was repaired and targets appeared on the screen to both sides of the ship. On one side the leading Japanese destroyer was at once taken under fire by all remaining guns; then fire was shifted to the leading ship of a column of cruisers closing on the opposite side. Approximately a hundred rounds were fired at these targets, though they were not actually seen at any time.

Steered manually from aft, the *Johnston* not only managed to remain afloat for two more hours but continued to fight as violent an action as was ever fought by a ship of her class. When the order for a concerted torpedo attack was received, her skipper, Comdr. Evans, was wounded in several places, his ship was severely damaged, her speed reduced, and all her torpedoes expended. Evans nevertheless maneuvered for position to give fire support to the two other destroyers while they ran in for a torpedo attack.

Steaming through the carrier formation at high speed to join up for the attack, the *Heermann* narrowly avoided a collision with the *Roberts* and had to back her engines emergency full speed to miss the *Hoel*. The destroyers joined up and headed north to attack. Observing that "the tactical situation required the stopping of at least two columns of enemy ships," Comdr. Kintberger of the *Hoel* ordered only a half salvo of torpedoes fired at his first target, the leading ship of the battle line. At a range of 14,000 yards the *Hoel* opened with her 5-inch guns on the leading battleship and almost immediately took the first of the scores of hits she sustained before going down. Some of the first shells struck the bridge and main battery director, knocking out much radar equipment and all voice radio communications. The destroyer was still taking one direct hit after another in various parts when at a range of 9,000 yards she launched a half salvo of torpedoes at her battleship target.

She was unable to observe the results, for immediately. after firing she was struck a series of shattering blows. Her after fireroom and engine room took 8-inch shells from the port side, and her port engine was put out of commission by a direct hit on the after turbine. Her No. 3 gun was untenable because of steam escaping from the engine room and a fire in the handling room; half of the barrel of No. 4 gun was shot off by a direct hit, and No. 5 gun was frozen in train by a near miss. Casualties were very high. The only reason the *Hoel* kept afloat as long as she did was the fact that the enemy was using armor-piercing shells that for the most part passed through the thin plates of her hull without exploding.

While the *Hoel* was turning away from her torpedo attack, her rudder jammed right and the vessel came slowly around, heading for the battleship that had been her target. Within two minutes this perilous course was corrected by shifting to hand steering with the trick wheel in the steering engine room. Using one engine and steering by hand, the crippled destroyer then gained position for an attack upon the cruiser column on her other side. At a range of about 6,000 yards she launched her remaining half salvo with manual train at the leading heavy cruiser. All torpedoes ran "hot, straight, and normal," and at the end of the scheduled run, tall columns of water were reported to have risen from the side of the cruiser.

Comdr. Hathaway of the *Heermann*, the third destroyer, reversed the order of the *Hoel*'s targets, attacking the cruiser column first and the battle line second. During his approach he fired 125 rounds from his main battery at a *Tone*-class cruiser, then at 0754 launched seven torpedoes at a range of 9,000 yards. While the launching was in progress the ship's gunnery officer sighted the battleship *Kongo* on his port bow followed by three other battleships. Course was immediately changed and gunfire shifted to the leading ship in the column. The way in which the *Heermann*'s guns raked the superstructure of her target was pronounced by Hathaway "a joy to behold." Although the battleship returned her fire with both main and broadside batteries, the destroyer suffered only minor damage during her approach, possibly because of the effectiveness of her gunfire. She steamed on through towering splashes until the range had closed to a mere 4,400 yards, then fired her three remaining torpedoes. The gunnery officer believed he scored one torpedo hit on the starboard quarter of the *Kongo* under her No. 4 gun turret, but since the depth setting of the torpedoes had been only six feet and there had been no time to change it, the effectiveness could hardly have been great. The action was at once broken off as the ships entered a blinding rain squall.

The slower destroyer escorts were also prevented by low visibility from coordinating their attack successfully, so that their efforts were largely individual. Advancing under the cover of the destroyer smoke screen, the *Samuel B. Roberts* withheld fire during her approach on the cruiser column and was able to advance undetected to within 4,000 yards of an *Aoba*-class cruiser before launching her three torpedoes. Three or four minutes later fire, smoke, and a column of water were seen to rise from the water line of the target ship. The *Dennis* and *Raymond* also launched their torpedoes at about the same time, around 0800, and possibly at the same ship, so that the hit may have been scored by any one of the three. The *John C. Butler* made no torpedo attack, but engaged a cruiser and destroyer with gunfire.

All four DE's retired on a southwesterly course, laying smoke to the rear of the carriers, engaging in gunfire exchanges with the cruisers on the left flank of the formation, and eventually interposing themselves between the carriers and flanking cruisers. All of the little vessels were under heavy fire and only the *Raymond* and *Butler* escaped without serious damage. The *Dennis*, with both her 5-inch guns inoperative, retired behind the *Butler*'s smoke screen.

Attempting to retire after her torpedo attack, the badly crippled destroyer *Hoel* found herself boxed in on both sides by enemy ships. With Japanese battleships 8,000 yards on her port beam and cruisers 1,000 yards on her starboard quarter and each column pouring broadsides at her, the *Hoel* managed by dint of violent "fish-tailing" and "salvo-chasing" to remain afloat long enough to fire 250 rounds from each of her remaining guns. After taking many additional hits, the ship lost power in her starboard engine and discovered that all her engineering spaces were flooded and her No. 1 magazine was on fire. Comdr. Kintberger ordered all surviving hands to abandon ship. The *Hoel* rolled over on her port side and sank stern first a few minutes later after some 300 salvos had been fired at her while she lay dead in the water.

Firing first on one side then on the other, the remaining vessels of the screen plunged southward through smoke curtains laced with tall splashes containing tons of water, zigzagging radically at high speed to avoid salvos—and sometimes to avoid collisions. The *Heermann* was slamming through the formation at flank speed, firing at targets of opportunity and laying smoke as she came. Receiving orders from Admiral Sprague to engage enemy cruisers firing on the carriers from the port quarter of the formation, she turned left to gain station and suddenly saw the *Fanshaw Bay* cutting across her bow from port to starboard. She backed her engines emergency full speed to miss the carrier, then plunged ahead at flank speed again. Five minutes later the crippled *Johnston*, which was having steering trouble, rose out of the murk dead ahead and the *Heermann* again threw her engines into reverse at emergency full speed. When she missed the destroyer's bow "by about three inches," a loud spontaneous cheer went up from topside hands of both ships. It was the last time the *Heermann* saw the *Johnston*.

The *Heermann* soon sighted a *Tone*-class heavy cruiser pumping full salvos at close range into the *Gambier Bay*. The destroyer immediately opened fire on the Japanese cruiser, which was leading a column of six ships, four of which were heavy cruisers. The cruiser shifted fire to the *Heermann*, upon which three other vessels quickly concentrated their guns. So thick were the splashes from near misses drenching the director platform deck, that Hathaway wished for "a periscope with which to see over the wall of water." Yet "everything looked rosy": the splashes were colored red by dye loads! At 0845 a shell struck the destroyer's pilot house, which the captain had just left, killing three men and fatally wounding a fourth. Chief Quartermaster John P. Millay, wounded and knocked to his knees, took the wheel from the dead steersman and carried out an unexecuted order from the captain, who was busy chasing salvos. Damage control parties were kept busy from keel to pilot house.

The destroyer escort *Roberts*, with one engine room knocked out and her speed reduced to seventeen knots, was perforated by many heavy-caliber shells that failed to explode, in all more than forty direct hits. About 0900, however, two or three 14-inch shells, apparently of high capacity, struck with a tremendous explosion that tore a hole thirty to forty feet long and about ten feet wide in the port side at the waterline. No. 2 engine room was wiped out, fires were started on the fantail, and all power was lost. The ship abaft her stack was described as "an inert mass of battered metal."

Even after all power was lost the crew of the *Roberts'* No. 2 gun continued to fire. This crew loaded, rammed, and fired six charges entirely by hand, with full knowledge of the risk they ran in operating without air supply for gas ejection. While they were attempting to fire the seventh and last charge in the mount, an internal explosion occurred in the gun which killed all but three members of the gun crew; two of the three later died. A petty officer, the first man to enter the mount after the explosion, found Gunner's Mate 3/c Paul Henry Carr, the gun captain, standing on the deck of the mount holding the last shell, a 54-pound projectile, above his head. The breech of the gun was an unrecognizable mass of steel. Carr, his body torn open from neck to groin, begged for help to get off the shell. The petty officer took the shell from him and dragged a wounded and unconscious man from the mount. When he returned he found Carr attempting to get the projectile on the loading tray. Carr died within five minutes.

Because of the large number of wounded who had to be lowered over the side, it required some twenty-five minutes, under heavy fire, to abandon ship. The hope of many of the survivors depended upon a raft which four men were edging along the port and windward side of the sinking vessel. When the raft reached the large hole blasted in the side of the ship at the waterline, the pressure of water rushing into the hole carried the raft inside the No. 2 engine room where fires were raging from ruptured fuel tanks. By some means the men were able to push the raft back through the hole and use it to pick up survivors.

In the last glimpse her sister ships had of the *Johnston* the destroyer was under heavy fire, her speed greatly reduced, and her mast shot away and dangling down over her superstructure. Nothing was known of her fate until some time after the battle. From her senior surviving officer, Lieut. Robert C. Hagen, it was then learned that the *Johnston* remained in the thick of the melee throughout the surface action, engaging an almost incredible number of ships. "In a somewhat desperate attempt to keep all of them from closing the carrier formation," said Hagen, the destroyer had in succession engaged a heavy cruiser to her starboard, a battleship 7,000 yards off her port beam, another heavy cruiser which was firing on the *Gambier Bay*, and a column of destroyers which was closing the formation rapidly with the apparent object of launching a torpedo attack. The *Johnston* claimed hits on all of these targets and believed that she turned back the torpedo attack.

The destroyer finally found herself with two enemy cruisers dead ahead, several destroyers on her starboard quarter, and two cruisers on her port quarter—all pouring fire into her from ranges of 6,000 to 10,000 yards. "Killed and wounded littered our decks," reported Hagen. Under "an avalanche of shells" her remaining engine room and fireroom were knocked out, all communications were lost, and all but one of the guns were put out of commission. Comdr. Evans gave the order to abandon ship, and a few minutes later the

Johnston, dead in the water and under point-blank fire, rolled over and sank.

The loss of the *Johnston*, *Hoel*, and *Roberts* is less surprising than the survival of the other vessels of the screen, for none of them could have reasonably expected to come through the ordeal afloat. "It hardly seems possible," remarked the skipper of the *Hoel*, "that during daylight a destroyer could close to ranges of 6,000 to 10,000 yards of a battleship or cruiser, launch torpedo attacks, and then remain afloat for more than an hour." Loss of life was very high among these ships, and not all who survived the battle were able to survive the exposure and torment of two days and nights in the water before rescue appeared. Admiral Kinkaid called the attack of these vessels "one of the most gallant and heroic acts of the war."

The effectiveness of the destroyer attack is admitted and emphasized by the Japanese accounts of the battle. "This attack greatly delayed our advance; it slowed us down," said Admiral Koyanagi. The smoke screen was especially effective in interfering with gunfire and concealing our maneuvers. "It was very serious trouble for us," said Admiral Kurita. "It was exceedingly well used tactically." This is borne out by an entry in the log of one of the Japanese destroyers which contains the command, "Fire into the smoke screen 80° to port." The Japanese command knew of only one torpedo hit scored by the screen. This was made on the heavy cruiser *Kumano*, reducing her speed to sixteen knots and forcing her to withdraw from the battle. It seems very probable, however, that the destroyers and destroyer escorts contributed something to the damage that proved fatal to three other heavy cruisers that were lost in the battle and about which the enemy information was not complete. Koyanagi sighted seven or eight torpedo tracks approaching the *Yamato* and maneuvered the flagship to avoid them. These evasive maneuvers scattered the formation, however, and threw the battleships behind. "The major units," said Kurita, "were separating further all the time because of your destroyer torpedo attacks."

The determined attacks of the screening vessels, however, did not prevent the enemy from continuing to extend his cruiser group around the left flank of the carriers. Forging ahead, these cruisers cleared our smoke screen shortly after 0800 and closed on the port quarter, pulling abeam of the carriers. The effect was to alter the carriers' course constantly, so that their track described a semicircle from east, through south, to the southwest, on which course they were retiring toward the eastern entrance of Leyte Gulf. Because of individual maneuvers and differences in speed, they became scattered out along a southwesterly course with the *Fanshaw Bay*, *White Plains*, and *Kitkun Bay* in the lead and the *Gambier Bay*, *Kalinin Bay*, and *St. Lo* trailing. It was the trailing vessels that took most of the punishment.

The tall columns of water caused by shell splashes were becoming familiar features of the seascape to the CVE's. They soared up suddenly, those of the major-caliber 18-, 16-, and 14-inch shells, to a height of 150 feet or more, easily distinguishable from the shorter 8-inch and 5-inch shell splashes. The carriers twisted in and out among them as through a forest of water spouts.

Few of the enemy's armor-piercing shells exploded, but enough direct hits were registered to cause considerable damage. The *Fanshaw Bay* took six hits from 8-inch shells, one of which landed on the flight deck and wrecked the catapult track, while another demolished the anchor windlass, and a third knocked a one-foot hole in the hull eight feet below the water-line, and still others severed twenty structural beams and stiffeners supporting the flight deck. One shell exploded in the flag office, wrecking it, killing one man and wounding two. Fifteen 8-inch hits, many of them on the flight deck, were received by the *Kalinin Bay*. One of these passed through the flight deck just outboard of the forward elevator and exploded upon striking a corner of the elevator, causing tremendous damage. The elevator platform was completely wrecked along with much equipment. Considerable flooding of compartments was caused by this and additional hits. The

Gambier Bay took the first of her many hits at 0810 on the after end of her flight deck, where fires were started.

Although personnel on topside assignments and in the combat information centers of the CVE's were aware of the gravity of the situation and could see little reason for hope, there was no evidence of panic among them. Repair parties made their rounds religiously; rearming crews loaded and armed bombs and torpedoes while shells were splashing on every hand, and plane-handling and repair crews performed their tasks as usual. When straddles rocked the *White Plains* from stem to stern, the black gang below found themselves in semi-darkness with fragments of lagging falling about, soot and dust filling the engine room, loose deck plates up-ending, and one of the engines vibrating heavily. Many thought the ship was hit and ruptured, but all stuck by their job.

The CVE's returned the enemy fire with all they had—which was one 5-inch gun to the carrier. The officer in tactical command had instructed the carriers to "open with peashooters," and each ship took a target under fire as soon as one came within range. Most of their fire was directed at the cruisers on the port flank. The *Fanshaw Bay*'s gunners commenced firing on the leading cruiser when range closed to 18,000 yards and continued to fire as long as these vessels were within range. When the target closed to less than 12,000 yards approximately five hits were believed registered, including one in the cruiser's superstructure amidships which caused smoke. The *Kalinin Bay* took as her target a *Nachi*-class heavy cruiser, which immediately shifted fire to her assailant and scored two direct hits on the CVE forward and many near misses. At a range of approximately 16,000 yards a direct hit was claimed on the No. 2 turret of the enemy cruiser, and another hit just below the previous one. The turret was slowly enveloped in flames after the first hit, and the second caused a quick burst of flame which completely obscured the turret. After this the cruiser turned hard to port and withdrew temporarily from the formation. The *Gambier Bay*'s gunners spotted three explosions on the enemy cruiser which was their target, and claimed at least three hits. The *White Plains* reported hits on several targets, two between the forward stack and superstructure and one on the No. 1 turret of a heavy cruiser on the port flank.

Japanese gunners used a slow rate of fire, with more than a minute between salvos, and salvo patterns were characteristically small. Their shooting was in the early phase good, but it certainly was not lucky, since there were relatively few hits in proportion to the number of straddles and near misses. In view of the overwhelmingly superior gun power and speed of the enemy, it is remarkable that all of our carriers were not swiftly overtaken and sent to the bottom. Only the enemy's failure to close aggressively and his use of armor-piercing ammunition, which often passed through the unarmored carriers without exploding, can account for the outcome.

The southwesterly course of the formation left the *Gambier Bay* on the exposed windward flank, where her smoke, drifting to the starboard and aft, afforded little or no protection. Three enemy heavy cruisers maintained a dasastrous fire on the exposed carrier, while salvos of major-caliber shells from the battle line fell dangerously close to the ship's side. After 0810 the ship was hit almost continuously in the flight deck and in spaces above the water line. Although few of these shells reached any vital part of the ship, they killed and wounded numbers of officers and men and started several small fires. Word was passed to sprinkle the magazines, though the fires were soon brought under control.

At 0820 a shell hit the port side of the *Gambier Bay* at the forward engine room and exploded upon impact without penetrating, opening a gap in the skin of the ship approximately four feet square and twelve feet below the waterline. So rapid was the flooding that water was up to the firebox of the boilers in five minutes and the engine room had to be abandoned. The ship then slowed to eleven knots and dropped astern of the formation. Ten minutes later steering control was lost as a result of a hit near the island structure. Hit number twelve entered a boiler in the after engine room and split a ten-foot hole in the ship's skin below the waterline. With all power lost, the *Gambier Bay* was dead in the water. Water was rising rapidly below the second deck, the ship was listing badly to port, and many fires were burning at 0850 when Captain Vieweg gave the word to abandon ship. Many men were killed by the explosion of the gasoline tanks of a torpedo plane, or wounded while going over the sides from the hangar.

The ship capsized and sank while an enemy cruiser fired into her from a range of less than 2,000 yards.

The running battle swept on past, leaving the survivors of the carrier as well as those of the three sunken vessels of the screen in scattered groups clinging to rafts, floater nets, and wreckage.

For the first hour and a half of the surface battle the CVE's were not able to bring to bear with any great degree of concentration or effectiveness their chief weapons, their air squadrons. It is true that almost as soon as the Japanese Fleet was sighted it was attacked by local antisubmarine patrol planes, but they could only drop depth charges and strafe. A large part of the planes of all three CVE groups had departed on missions over Leyte by the time the battle opened, and an hour or two elapsed before they could make rendezvous, return, and locate the enemy. Few of them were suitably armed when they did attack.

The Northern Group had to launch all available planes remaining aboard under heavy gunfire and as rapidly as possible. There was little or no time for briefing, fueling, or rearming. Planes took off through shell splashes while the decks were rocking from explosion and the carriers were maneuvering violently to avoid salvos. The six carriers under fire managed to launch sixty-five fighters and forty-four torpedo planes within the first thirty minutes of the action, but few of the torpedo planes were adequately armed for the task ahead of them. Of the nine Avengers launched by the *Gambier Bay*, two had no bombs at all, two were armed with depth bombs inappropriately fused, and of the two which carried torpedoes one was launched with only thirty-five gallons of gasoline and was forced to make a water landing within a few minutes. Many of Sprague's Avengers carried no greater threat to Japanese battleships than 100-pound bombs which were capable of nothing more than superficial topside damage.

The critical danger of their situation inspired pilots as well as crews to surpass themselves. Loading crews exceeded their practice records in many cases, and flight decks launched strikes under conditions normally considered impossible. Time after time planes were successfully landed and launched in strong cross winds. Since one of the carrier groups was under heavy gunfire for two and a half hours, two were subjected to heavy air attacks, and two carriers were lost and many damaged, pilots were compelled to change their bases often. In the course of the strikes against the enemy the *Manila Bay* of the Middle Group serviced and launched eleven visiting planes and at one time had on her flight deck aircraft from the *Sangamon, White Plains, Kitkun Bay,* and *Gambier Bay.* It fell to the lot of the Middle Group CVE's to bear the brunt of landing, rearming, and refueling visiting planes, since they were the only carriers to escape damage during the battle. Admiral Stump's group not only accomplished this additional work, but on top of it launched by far the heaviest air attacks against the enemy. Probably three-fourths of the planes striking Kurita's ships were launched from his group.

Pilots were ordered to damage as many of the major ships as possible and not to concentrate on any one ship to attempt a kill. When possible, planes from different ships formed up for attack after rendezvous, the senior officer took charge, gave his instructions, and led a coordinated attack. It was not uncommon for a strike group of eight planes to be made up of aircraft from four different ships. Rain squalls, smoke, confusion, and lack of time for briefing, however, very often hampered or prevented the coordination of strikes and forced pilots to attack in small groups, often without fighter cover. This was especially true of the earlier attacks.

A marked exception and one of the most successfully coordinated attacks of the day was one led by Comdr. Richard L. Fowler, who was in the air eight hours during the day. Six Avengers loaded with 500-pound semi-armor-piercing bombs were launched from the *Kitkun Bay* of the Northern Group during the first moments of action. Fowler led them toward the enemy, climbing rapidly to gain altitude. At 9,500 feet the planes met heavy antiaircraft fire of all kinds which knocked down one of the torpedo planes and damaged others. Thick clouds completely obscured the enemy formation, and twenty minutes of searching at this altitude revealed no hole through which an attack could be made. Fowler turned his group to the east and let down to 1,500 feet where he sighted the entire Japanese force. He then climbed back to 7,500 feet and gained a favorable position for an attack on a column of heavy cruisers. Another TBM had dropped out because of engine trouble, and the fighter cover had been lost in the clouds. Diving out of the sun and through a cloud at 0905 the four Avengers caught a *Mogami*-class cruiser, the second in column, by surprise and delivered their attack without meeting any antiaircraft fire. Five hits were scored amidships on the stack, one hit and two near misses on the stern, and three hits on the bow—nine 500-pound bombs in thirty-five seconds. The cruiser took a sharp right turn and went a few hundred yards while three heavy explosions sent clouds of steam and black smoke more than 500 feet in the air. She blew up later and sank.

Strikes which had been launched for direct support of Leyte ground forces before the Japanese force was reported and were consequently loaded with light bombs and rockets, returned and threw everything they had aboard at the enemy ships. Lt. Comdr. Percival W. Jackson, air coordinator for a strike from the *Savo Island*, brought his group back from Leyte Gulf to search for the Japanese task force. His TBM was loaded with ten 100-pound bombs and eight rockets. The first target that presented itself was a Japanese reconnaissance float plane of the Jake type which he encountered in a clear space between cloud layers. With tail shots from his wing guns, Jackson sent the Jake down enveloped in flames. He then led his group through a cloud gap in a dive on two heavy cruisers and scored two hits with 100-pound bombs on the stern of a heavy cruiser, starting small fires. While he was pulling out of heavy flak, one of his crewmen sighted a submarine directly below. With a steep turn Jackson came about for a run on the submarine's persicope and released eight rockets from a height of 600 to 800 feet. Six of them exploded near the periscope. With a score of one Jake destroyed and one cruiser and one submarine damaged, Jackson's day had only started. In later strikes he claimed one torpedo hit on a battleship, two rocket hits on a heavy cruiser, and one direct hit with a 500-pound bomb on another cruiser.

The Japanese did not feel the weight of the heavily armed strikes of the Middle Group of CVE's during the first hour and a half or more of the battle. Although Admiral Stump's carriers launched their first strike at about 0745, the planes were held up by difficulties in making rendezvous and in locating the enemy. As a consequence, Stump's second strike, launched at 0833, overlapped the first. These two strikes contained twenty-eight fighters and thirty-one Avengers, the latter armed with torpedoes. All of these planes attacked between 0850 and 0930 and probably had much to do with turning the tide of battle.

Four Avengers from the *Natoma Bay* loaded with torpedoes missed their rendezvous with fighters from another carrier and went in for attack alone at 0850. Starting their runs from the southwest at 7,000 feet, one two-plane section dived through cloud at a 45-degree angle making 310 knots and leveled off at 1,500 feet altitude for a run on three heavy cruisers which were shelling the CVE's of the Northern Group. The nearest cruiser turned into the planes to "comb" their torpedoes. The ship was strafed but passed up and the torpedoes were dropped at the two cruisers following her. One hit was believed scored on the stern of one of the targets and another just forward of the beam of the third. The two remaining Avengers of this flight joined up with three TBM's of another ship which were maneuvering for an attack on the leading battleship. The two *Natoma Bay* planes selected the second one. This ship turned suddenly and skillfully combed the two torpedoes, which passed to either side. While the pilots were asking each other how they could have missed such a large target, one of the radiomen saw the two projectiles continue past the battleship headed directly for an *Atago*-class cruiser. Two almost simultaneous explosions followed, the first amidships and the second on the fantail of the cruiser. The ship turned sharply and slowed her speed. One of the four Avengers took a 20-mm. hit in the instrument panel that forced a water landing, while another returned to her base with a 12-inch hole in one wing.

For a time it looked as if the Japanese might succeed in bringing the Middle Group as well as the Northern Group of CVE's under fire from close range and destroying both of them. Although Stump's group was about thirty miles to the southeast of Sprague's when the action opened, he had turned into the wind on northeasterly courses repeatedly to launch strikes and had failed therefore to maintain this distance. A column of Japanese heavy cruisers and a battleship were deployed to the east to flank the group at about 0845 and soon began to straddle screening Vessels astern with salvos. Splashes also began to creep up on the carriers. Pilots diverted by Stump against the threatening ships attacked with an inspired daring.

Lt. (jg) Clark W. Miller, of the *Ommaney Bay* squadron, finding that he was unable to release his torpedo during an attack which his group made upon a cruiser, retired alone and requested instructions from his base. At that moment the *Ommaney Bay* and other carriers of the group were being approached by the Japanese battleship which at a range of fifteen miles was firing salvos that were landing about 1,700 yards short. The pilot was ordered to attack. Circling between the carriers and the battleship until he gained an altitude of 6,000 feet, Miller started his lone attack, dived at a speed of 260 knots, released his torpedo at about 750 yards, and pulled out in "terrific" AA, so close to the stern of the battleship that he could hear her guns. He thought he got a hit. At any rate the ship turned and broke off the attack.

Shortly after 0900, when it seemed that the cruisers on the port flank of the Northern Carrier Group were threatening to turn the CVE's back to the northward and into the jaws of the main enemy force, the commander of Carrier Division 26 ordered the Avengers over the enemy force which had expended their bombs to make dummy torpedo runs on the cruisers in the hope of turning them back. Several TBM's complied, making "dry" runs on the cruisers repeatedly, though with what effect is not known. Throughout the air action Hellcat fighters strafed the superstructure of battleships, cruisers, and destroyers, silencing antiaircraft batteries for the torpedo planes, and doing such damage as they could. These strafing runs were usually made in the face of heavy AA fire, which inflicted much damage and several losses among the fighter planes. One Avenger pilot, forced to take off from the *St. Lo* without bombs or rockets, made repeated strafing runs on the *Nagato* without any fighter support. After his port wing was hit and its gun jammed, he continued his strafing attack until the ammunition in his remaining wing gun was exhausted.

Twice during the earlier phase of the engagement screening vessels had reported sighting enemy torpedoes. Both of these attacks, if they were attacks, proved ineffective, but the enemy destroyers were believed to have a dangerous load in their tubes yet. At 0920 the destroyer group that had been paralleling the carrier formation on the starboard side closed at high speed and launched its torpedoes at a range of 10,000 yards. The enemy was known to possess excellent long-range torpedoes, but his destroyer commanders failed in this attack to show the skill and daring which they had demonstrated in previous engagements.

Lt. (jg) L. E. Waldrop, piloting a torpedo plane from the *St. Lo,* was returning to his ship after making eight runs on four heavy cruisers and one on a destroyer, when he sighted the wakes of the enemy torpedoes approaching the carriers. Making a steep glide, Waldrop began to ride herd on the torpedo salvos. Diving astern of the formation, he strafed and exploded one of them in the wake of the *Kalinin Bay*, only a hundred yards astern of that vessel.

The explosion of the torpedoes was the first warning of the attack to reach the *Kalinin Bay*, which immediately spotted another torpedo directly astern in her wake. She opened fire upon it with the 5-inch gun on her fantail depressed to an elevation of 2°. One shell exploded ten feet ahead of the torpedo, which then veered off to port. The ship sighted at least twelve other wakes on parallel courses to both sides. Any one of these giant 24-inch projectiles was capable of finishing off a CVE, but fortunately none of them found a mark in the carrier formation.

At the time of the torpedo attack the enemy had maneuvered our formation into the most perilous position it had yet occupied. On the left flank his cruisers had advanced abeam of the carriers and closed range at will to as little as 10,500 yards, while on the right flank his destroyers had closed to less than that range. While the battleships had fallen far astern and were scattered, shells were still pouring in at a great rate from port and starboard and many were hitting. It was the constant fear that the enemy's next step would be to advance his cruisers farther and turn the carriers either into land or back into the battle line—a maneuver of which his advantage in speed made him entirely capable. None of our counter offensive measures, whether torpedo attack, gunfire, or air strikes, seemed to be able to stop the Japanese. Admiral McCain, whose aid had been promised the CVE's, was steaming westward at high speed but would not gain position from which to launch his first strike for more than an hour. Admiral Halsey's battleships were at that time still steaming northward in pursuit of Ozawa's carriers.

Then at about 0925, when it seemed only a matter of time until the entire Northern Group would be wiped out and the Middle Group overtaken, a completely unexpected thing happened. The advanced vessels on the flanks ceased fire, turned about, and retired northward, breaking off the action.

This maneuver, inexplicable at the time, marked the end of the surface phase of the Battle off Samar.

The reason for the decision of the Japanese to break off an engagement with a greatly inferior force has been a subject of much speculation and theorizing. The mystery has been dispelled in part by the postwar interrogation of officers in command of the enemy fleet. In the first place they draw a distinction between the decision to break off the action with the carriers and the more important later decision with regard to carrying out the assigned mission in Leyte Gulf.

According to Admiral Kurita and his Chief of Staff, the decision to abandon the pursuit of Sprague's carriers was dictated in part by the need for closing up the widely scattered units of the fleet in anticipation of large air attacks. In taking evasive action under the persistent attacks of our destroyers and aircraft, the ships of the fleet were permitted to maneuver individually, each at her best speed, instead of maneuvering together by signal. Differences in speed as well as in maneuvers contributed to the wide dispersion of units. While the *Yamato* was capable of twenty-six knots at that time, the *Nagato* was limited to twenty-four, and the cruiser *Kumano,* which had taken a destroyer's torpedo, was reduced to sixteen knots. Two other cruisers crippled by our destroyer and aircraft attacks were having trouble maneuvering at all. The Japanese destroyers and left flank cruisers, moving at high speed, advanced far ahead while other units were being left farther and farther behind, scattered over a wide area. Kurita soon lost sight of our carriers and of his advanced units and seems also to have lost his grasp of the tactical situation. Koyanagi professed to be ignorant of the fact that the advanced cruisers were within five miles of our carriers when they were ordered back. "We did not know on account of the squall and smoke," he said.

While the CVE's enjoyed some advantage from steaming on the inside of the wide arc through which the battle track passed, they were never able to make better than eighteen knots. Believing that he was pursuing fast carriers, overestimating their speed, and being entirely unable to discern their maneuvers, Kurita feared that his destroyers would exhaust their fuel supply in an extended stern chase at high speed and thus jeopardizing his whole mission. This was an additional reason for abandoning the pursuit.

It is still difficult to understand why this powerful force of battleships, cruisers, and destroyers, after two and a half hours of gunfire, had been able to sink only one of the slow CVE's and three of the smaller vessels. Kurita attributed the ineffectiveness of his gunfire to a combination of smoke screen, rain squalls, and the zigzagging of the carriers. After the targets were lost to view by the major vessels early in the action, the enemy gunners shifted from visual to radar controlled gunfire, which was poorly developed and unreliable. It has already been observed that armor-piercing shells were ineffective against our light vessels. This explanation still leaves room for the suspicion of poor tactical judgment and bad shooting.

The abandonment of the pursuit did not mean abandonment of the mission of the fleet. "I then intended [after reforming] to enter Leyte Gulf," said Kurita, "and passed through the damaged or sinking ships of your formation, aircraft carriers and cruisers [sic] of your formation." The determined attacks of our destroyers and aircraft, however, had left the Japanese columns in such condition that Kurita could not continue immediately with his mission. Before setting course for Leyte Gulf he would have to take care of his cripples, assess the damage, and re-form his fleet.

The surviving ships of Sprague's Northern Group, still unable to believe their good fortune, slowed to fifteen knots after the enemy broke off and limped southward out of immediate danger for the time being. Damage control parties slaved to shore up gaps, pump out water, and put splintered flight decks in shape to resume flight operations. Hundreds of wounded and dying men required immediate attention.

In seeking to explain his escape from what had seemed to be certain destruction, Admiral Sprague paid tribute to the self-sacrificing attacks of the destroyers and aircraft, but also added a note to his report concerning "the definite partiality of Almighty God." A signalman aboard the flagship was heard to remark, "Oh Hell, they got away!"

The enemy enjoyed a brief lull in the air attacks after 0930, but it did not last long. Every effort was made by all three carrier groups to launch new strikes and keep the Japanese under attack. While the enemy was still too close to permit a turn into the wind, Admiral Stump's Middle Group took the risk of launching its third strike at 0935 while steaming on a southerly course in a cross wind. Somehow the planes managed to take off without casualties. Twelve Avengers, one with a torpedo and the rest with four 500-pound bombs each, and eight fighters immediately headed for the enemy. They threw their weight against the Japanese within the following hour, claiming three bomb hits on heavy cruisers previously damaged.

In the Northern Group the *Kitkun Bay* launched five Avengers at 1013, all but one of them loaded with torpedoes, and at 1020 the *White Plains* got off two Avengers which had been loaded with torpedoes while the ship was under fire.

Admiral Thomas L. Sprague's Southern Group of four carriers had launched a strike of sixteen torpedo planes and twenty-eight fighters at about 0730. Since the carrier group was brought under air attack (described below) immediately after the launching, however, the Avengers were ordered to retire southward while the fighters were detached to defend the CVE's. When the strike eventually headed north the gas supply of the planes was dangerously low and the fighter cover was reduced to six Hellcats. A damaged light cruiser, which hit one of the planes with flak, was sighted on the way north and proposed as the target for the group because of gas shortage. Although the strike had been airborne for nearly three hours, Comdr. James W. McCauley, leader of the group, ordered all planes to press forward in search of the Japanese fleet. When the battleships were at length discovered and the strike pushed over for the attack at 1050 some planes did not have sufficient fuel to return to their bases. Diving through extremely intense flak and retiring at once into a rain squall, the pilots could not see the results of their torpedo runs but claimed four probable hits on three battleships, two of them on the *Yamato*. One Avenger spun into the water alongside a battleship, one was forced to make a water landing when fuel was exhausted, and three landed aboard carriers with their tanks almost empty.

Unable to return to their ships or to find carriers which could take them aboard, pilots from various carriers attempted landings at the Tacloban strip on Leyte, which the army had been able to put in barely usable shape. Some were refused permission to land and compelled to ditch their planes in the gulf. Others were able to land, refuel, reload and return to the battle, although of one hundred emergency landings made during the day twenty-five resulted in crashes and total loss of planes. Four pilots from the *St. Lo*, their planes damaged by flak and their ship sunk, landed at the Dulag strip. Three of them were promptly issued carbines, assigned a fox hole, and instructed to fire on a Japanese counterattack. The pilots eventually refueled, largely by means of buckets, re-armed and repaired their own machines, and returned to other carriers. By some unknown means one pilot managed to get a new wing on his plane.

Admiral Kinkaid was completely puzzled by the maneuvers of Kurita's fleet after it broke off action with the CVE's. Contact reports from attacking pilots, while containing obvious errors, indicated that for more than two hours the Japanese ships remained within a short radius of their position at the end of the surface action, steaming on various courses. They did not retire toward San Bernardino Strait during that period, though they were sighted on northwesterly courses at various times. But on the other hand, neither did they consistently steer a course toward the entrance to Leyte Gulf. They seemed to be milling about aimlessly in the same waters without accomplishing anything, wasting invaluable time in the face of an unprecedented opportunity.

"We were collecting, assessing our information, and preparing to undertake the attack [on Leyte Gulf]," explained Admiral Koyanagi later. "All during these two hours we were assembling and assessing the information and taking account of the situation, including fuel, etc. . . ." Kurita also had the problem of his cripples to deal with. Four heavy cruisers had been badly damaged, the *Kumano, Suzuya, Chokai,* and *Chikuma.* The *Kumano* withdrew at slow speed, accompanied by the destroyer *Hayashimo,* also damaged; one of the three other damaged cruisers, other accounts differ as to which, sank after internal explosions resulting from bomb hits. The other two became unmaneuverable as the result of damage from air attack, dropped behind the formation, and eventually had to be sunk by torpedo from Japanese destroyers. Other destroyers were detached to pick up survivors.

Granting that the Japanese admiral had his hands full, his momentary difficulties do not adequately explain his maneuvers. Poor communications and lack of information help explain them, but they look more like the result of a feeble grasp upon fundamental strategy and a lack of firm resolution—symptoms of the deteriorating morale of a once great naval power.

At least twice during the period of confused maneuvers off Samar Admiral Kinkaid was informed by aircraft that the enemy had taken a course toward the entrance of Leyte Gulf. The admiral was convinced until noon, and for an hour afterward, that the enemy intended to force entrance to the gulf and fall upon our weakened forces. His situation appeared to be as desperate as it had been when the CVE's were surprised early that morning; even more so, since the attacks on the carriers had disrupted his air support. In the absence of air cover for the beachhead, the enemy drove home twelve air attacks on Tacloban, sinking two LST's and destroying a warehouse and a concrete dock. While Kinkaid had ordered a detachment of battleships and cruisers to rendezvous and defend the entrance, these vessels had not been able to refuel and replenish their ammunition and were not in condition to engage the Japanese battle line.

The Seventh Fleet commander dispatched some of his most strongly worded appeals for assistance to the commander of the Third Fleet after the surface battle had ended. Admiral Halsey did not reverse course with his fast battleships, however, until 1115, too late for them to have any effect upon the tactical situation. It would also have been too late had he set course for Samar upon receiving the first appeal. Admiral McCain launched the promised air strike at 1030, but it did not arrive for two and a half hours. Kinkaid could do little more than await developments and attempt to slow the Japanese if they forced an entrance.

Admiral Kurita was prepared to lose half of the ships of his fleet, so he said, in order to carry out his mission. By noon of the 25th he had lost one of his five battleships, and of the ten heavy cruisers of his original force five had been sunk or were in a sinking condition and three had been sent back damaged. His four remaining battleships were in good fighting condition, he said, and they were supported by at least two heavy cruisers, two light cruisers, and some ten destroyers. With more than half of his original fleet intact, Kurita still had a powerful force under his command and was in a position to use it. As the Japanese operation plan had envisioned, Ozawa's force had diverted the powerful Third Fleet beyond striking distance of the gulf. As the plan could not have foreseen, the destruction of Nishimura's force in Surigao had almost exhausted the ammunition of the surface forces of the Seventh Fleet defending the gulf. The two diversionary movements had resulted in the almost total destruction of two Japanese fleets, but the cost of that sacrifice had been counted.

Having forced his passage through the narrow interisland waters of the Philippines under almost constant attack for three days—by our submarines on the 23rd, by heavy air strikes on the 24th, and by a combination of surface and air strikes on the 25th—Admiral Kurita had obstinately fought his way to within two hours of his objective. Then after hesitating for two hours or more on the threshold of the gulf, the objective of the mission for which the Imperial Fleet had been gambled and terrible losses had already been suffered, Kurita turned north and abandoned his mission.

"Why did Kurita turn back?" The question has been asked many times and there have been many answers. It is the sort of question which provokes more argument than agreement and it is doubtful that there will ever be complete agreement on the answer.

Admiral Kurita himself had difficulty answering the question in two days of interrogation by American naval officers. He gave his reasons, to be sure—perhaps too many reasons. But he left enigma as thick as a smoke screen in the wake of some of them.

The decision to turn back, perhaps the most important made by the Japanese during the three days' battle, was made entirely on the responsibility of Kurita after consultation with his staff. There had been no further instructions from Admiral Toyoda, whose last orders had been to proceed with the mission. Kurita adhered to his mission until "about two hours" after he broke off the engagement with the CVE's. "I am not sure about the exact hours," he admitted, but thought that it was surely less than three hours.* His official action report, not completely reliable as to chronology, fixes the time at 1236. It therefore appears that the two most critical decisions of the day on both sides were weighed and made at about the same hour—that aboard the flagship *New Jersey* off Cape Engaño and that aboard the *Yamato* off Samar.

"I held to [my] intention until I received the second bombing attack," said Kurita. Since the fleet was under intermittent attack by small groups of aircraft throughout the morning, it is not entirely clear to which attack the admiral was referring. It seems probable, however, that this was the fourth strike of Admiral Stump's Middle Group, easily the largest

---

* Admiral Koyanagi, his Chief of Staff, testified independently that it was "an interval of about two hours." This would mean about 1130, or at any rate before 1230. The decision, therefore, could hardly have been influenced by the air strike from Admiral McCain's task group, which arrived after 1300.

launch by any CVE group during the day. The strike began at 1140. It consisted of thirty-seven torpedo planes and nineteen fighters, and included planes from the other two groups. The pilots claimed several bomb hits on a cruiser and one bomb and one torpedo hit on a battleship. The enemy was reported to be headed for Leyte Gulf (course 225°) when brought under attack, but afterward, according to the pilots, "there was no doubt as to his heading, which was north, at top speed." Substantially the same claim was made by other units, who were also sure that *their* men turned the tide. Exclusive credit is due no one unit, and some was due to all.

The cumulative effect of the morning's attacks of all types rather than the results of any one attack seems to have introduced an eleventh-hour reconsideration of the whole mission. Kurita was convinced, so his action report reveals, that American "preparations to intercept our force were complete, where-as we could not even determine the actual situation in Leyte Gulf." He also feared that he "would fall into an enemy trap," should he continue with his mission. "The conclusion from our gunfire and antiaircraft fire during the day had led me to believe in my uselessness, my ineffectual position, if I proceeded into Leyte Bay where I would come under even heavier aircraft attack." But, it was pointed out, he would be under attack by the same planes and probably additional ones from the Third Fleet while proceeding northward, and he had broken off pursuit of the source of those attacks, the CVE's. "In the narrow confines of Leyte Gulf," replied the admiral, "I couldn't use the advantage that ships had of maneuvering, whereas I would be a more useful force under the same attack with the advantage of maneuver in the open sea."

It would seem that this was a consideration which should have been taken into full account at the outset, instead of this late hour. But Kurita believed that an additional factor had entered the picture. He had intercepted instructions from the CVE's telling pilots whose ships were sunk or under attack to land at the Tacloban and Dulag strips. This was a desperate expedient and not a plan, for the strips were in no condition to receive and care for the planes. But Kurita concluded that carrier planes were shuttling to land bases (a scheme favored by the Japanese) and would combine with army planes from Leyte to attack him in the gulf from both land and carrier bases. Japanese land-based planes should have been well-informed of the poor state of our air strips, but Kurita received no intelligence from them, incredible as that may seem.

A more serious failure of Japanese communications and intelligence left Kurita in the dark as to the outcome of the two coordinated operations upon which the success of his own to a large extent depended—that of the Japanese Northern and Southern Forces. The admiral dispatched two planes from the *Yamato* during the morning, one to the north and one to the south, to learn what had happened to those forces. Nothing more was heard from the plane sent south, and the other reported that nothing could be found to the north. At the time the decision was made to go north information regarding Nishimura's fate in Surigao Strait was fragmentary and nothing whatever was known of Ozawa's progress or location. While Admiral Ozawa, contrary to his expectations, had been remarkably successful in diverting the Third Fleet to the north, he had been unable to inform Kurita or Tokyo of the success of his mission. The heroically conceived diversion that resulted in the sacrifice of the Japanese carriers proved to be largely in vain, therefore, simply because Kurita was unaware of its success. Kurita went so far as to say that "the lack of success of the entire operation depended upon that failure of communication." This view is open to serious question, though the Japanese suggest that had Kurita been informed of the situation to the north he might well have continued with his mission, spread destruction in Leyte Gulf, and escaped through Surigao Strait. As it was, he assumed all along that the Third Fleet task force lay northeast of San Bernardino Strait, within striking distance of the Gulf, instead of some 250 miles farther to the north off Cape Engaño.

While admitting that before he decided to turn back he probably received reports from a surviving destroyer of Nishimura's force indicating the failure and possible destruction of that force,* Kurita denied that this information influenced his decision. On the other hand, his Chief of Staff said positively that news of Nishimura's disaster did influence the decision. Whatever the testimony on this point, it is obvious that Kurita had been thrown six hours behind his schedule by the Third Fleet air strikes on the 24th and several hours more by the determined resistance of the CVE groups on the 25th, and that he was fully aware that, entering the gulf in the afternoon instead of at dawn as planned, he would be unable to coordinate his attack with Nishimura's and would probably reap few of the diversionary benefits of the latter's attack.

Lack of fuel was no consideration, according to the admiral, nor was it fear of destruction. "It wasn't a question of destruction; that was neither here nor there. It was question of what good I could do in the bay. I concluded that . . . I could not be effective. Therefore, on my own decision I concluded it was best to go north and join Admiral Ozawa."

The turn north, then, was not a retirement but the undertaking of a new mission! The kind of logic which dictates the abandonment of the primary mission of an operation in order to go to the aid of a force admittedly sacrificed to create a diversion for the primary mission calls for no comment. "Yes, but was there a choice?" was the difficult question put by an American officer who had been under Kurita's fire off Samar. "By the time the question arose," was the reply, "your landing had been confirmed and I therefore considered it not so important as it would have been before." Warned of his approach, the transports would probably have escaped, he thought.

It later appeared that Kurita's intention was "not primarily to join Admiral Ozawa but to go north and seek out the enemy"—that is, the Third Fleet! "Do you mean that you felt it more profitable to attack our task force than to attack our

---

* The admiral first denied that he had this information before the decision, then later said that he did have it. The captain of the destroyer *Shigure* said that he dispatched a report of the disaster at about 1200 and believed this was the first report made after the battle.

transports and invasion shipping in the gulf?" The admiral evidently did think so. He did not know the location of either Halsey or Ozawa, but hoped to join attack on his way north. "The point was the immediate objective to hit the enemy," he declared. But this was not the last of the admiral's multiple motives!

"Secondarily or over-all," he said, "I wanted to be at San Bernardino at sunset to get through and as far to the west as possible during the night."

"Which was the most important?" he was asked.

"I won't say which was more important," he hedged; "because if I did not get into the strait by night, the next day was hopeless for me, because I could be brought under attack by land planes and by this [carrier] force."

It is easy, and not very gracious, to pass judgment upon the vanquished, and it might be a mistake to accept too literally the groping memory of an elderly admiral seeking to explain his failure to a delegation of his conquerors. It is only fair to recall that at the time of the crisis off Samar, Kurita and his fleet had been under heavy attack for three days. On the first day he had his flagship sunk under him by submarine attack and he was ignominiously fished out of the drink by a destroyer— hardly an auspicious beginning. On the second day he had witnessed the destruction by our aircraft of what he assumed to be, and what probably was, one of the two most powerful battleships in the world. The *Musashi* was the first Japanese battleship ever sunk by aircraft alone. On the third day the general breakdown of Japanese communications and intelligence seemed to frustrate the coordination of fleet actions upon which Kurita's mission depended. By that time, also, the poisons of nervous strain and fatigue must have begun to tell upon Japanese admirals as they would upon any human flesh. And our attacks continued relentlessly.

After all these considerations are taken into account, the strange maneuvers off Samar are still not fully explained. The multiplicity of alternate plans and missions, the eleventh-hour changes in objective, the vacillation of purpose, the confusion

of ends and means all indicate a general weakening of grasp
that marks the failure of a man, but at the same time is probably significant of more than the failure of an individual.

It was characteristic of the lack of coordination between
Japanese forces, commands, and services that Admiral Kurita
was not informed of the plans of the commander of land-based
naval planes to inaugurate the spectacular and long-promised
Kamikaze campaign in coordination with the naval effort off
Leyte Gulf. According to Admiral Toyoda, the decision was
made upon the spur of the moment by the commanders of
the First and Second Air Fleets, Admiral Onishi and Admiral
Fukudome. Upon learning of Kurita's mission, these admirals,
whose planes were stationed in the Philippines, "decided that
if the surface units are taking such desperate measures we too
must take similar desperate measures, and started the first
operation of the so-called Special Attack Force."

While the surface action was in progress to the north, the
Southern Group of CVE's, consisting of the *Sangamon, Suwannee,
Santee,* and *Petrof Bay,* was subjected to the first of a series of
suicide-plane attacks, which during this and the following
day was to inflict severe damage upon four of the CVE's
and result in the sinking of a fifth among two of the carrier
groups.

The attack marked the opening of a new and dramatic
chapter in the history of desperate Japanese tactics. It is true
that Japanese pilots had crashed their planes into our ships on
several previous occasions, but these were individual actions
and not coordinated, planned attacks. Moreover, there was no
conclusive evidence that earlier suicide dives were premedi-
tated and deliberate. They had usually been carried out by
planes that had been hit and damaged by antiaircraft fire and
were already doomed, or were the result of uncontrolled and
apparently accidental crashes. It was in the Battle off Samar
that the first deliberately planned and executed suicide attack
was carried out by several planes acting in coordination.

The Southern Carrier Group was launching planes for a
strike against the Japanese Central Force when at 0740 enemy

planes were picked up by radar at a distance of about ten miles. In this, as in later attacks, the approach of the enemy planes was shrewdly timed to coincide with periods when our carriers were launching or landing planes and thus when the radar screens were cluttered with indications of our own aircraft and it was difficult to distinguish and identify attacking planes. Shortly after the radar contact, however, lookouts on the *Sangamon* spotted a group of four "Zeke" fighter planes through an overcast of altostratus clouds at about 10,000 feet overhead on the starboard beam. Three of the Zekes immediately went into an almost vertical dive, each apparently selecting one of the ships as a target. The fourth delayed its attack for several minutes.

The first plane circled to port and dived out of the sun at the *Santee*. That ship did not have time to bring her guns to bear, nor to take evasive turns. The Zeke, bearing down fast from astern, strafed the decks for about five seconds as it dived, then crashed into the flight deck on the port side forward and outboard of the after elevator, smashed through the deck blowing a hole approximately twenty-four feet long and ten feet wide, and stopped on the hangar deck. The plane carried a bomb estimated to be about 300 pounds in weight. The resulting explosion, besides blasting the hole in the flight deck, started fires there and on the hangar deck directly below. Sixteen men were killed and many wounded. Gasoline tanks in planes on the flight deck were set on fire and the contents of depth charges, split open by the explosion, started burning below. Life preservers knocked to the deck were aflame and the clothing of dead and wounded also caught fire. In the immediate vicinity of the flames, and more of a menace than the fire itself, were stored eight 1,000-pound bombs. Men set furiously to work in and about the flames to jettison the bombs and depth charges and put out the fire.

The second Zeke circled astern the *Suwannee* and was hit by antiaircraft fire. It spiraled down, smoking slightly, then rolled over into a 45° dive and headed for the *Sangamon*. With the only shell fired by her 5-inch gun, the *Suwannee* hit the diving plane when it was about 500 feet from its target, causing it to swerve slightly and miss. It crashed into the water close aboard off the port bow of the *Sangamon*. Its bomb exploded as it struck the water, killing one man on the forecastle and knocking a few small shrapnel holes in the side of the vessel. The third Zeke was also diverted by antiaircraft fire and crashed into the water near the *Petrof Bay*.

In the meantime the crew of the *Santee* had brought her fires under control, when, at 0756, just sixteen minutes after being hit by the Kamikaze plane, the carrier was shaken by a violent underwater explosion from the torpedo of an unseen submarine. The torpedo, which struck amidships on the starboard side, blasted a large hole in the skin of the ship and flooded several starboard and center compartments, causing a six-degree list to the starboard.

Startled by the torpedo explosion on the *Santee*, the gun crews of the formation nevertheless kept watching for the fourth Zeke. It was spotted slightly astern at 0758 circling in the clouds at 8,000 feet. Suddenly it was caught by antiaircraft fire and started smoking. At that instant, a Hellcat fighter came in fast from the left, apparently attempted interception and was gaining when the Zeke rolled over, dodged the pursuing Hellcat, and came straight down toward the *Suwannee*. The plane, carrying a 250-kilogram bomb slung under its belly, struck the flight deck of the *Suwannee* about forty feet forward of her after elevator slightly to the starboard side. The plane's engine penetrated to the main deck, and the bomb exploded between the flight and hangar decks, tearing a great hole in the latter. The explosion knocked many of the crew over the side, temporarily put steering out of commission, and made the after elevator inoperative. Emergency repairs enabled both the *Suwannee* and the *Santee* to keep their stations in the formation and even to resume flight operations within a few hours.

The torpedo attack on the *Santee* came at a moment when all attention was directed aloft and a periscope was least likely to be observed. This was taken by some officers as an indication that submarines were operating in conjunction with the Kamikaze planes, although it may have been a coin-cidence instead of a plan. Immediately after the explosion, the destroyer *Trathen* of the screen came about sharply to run down the track of the torpedo, and a minute later sighted a periscope at 1,000 yards range. She attacked with depth charges but without any apparent success. Another submarine was sighted about the same time by carriers to the north.

After Kurita's force broke off the engagement, the surviving carriers of the Northern Group, nearly all of them damaged or crippled, were landing planes and the air was filled with friendly aircraft, when at 1049, without any radar warning, lookouts suddenly sighted six Zeke fighters coming in fast on the port bow. The screen and one carrier opened fire at once. Crossing ahead of the *Kitkun Bay* from port to starboard, one Zeke climbed rapidly, rolled over, and started a suicide dive directly at the bridge of that ship, strafing as it came down. Passing over the island structure, the plane crashed into the port catwalk and fell into the sea about twenty-five yards off the port bow. The fragmentation bomb it carried exploded as the plane crashed, causing fires and other damage.

The *White Plains* opened fire on two planes which started a dive on her from ahead. When the Zekes reached an alti-tude of 500 feet they pulled out and turned to port, one of them heading for another target while the second circled and started a run on the *White Plains* from astern with the apparent intention of landing on the after end of the flight deck and crashing forward the length of the ship. To avoid the crash, the ship turned with a hard left rudder, her guns sending a torrent of fire into the fuselage and wing roots of the plane. Only a few yards astern the Zeke rolled over and dived toward the water, missing the port catwalk by inches, exploding between the level of the flight deck and the surface of the sea, and showering debris and fragments of "metal and Jap" over the flight deck and catwalk.

Simultaneously another plane with a bomb under each wing turned right when abeam of the *St. Lo,* continued around and over her after ramp at very high speed, then pushed over sufficiently to hit the flight deck near the center line. There was a tremendous flash as one or both bombs exploded and flaming gasoline and fragments of the plane were scattered down the length of the deck and over the bow. From the bridge of the *St. Lo,* Capt. McKenna's first impression was that the damage was not serious. Then a minute or two later a minor explosion on the hangar deck sent up clouds of smoke. No communication could be established with the hangar deck from the bridge. A few seconds later occurred a much more violent explosion which rolled back a large section of the flight deck for its entire width. This was followed by another heavy explosion that tore out more of the deck, sending plating hundreds of feet in the air, and blowing the forward elevator out of its shaft and landing it upside down on the deck. Many men were blown overboard and many killed. Smoke and flames were so thick that the captain remarked that he was "uncertain as to whether the after part still was on the ship." The blaze seared men at the guns and forced several over the side. By that time the fire fighting equipment was inoperative and it was apparent that the *St. Lo,* now listing to the port, could not be saved. At about 1100, Captain McKenna ordered all engines stopped and passed the word, "stand by to abandon ship."

From the forecastle of the sinking vessel large numbers of wounded were lowered into the water. While the crew was abandoning ship, heavy explosions continued below, one of them seemingly blowing out a large section of her bottom on the starboard side, since the ship shifted from a list to port to a sharp list of thirty degrees to the opposite side. Capt. McKenna, the last man to leave the ship, had been in the water only a few minutes when the *St. Lo*'s bow turned up almost vertically in the air and at 1125 she sank by the stern. So carefully were the casualties handled on abandoning ship that four hundred wounded men, including seventy-five stretcher cases, were saved and later picked up by the *Heermann.*

While explosions were tearing apart the *St. Lo,* two suicide divers crashed into the *Kalanin Bay.* One of these, coming in from astern and smoking from antiaircraft shells of that ship, crashed on the port side of her flight deck, wrecking it badly and starting numerous fires. Aflame from hits, the second plane approached in a steep glide from the starboard quarter and crashed amidships on the port side and into the after stack, wrecking it as well as a long section of the catwalk. Fires were quickly extinguished.

A second and larger group of planes, apparently "Judys," was sighted at 1110 approaching from astern. Only one of these attempted a suicide dive. By this time the screening vessels had been detached and left behind to pick up survivors of the *St. Lo.* The remaining carriers made evasive turns to confuse the diver's aim and brought the plane under concentrated fire. With boths its wings shot off, it struck the water about fifty yards off the port bow of the *Kitkun Bay.*The plane's bomb entered the water about twenty-five yards off her port bow, and parts of the plane landed on her forecastle.

The Southern Group had in the meanwhile been left unmolested since about 0800, and at 1115 launched all available fighters to go to the assistance of the Northern Group, which at that time was under air attack. After the fighters had departed, three or four single-seat Japanese fighter planes carrying bombs came in at 1154 to make a low level strafing attack. They were driven off by gunfire, but not before they had caused a few casualties by strafing. One plane aimed a bomb at the *Petrof Bay*, but missed and did no damage. Twenty minutes later the gunners drove off another air attack after one suicide dive missed the *Santee.*

From a fueling rendezvous far out in the Pacific to the northeastward Admiral McCain's task group had been rushing toward Samar at high speed since 0940. Although the distance was still extreme, the order was given at 1030 to launch the strike, and within the next fifteen minutes the *Hancock, Hornet,* and *Wasp* got off forty-six fighters, thirty-three bombers (Helldivers), and nineteen torpedo planes, a 98-plane strike. Two of the Helldivers were lost in launching, but all the others made the rendezvous and set course for Samar.

From the launching point to the position of the enemy fleet it was a distance of 340 nautical miles—"extreme range, and then some," as one report put it. It was one of the longest strikes of the carrier war. Since there was no assurance that the planes could refuel or even land safely at the air strips on Leyte, they had to be lightly loaded in order to conserve fuel. No planes carried torpedoes, and since the strike had been armed for an attack on the enemy carrier force to the north-west (which had been called off at the last moment) there were not as many armor-piercing bombs as were needed against the heavier ships off Samar. Nor had there been time to install disposable wing tanks to supplement the normal fuel supply. Prospects for completing the return leg of the mission and landing back aboard were consequently slim for the more heavily loaded bombers. In spite of this there was no hesitation in undertaking the strike, and two pilots whose planes were loaded with torpedoes even petitioned to join the strike, knowing that they could not return. They were given a "negative."

The strike was a little more than three and a half hours en route to the target and the pilots were not so fresh during the attack as they might otherwise have been. Admiral Stump's fighter director gave the strike leader from the *Wasp* the loca-tion of the enemy force, which was sighted at about 1310 steaming on a northerly course at a speed of about twenty-four knots. The ships this time maneuvered together in good style under attack instead of individually. The Third Fleet pilots were unanimous in their opinion that the antiaircraft fire was the "fiercest" they had ever encountered, "exceeding in volume even the well defended land installations around Manila." Three planes were shot down and several were dam-aged. For the first time during the day Japanese fighter planes came out to offer resistance. While they were able to cause the bombers some trouble, two of the six Zekes sighted were shot down and the rest driven away by our fighters.

The three carrier groups attacked individually instead of in coordination, thereby losing some of their effectiveness.

Claims of hits were surprisingly light for a strike of this size, though some damage, none of it very serious, was claimed upon battleship and cruiser targets.

The return flight was a nightmarish race against dropping fuel indicators, in which there were several losers. Of the twelve Helldivers in the *Hancock* bombing squadron, for example, only three were able to return to their ship before dark. One was knocked down by flak; two ran out of fuel and made forced water landings forty-five and thirty-four miles short of their bases; four landed aboard CVE's of the Middle Group, and two made difficult landings at Tacloban, one of them cracking up.* Nine planes from McCain's group landed on the rugged strips on Leyte, and eleven planes were reported missing by the end of the day.

A second strike was launched from the *Hancock* and *Hornet* at 1245, after the carriers had closed for two hours at high speed. A smaller strike, this one consisted of twenty fighters, twenty bombers, and thirteen torpedo planes. Although they were given a vector by the CVE's, their formation became confused and strung out during the approach at about 1500, and their attack was not well coordinated. In the course of both strikes McCain's air groups dropped sixty-five tons of bombs and fired sixty-four rockets. In all they claimed four bomb hits on the *Yamato*, an equal number on one of the *Kongo* class battleships, one on the *Nagato*, five on unidentified battleships, and other hits on several cruisers and destroyers.

During the course of the afternoon strikes, a large part of them by CVE planes, the bulges or blisters of all the major Japanese ships were perforated by bomb damage, according to Admiral Kurita. "The ability of the ships wasn't seriously

---

* One of the *Hancock* bombers, piloted by Lt. (jg) Alders, after severe damage from flak, ran out of gas and made a difficult water landing. Pilot and gunner had spent fifty-six hours in a raft when they were sighted and picked up by a patrol plane from Palau. The PBM unfortunately sprang a leak in landing and sank, leaving no provisions or water afloat for rescued or rescuers. Then twenty-four hours later the two crews were sighted by the *Cushing*. While the destroyer was hauling the half-dead crews aboard she was attacked by a Japanese submarine which narrowly missed with a torpedo. "The remainder of the trip was uneventful," it is gratifying to learn.

interfered with, but they left a long, conspicuous trail of oil in the water," he said. Still, there was no vital damage. "They could maintain speed and they were able for battle all the way through it." This seems to be corroborated by our pilots.

By noon the limited supply of torpedoes and armor-piercing bombs aboard the escort carriers was all but exhausted and they were scraping the bottom of their bomb stage for contact bombs and rockets. These were of limited effectiveness, but the indefatigable crews and pilots of the CVE's continued throwing whatever they had at the enemy as long as daylight lasted and they could get planes in the air. Admiral Stump's group launched two more strikes in the afternoon, making a total of six from the Middle Group during the day, while those carriers of the Northern and Southern Groups that remained capable of it continued intensive air operations.

The last strike from the escort carriers attacked Kurita's fleet at 1723 off the northeastern tip of Samar Island. Pilots reported sighting four battleships, three heavy cruisers, two light cruisers, and some seven or more destroyers present on a northwesterly course (300°) at low speed. Kurita had left behind him three heavy cruisers sunk off Samar and was retiring with several cripples. While he probably had not yet set course for retirement through San Bernardino Strait, he was unquestionably eliminated as a threat to our forces in Leyte Gulf. In that sense, at least, the Battle off Samar was our victory.

It would be a mistake to minimize the contributions of the Third Fleet forces to this victory, both by their air strikes which weakened the enemy fleet in the Sibuyan Sea on the 24th and by the strikes off Samar on the 25th. With due credit assigned to those forces, however, it remains clear that the chief credit belongs to the CVE groups of the Seventh Fleet, to the sacrificial attack of the small screening vessels of the Northern Group, and to the air squadrons of all groups. In the course of the day's attacks there were 252 sorties made by torpedo planes and 201 by fighters. They dropped a total of

191 tons of bombs and 83 torpedoes and destroyed more than 100 enemy planes.

The cost in lives, ships, and planes had been high. The escort carriers *Gambier Bay* and *St. Lo,* the destroyers *Johnston* and *Hoel*, and the destroyer escort *Roberts* were sunk. In addition, seven CVE's, the *White Plains, Fanshaw Bay, Kitkun Bay, Sangamon, Suwannee,* and *Santee*, as well as the destroyer *Heermann* and the destroyer escort *Dennis*, were seriously damaged. Some 128 planes were combat or operational losses. Among all ships' personnel 473 were reported killed, 1,110 missing, and 1,220 wounded, a total of 2,803 casualties.

Clutching rafts, nets, and wreckage, the survivors of the *Gambier Bay* and the three vessels of Sprague's screen sunk in the surface engagement watched anxiously while passing Japanese destroyers took motion pictures of them. They were not strafed, as they expected, but they were not picked up.

First aid was administered to the wounded, and the men began the long wait for rescue that was to last for two days and two nights, and for some never came at all. Friendly planes "buzzed" the rafts to let the men know they were spotted on the afternoon of the action, but nothing happened. The following morning two friendly planes passed five miles to the east, but apparently did not see the Very stars and dye markers used to attract their attention. After thirty hours in the water many of the wounded and unwounded survivors of the *Gambier Bay* had to be restrained from drinking salt water. Some became delirious and were prevented with difficulty from drowning themselves or injuring other members of their groups.

The second day went by without aid appearing. Suffering from sun, immersion, and exhaustion, many died from wounds, shock, and exposure. Forty-five officers and men of the *Johnston*, including her captain and executive officer, all of whom were seen alive in the water, died or were not seen again. Fifteen survivors of the *Gambier Bay* also died. Morale was not improved by the presence of sharks in the vicinity, especially after two men died as the result of attacks by the fish.

In the early morning hours of the 27th, two submarine chasers and five LCI's from Leyte Gulf located and picked up approximately 700 survivors of the *Gambier Bay*. The search for the survivors of the three other vessels was continued through the morning, during which those who had survived the ordeal from the crews of the *Johnston*, *Hoel*, and *Roberts* were rescued.

VI

THE END OF THE NAVAL WAR

Since about 1630 on the afternoon of the 25th Admiral Halsey had been steaming southward at twenty-eight knots in a dash for the entrance to San Bernardino Strait, where he hoped to intercept Kurita's fleet. Leaving behind with Bogan's carrier group four of his battleships and the bulk of the supporting ships of Task Force 34, Halsey took with him only the two fastest battleships, *Iowa* and *New Jersey*, the three light cruisers, *Vincennes*, *Miami*, and *Biloxi*, and eight destroyers. His plan was to arrive at the earliest possible time off the entrance to the strait, then sweep eastward along the northern coast of Samar, destroying any forces encountered, and steam south off the eastern coast of the island as far as Leyte Gulf in search of stragglers and cripples.

The "time-honored principle of concentration," in the name of which the decision had been made the night before to leave San Bernardino Strait unguarded, had now gone by the board under the exigencies of battle and high strategy. Twenty-four hours after the historic decision was made, the component parts of the Third Fleet which had gone northward concentrated as one force were scattered over 200 miles of sea off the eastern coast of Luzon, while Admiral McCain's task group was still more than 300 miles to the eastward of San Bernardino Strait. Admiral Mitscher, with two carrier groups, was about 250 miles east of the northern tip of Luzon; Admiral Halsey, with his small force, was more than 200 miles to the southwest, of Mitscher, while Bogan's carrier group and the bulk of the battleship force were some forty miles astern of Halsey's group.

In spite of the Third Fleet's great superiority of gun power over that of the enemy, neither of our groups in contact or seeking contact with the enemy enjoyed a preponderance, or for that matter an equality of fire power on the night of the 25th. Mitscher, facing a Japanese force containing two battleships, had been left with no heavy ships in his carrier groups to the north. The attempt of Admiral Ozawa's battleships to intercept Mitscher's cruisers has already been reviewed. Admiral Halsey at the same time was steaming south with two battleships and three light cruisers in pursuit of an enemy force containing four battleships, two or three heavy cruisers, two light cruisers and a probable superiority in destroyers.

A successful interception of Kurita by Halsey would have resulted in the third battleship action of the Pacific War and might have settled some interesting questions regarding enemy ordnance and comparative fire power. The *Yamato's* 18-inch guns, concerning which our Naval Intelligence was not informed at that time, had never been trained upon an American battleship. Had the enemy's shooting been no better than it proved off Samar that morning, he might have fared badly. But the battleships do not appear to have been fully committed in that action and the test was not conclusive. Our heavy ships enjoyed an advantage of about four knots in speed. Whether Halsey's advantages in speed and radar would have compensated for Kurita's advantage in ships and ordnance, however, remains a debatable point. Much would depend upon the extent and effect of the damage Kurita's ships had sustained.

At about 1730, when Kurita had reached a position off the northeastern coast of Samar, he sighted a Japanese plane which led him to expect to find American forces to the northward. To top off a very bad day, two Japanese bombers proceeded to attack him. It may have been about this time, or probably later that Kurita heard from some source, not from Ozawa directly, that the Northern Force had been heavily engaged and that a night torpedo attack upon our force was planned.* The extent of the losses Ozawa had suffered was

---

* The admiral did not remember the time he received the information, but it was obviously received at a later time than he thought, since the attack was not ordered by Ozawa until after dark.

not indicated, nor was his position given. Kurita still assumed that part of the Third Fleet was operating not far northeast of San Bernardino Strait. At any rate he sent a message to Ozawa (which was never received) saying that he was coming north to join him in a coordinated attack. Then, he said, "if I didn't find anything up in here [indicating a point east of the northern tip of Samar], I would withdraw through San Bernardino Strait." If he could make contact with our force, however, he declared that he was prepared to fight it out.

Just how eager Kurita was to make contact with our force and how far north he went in search of it is not clear, although it seems that he did not go very far north of Samar. At 1727 he sent a message saying that he would head for the strait at dusk, and a few minutes later he increased speed to twenty-four knots. "I tried to seek out the American forces but couldn't find them," he said. It seemed to the admiral that in view of the inevitable air attacks of the following day it was highly important to put as much distance between himself and our carriers as possible—especially important that he should not be caught by daylight in the Sibuyan Sea. Toyoda had already approved a retirement through the strait if no action developed. The matter of his fuel supply, which had been "no consideration" in his decision to turn back from Leyte Gulf, had now become "a very important consideration," in fact "the basic one." Kurita therefore set course for San Bernardino Strait. At 2115 a dispatch was sent from one of the vessels of his fleet saying that he intended to go through the strait at midnight. At 2145, however, a search plane from the *Independence* sighted him at the entrance of the strait.

Midnight found Admiral Halsey steaming at high speed on a course directly for the strait and only about forty miles off the entrance, in position at last to cover the approaches. He was too late, for by this time Kurita was already through the strait. Halsey apparently missed an interception by about two hours. Thus the opportunity which the fast battleships lost when Kurita sortied from the strait on the previous midnight was not retrieved when he retired through the same strait

the following night, in spite of Halsey's abandonment of the
opportunity of destroying Ozawa's force to the north in order
to attempt the interception. The fast battleships of the Third
Fleet therefore spent the twenty-four most critical hours of
the three-day battle steaming 300 miles up the coast of Luzon
and 300 miles back between two enemy forces without firing
a shot at either, though narrowly missing contact with both.

A report from an *Independence* night plane indicated that a
straggler, probably a destroyer, might be intercepted off the
entrance to the strait about 0100. The destroyer *Lewis Hancock*
was assigned picket duty and stationed twelve miles in
advance of the battleships and cruisers. The night was dark,
the sky partially overcast, but visibility was good and the sea
was smooth.

At 0025 Halsey's force turned southeast, course 135°, and
three minutes later the *Hancock* reported a radar contact to the
southward, bearing 188°, at a distance of 23,900 yards or more
than twenty miles from the main force. The target was on a
westerly course, making about twenty knots. Rear Admiral
F. E. M. Whiting, in the *Vincennes,* was ordered to close with
the three light cruisers and three destroyers, while the battleships and remaining destroyers turned to course 90° to stay
clear of their line of fire.

Whiting took the light force south, then at 0054 turned to a
westerly course and opened fire with the main batteries of the
cruisers at a range of about 17,000 yards. After about five minutes they checked fire for a look at the target. It had slowed
to about thirteen knots, presumably as a result of the firing,
and a dull red glow appeared. Firing was resumed, and by
0103 the target, apparently a large destroyer, had broken out
in flames from bow to stern and was soon dead in the water.
The cruisers were ordered to cease fire and the destroyers to
open when ready. The *Miller* and *Owen* closed to 4,400 yards
and at that range the *Owen* fired a half salvo of five torpedoes.
There was no definite evidence of hits. The two destroyers
then opened rapid and accurate fire with their main batteries
at close range. Tracers could be seen entering the blazing hulk,

causing flashes and showers of sparks. No return fire was observed from the enemy vessel. The two destroyers reversed course and continued to pour rapid fire into the target until 0132. At that time the vessel flared up in a tremendous explosion that sent flaming debris high in the air and illuminated the whole area. All flames subsided, only to reappear soon afterward. The destroyers maintained their gunfire. Then after a second enormous explosion at 0135 the target disappeared from view and from all radar screens. The *Miller* closed and while passing through the waters where the target was last seen struck some object. Two heavy underwater explosions were felt later by both destroyers. Just to make sure, the *Owen* fired three star shells. Nothing was seen and the target was reported definitely sunk. The ship was later identified as the new destroyer *Nowake*, which was packed with survivors of the heavy cruiser *Chikuma*.

After the destroyers and cruisers rejoined, the sweep around the north coast of Samar was continued. The force rounded the island and continued down the east coast after dawn, searching for cripples. Large oil slicks and several patches of Japanese survivors, a few of whom were picked up by destroyers, were passed on the way south. Nine pilots and crewmen of the CVE planes were also picked up, but no further targets were discovered.

In the meanwhile a night plane from the *Independence* had been shadowing Kurita's force and making periodic reports of the progress of the fleet as it threaded its way through the narrow waters west of San Bernardino Strait. The plane was relieved on station before midnight by a second night plane, which kept the fleet under observation as it continued toward the Sibuyan Sea. About 0315 on the morning of the 26th the *Independence*, hoping to catch the enemy in the narrow passages, launched a night strike consisting of four Avengers, loaded with torpedoes, and five Hellcats, each with one 500-pound bomb. In the meantime a severe and widespread thunderstorm had broken over the Sibuyan Sea and at 0230 the plane that had been shadowing the enemy fleet lost contact and never regained it. The night strike nevertheless flew on through the raging storm to deliver an attack. The five fighters actually reached the target area but were unable to locate the enemy fleet and had to turn back.

There would be one more opportunity for a blow at the retreating enemy, for even at best speed from the position last sighted he could not escape beyond the extreme range of a dawn strike from our carriers. On the evening of the 25th Admiral Halsey had ordered Admiral Bogan's carrier group and the remaining units of Task Force 34 with it to make rendezvous with Admiral McCain's carriers northeast of San Bernardino Strait at 0600 the following morning. There McCain was to take charge and launch searches to locate targets and strikes against the enemy.

At 0800 on the morning of the 26th two search planes from the *Wasp* spotted, through a cloud gap, the main body of Kurita's fleet steaming southward at good speed ten miles northwest of the northern tip of Panay Island in Tablas Strait. Kurita had made good time during the night and given a few more hours would be beyond striking range. His force when sighted by the search planes consisted of four battleships, two heavy cruisers, two light cruisers, and several destroyers. A few stragglers to the rear were sighted later.

Strike groups from the *Wasp*, *Hornet*, *Hancock*, and *Cowpens* in McCain's group and from the *Intrepid* and *Cabot* in Bogan's group had been launched at dawn and sent westward to await a report of contact by the search. The *Intrepid* group of sixteen bombers, seven torpedo planes, and twelve fighters, accompanied by three torpedo planes from the *Cabot*, delivered the first attack, beginning about 0830. A heavy cloud cover gave the strike leader difficulty in assigning targets and prevented a well coordinated attack. The enemy ships still had plenty of fight left in them, if the quantity of flak was any indication. This being their last attack, the planes went for the heavy ships. The pilots claimed two torpedo hits on the *Nagato* and one on the *Kongo*, five half-ton bomb hits on the *Kongo*, and one hit with a 500-pound bomb on the *Yamato*. The hits seemed to have no effect on the speed of the battleships. The number of direct hits was no doubt overestimated, since the Japanese reports indicate no serious damage to their heavy ships.

The air groups in this strike suffered severe losses due to flak and shortage of fuel. One was shot down over the targets, and four were forced to make water landings as a result of fuel shortage or damage.

Flying south at high altitude down Tablas Strait east of Mindoro Island, the large strike of eighty-three planes from the carriers of McCain's group sighted a single vessel, a light cruiser or large destroyer, in the northern part of the strait. Not knowing whether his gas would hold out until the main fleet was sighted, the flight leader assigned a division of *Hornet* planes to attack the straggler. Because of a misunderstanding of the order, all the *Hornet* bombers left the group and attacked this target. One bomb hit was scored but with undetermined results.

Farther down the strait the main strike group spotted a heavy cruiser of the *Mogami* class through cloud layers off the southern tip of Mindoro Island steaming west. This was the *Kumano*, damaged off Samar the previous day. The *Hancock* group of four bombers, seven torpedo planes, and twelve fighters was assigned this target and broke off at 14,000 feet to leave the other planes. Their attack was reported to have resulted in at least one 1000-pound bomb hit and perhaps two torpedo hits. Photographs taken during the attack show great billows of black and white smoke or steam rising from the cruiser. She was left dead in the water and, it was thought, sinking, though she later managed to get under way and escape.

Shortly after the *Hancock* group left to attack the cruiser the remaining planes of the strike sighted the main body of the fleet. Unfortunately only thirteen torpedo planes, three bombers and four fighters from the *Wasp* and *Cowpens* were present to take part in the attack on the fleet. The *Yamato*, which was leading the battleship column, was selected as the primary target. One unquestionable hit on her No. 1 turret was made by the bombers and two more bomb hits were claimed. The Avengers believed they scored one torpedo hit on the *Yamato* and one on the *Nagato,* although neither ship was visibly affected. Two confirmed torpedo hits were made on the light cruiser *Noshiro,* which was left dead in the water. This was the last shot our forces had at Kurita's four battleships, for they steamed south through the Sulu Sea beyond range of the later strikes.

Twenty-four B-24 bombers of the 13th Army Air Force attacked the enemy fleet later in the morning. They claimed numerous hits on the *Yamato* and one other battleship. According to Admiral Kurita the army bombers made no hits.

Two additional strikes were launched by McCain's group, one at 0815 and one shortly after noon. Because of the great distance to the targets the air groups from the *Hornet, Hancock,* and *Wasp* were ordered to attack individually instead of taking the time necessary to coordinate their attacks. Instead of pursuing the main body of the fleet, therefore, the reduced squadrons confined their attacks to stragglers and cripples. *Hornet* planes located the light cruiser *Noshiro* west of Panay, where she had been left badly damaged by the *Wasp* group in their first strike. She was finished off by a bomb, and sank at 1113. Torpedo planes from the *Wasp*'s second strike blew the bow off a Japanese destroyer. She was left afloat and under way, but later a destroyer with her bow missing was seen grounded to her deck level near the same area, presumably the same vessel.

In the afternoon the third and last strike from the Third Fleet attacked a group of five destroyers south of Mindoro and reported bomb hits on two of them. A special search of the Visayan Sea area by the *Hancock* group located no targets except one 5,000-ton landing ship off the eastern coast of Panay. It was hit by two bombs and disintegrated in a tremendous explosion.

McCain's strike groups encountered considerable opposition from land-based planes south of Mindoro and some on their return trips. In all, the fighters shot down twelve Japanese planes during the day. Eight of our planes were lost as the result of antiaircraft fire, and with them six pilots and five air-crewmen.

The last blow struck by the Japanese in the Battle for Leyte Gulf was leveled at the unfortunate escort carriers, and the enemy's weapon was again the Kamikaze planes. Leaving Admiral Stump's Middle Group to furnish air support for Leyte, the Northern and Southern Groups retired eastward with their crippled vessels on the evening of the 25th.

The Kamikaze planes put in their appearance over the Southern Group about noon of the 26th. By radar six or eight Zekes were picked up while they were at a distance of thirty-five miles, then spotted later through binoculars in a high overcast at about 10,000 feet. Local combat air patrol planes from the carrier group shot down three enemy planes before they reached the formation, and a torpedo plane returning from antisubmarine patrol splashed a fourth which had started a dive on the *Petrof Bay*, and as a result crashed astern of that ship. As usual, the attack developed while the carriers were landing planes.

The *Suwannee* had just landed an Avenger which had hardly come to a stop on the forward elevator when one Zeke crossed over the formation under fire from several ships, nosed over at about 4,000 feet, and started a 45-degree dive at the *Suwannee* through a torrent of tracers, strafing as it came in. The Zeke struck the parked torpedo plane, exploding it instantaneously and wrecking the elevator. Probably at the level of the bridge the suicide plane dropped a 250-kilogram bomb, which exploded on contact with the deck. A minute or two later another plane dropped a bomb that struck forward of the first hit, wrecked the catapult machinery, and caused heavy damage. Fires spread on the flight deck until they set fire to seven fighter and two torpedo planes. The planes started exploding, causing fires that raged for several hours. Flaming gasoline flowed over the side, into the gun buckets and over the men manning the guns.

Lt. C. J. Premo, navigator, severely wounded and burned, made his way through fires from the bridge to the after quarters to report that several wounded officers and men, including

Capt. W. D. Johnson, were trapped and threatened by fires on the bridge and needed help. Premo died a few hours later as the result of his action. Such acts became commonplace on the *Suwannee* as on other CVE's. An enlisted man, William S. Brooks, Chief Ship's Fitter, crawled forward along the hangar deck until he was knocked unconscious and injured in the abdomen by explosions. Regaining consciousness, he crawled under the planes to the valves controlling the water curtain and sprinkler system and opened them, thus preventing the fire from igniting the gas-filled planes on the hangar deck, which would probably have made the fires uncontrollable and doomed the ship. Brooks had performed the same duty the previous day under similar circumstances.

Unable to endure the sufferings of the many wounded trapped on the forecastle without medical supplies, one enlisted man who was never identified started climbing through the flames over the 20-mm guns toward the flight deck to get help. A torpedo plane directly in his path suddenly exploded. He was next seen clinging to the side of the flight deck with one leg blown off. A moment later he dropped into the water and was not seen again. Casualties aboard the *Suwannee* alone during this and the previous day were eighty-five killed, fifty-eight missing, and ninety-two wounded.

Gun crews on the *Petrof Bay* could hardly have failed to think of the planes parked just above their heads while they watched the Kamikaze plow into planes on the *Suwannee* and shower flaming gasoline over the gun buckets of the sister ship. A few seconds after that happened a Zeke attempted the same tactics on the *Petrof Bay*. His dive was well aimed and almost vertical, and with a 90-degree aileron roll to the left he kept his alignment perfectly while the ship turned to port to avoid him. The guns continued to fire incessantly, though the crews had before them an example of what would happen if they failed. When the Zeke was about 500 feet above the deck, its tail was shot off, and it went into a flat spin, though it kept on coming. Continuing a relentless fire, the guns tore the

Zeke "almost completely to pieces." Instead of crashing into the parked planes it fell into the sea about fifty feet astern.

This was the last of the Kamikaze planes in the Battle off Samar. In their first coordinated attacks the suicide planes ran up a score of one escort carrier sunk, four seriously damaged, and one slightly damaged. Enemy losses in planes, including both those shot down by our planes and by ships' gunfire were fifty-two planes, including fifteen Zekes and twenty other single-engine fighters. The conclusion of our airmen was that the new suicide tactics of the Japanese were "wasteful."

Early on the morning of the 26th, Seventh Fleet search planes spotted a light cruiser and four or five destroyers in the Camotes Sea to the west of Leyte Island. These ships were believed at the time to be units of the Japanese Southern Force which had survived the Battle of Surigao Strait. Actually they made up a transport force which had taken part in none of the battles, but under cover the three-pointed thrust at Leyte Gulf on the 25th, while our aircraft and ships were thoroughly occupied, had landed reinforcements in Ormoc Bay on the western side of Leyte.

Although Admiral Stump's CVE's were occupied with fighting off air attacks over Leyte Gulf, they also launched strike after strike at the transport force west of Leyte. Their attacks began before dawn and continued until late in the afternoon. With no torpedoes or heavy bombs left after the battle of the previous day, they were limited to the use of contact bombs, rockets, and strafing. They pounded away persistently, however, while the transport force steamed northward between Leyte and Cebu Islands toward the Visayan Sea. One of the destroyers, the *Uranami* it was later learned, was sunk largely by strafing south of Masbate Island early in the afternoon. The light cruiser *Kinu*, after absorbing many hits, went down in the same area at 1730. She was the last of twenty-six Japanese vessels sunk in the Battle for Leyte Gulf.

Admiral Halsey had announced "with assurance" on the evening of the 25th that the Japanese Navy had been "beaten,

routed, and broken." While the successful retirement of six of
the nine enemy battleships brought to action and the escape
of numerous supporting vessels somewhat qualifies the admiral's colorful statement of the case, it is nevertheless clear that
the Battle for Leyte Gulf was an overwhelming victory for
the United States Navy; somewhat less overwhelming than
it might have been and somewhat less than first appeared,
to be sure, but still an unquestionable victory of striking proportions. A recapitulation of losses sustained on both sides
between the 23rd and 26th demonstrates only one aspect of
the victory:

Reckoned in terms of standard tonnage the Japanese
losses were greater than the number of ships would indicate:
305,710 tons for the Imperial Navy as against 36,600 tons for
the United States Navy. Our losses therefore were approximately 12 percent of those suffered by the enemy. Of the tonnage of fighting ships committed in the battle by the Japanese,

JAPANESE LOSSES		AMERICAN LOSSES
3 battleships	*4 light cruisers*	*1 light carrier*
Musashi	Abukuma	Princeton
Yamashiro	Tama	*2 escort carriers*
Fuso	Noshiro	Gambier Bay
1 large carrier	Kinu	St. Lo
Zuikaku	*9 destroyers*	*2 destroyers*
3 light carriers	Wakaba	Johnston
Chitose	Yamagumo	Hoel
Chiyoda	Michishio	*1 destroyer escort*
Zuiho	Asagumo	Samuel B. Roberts
6 heavy cruisers	Hatsutsuki	———
Atago	Akitsuki	6 combatant vessels
Maya	Nowake	
Chokai	Hayashimo	
Suzuya	Uranami	
Chikuma	———	
Mogami	26 combatant vessels	

approximately 45 percent was sunk. The American losses, on the other hand, represented only 2.8 percent of the tonnage of our ships in the engagement.

The simple arithmetical ratio of these figures is deceptive as an indication of their real significance. In the first place the proportion of losses to surviving ships of the two navies must be taken into account to understand the meaning of these losses to the Imperial Fleet. While in view of the impotence of the enemy air groups at the outset of the action the importance of the sinking of the four carriers was overstressed at the time, the destruction of the enemy's entire operational carrier force dramatized conclusively the end of Japanese naval air power. The escape of four enemy battleships and two battleship-carriers becomes of less significance when the heavy loss of supporting vessels, without which the major ships are immobilized, is taken into account.

"Would you say that, to all intents and purposes, the naval war ended with the battle of October?" Admiral Ozawa was asked.

"After this battle," replied the Japanese Admiral, "the surface forces became strictly auxiliary, so that we relied on land forces, special [Kamikaze] attack, and air power." He added this significant obituary: *"There was no further use assigned to surface vessels,* with exception of some special ships."

Viewed in this light, Leyte Gulf becomes more than a victorious battle or a successful campaign. In many ways it was the death struggle of the Japanese Navy. While the United States Fleet fought many bloody actions in the following months, they were actions against land-based forces in direct support of our own ground forces—at Lingayen Gulf, Iwo, Okinawa. Leyte Gulf was the last battle fought between surface forces. None of the numerous beachheads which our operation plans had marked off in the area from Leyte to Tokyo would be menaced by battleships or carrier-based planes, and the network of interisland passages and seas lay open to our fleet. The command of seas was established.

Admiral Mitsumasa Yonai, Navy Minister of the Koiso Cabinet, said that he realized that the defeat at Leyte "was tantamount to loss of the Philippines." As for the larger significance of the battle, he said, "I felt that that was the end."

To account for this victory by simple reference to the numerical superiority of Allied ships would be a false emphasis. A more complete analysis would take into account that the battle was fought many thousands of miles from the continental home bases of the United States Fleet, within range of scores of enemy air fields, and within less than 1,000 miles of the Empire bases of the Japanese Fleet. For air support our forces had to rely almost entirely upon carrier-based planes, since we lacked so much as one fully operational air strip in the Philippines and our nearest land bases for planes were Morotai and Palau. A somewhat wider view of this struggle would take into consideration certain important contemporaneous naval commitments on the opposite side of the globe.

Victory is a palladium against critics, and victory of this magnitude and decisiveness may silence or discourage needed criticism until time eventually brings events into true perspective. It is already apparent, however, that not all the mistakes were made by the Japanese. On the American side much of the trouble was attributable directly or indirectly to division of the naval command. The Seventh Fleet, of course, remained subordinate to MacArthur. The lack of a common superior for the Third and Seventh Fleets short of Washington, however expedient under the circumstances, would find few defenders among sound naval strategists.

The command situation explains in part, at least, the difficulties and the slowness of communication between our fleets, the lack of complete coordination of their movements, the absence of information concerning the location of Task Force 34, and the lack of intelligence concerning the movements of the enemy Central Force during the night of 24th—25th October. Had there been a unified naval command it is scarcely conceivable that Admiral Kinkaid could have been left in any doubt whatever regarding Admiral Halsey's decision to leave San Bernardino Strait unguarded (if, indeed, that decision would have been approved), and it is likewise difficult to see how the escort carriers could have been surprised by a superior enemy force.

Of course the command situation was not the whole story. There was the failure to maintain an air patrol and to launch an effective dawn search over San Bernardino, and the tendency to overestimate damage to enemy ships inflicted by air strikes. It was not entirely Oriental cleverness that enabled the enemy to escape with six of his battleships while the six fast battleships of the Third Fleet steamed back and forth between Ozawa and Kurita; nor was it entirely American heroism that saved the escort carriers (those that *were* saved) and averted disaster at Leyte Gulf. Fortunately the enemy's mistakes were much more numerous than our own.

The more that is learned about the Japanese frame of mind at the time of the battle, the more it seems that the daring *Sho* Operation was undertaken less in a spirit of bravado than of desperation. "When this whole plan was in Tokyo," said a Japanese captain who had part in the planning, "we thought that there wasn't such a good chance, but if we did nothing, the whole Philippines would be seized. So we had to do something and we did our best. It was the last chance we had, although not a very good one." While Ozawa said that he was not surprised by the outcome, he still believed at the end of the war that "it was the best possible plan under the circumstances."

In retrospect the failure of the plan seems less remarkable than the relatively narrow margin by which it missed success. When asked for their explanation of the failure of the operation, the Japanese usually fixed upon weakness of air power. "The lack of planes, either for search or for attack," was considered the "main cause" by Kurita. "The lack of air power, I feel, was the weakest point," agreed Ozawa. The immediate shortage of aircraft was attributed mainly to the devastating air strikes against Formosa, Luzon, and the southern Philippines by the fast carriers of the Third Fleet in the period before the battle.

Another cause emphasized by the Japanese was failure of communications. The enemy's ineptitude in this respect and the consequent failures in coordination of fleet movements seemed to our commanders almost unbelievable at the time of the battle, and they still seem so. The major failures of this sort were numerous. Steaming less than fifty miles to the rear of Nishimura's force, Shima remained unaware that it had been brought under air attack on the morning of the 24th and failed miserably to coordinate his action in the Strait with that of Nishimura. Again, there was the failure of Shima as well as of the senior survivor of Nishimura's force to inform Kurita promptly of the disaster in Surigao Strait; or Ozawa's pathetic inability to inform either Toyoda or Kurita of the success of his sacrifice mission. The incompetence and ineptitude of these failures add up to something like general deterioration. By comparison, the delays and misunderstandings in communications between the two United States fleets, while serious enough in some respects, seem relatively minor.

In addition to technological deficiences in radar and other fields, the Japanese failure in coordination within and between branches of military service can not be overlooked. Throughout the period when Japanese naval forces were engaged in bitter struggles to the south and east of Leyte Island and were entirely lacking in air cover not once did the enemy's 4th Air Army, based in the Philippines, attempt to come to the aid of the ships. The army planes stuck doggedly to their assigned task of attacking transports in the gulf. Landbased planes of the Japanese Navy did attempt with some success to coordinate attacks with those of the surface forces, but communication between fleet and land-based planes was almost non-existent and the fleet seems to have received little or no intelligence from the planes.

Admiral Ozawa is reported to have considered committing suicide after the action and to have been dissuaded by a fellow officer who pointed out to him that of all the Japanese fleet commanders taking part in the battle he was the only one who succeeded in carrying out his mission. His mission was the sacrifice of his fleet as a diversion. The fleet was sacrificed and the diversion created. The fact that the sacrifice had been largely in vain was a bitter reflection to take into retirement, but that was a failure of communications, not of honor.

The reactions of Admiral Nishimura to his disaster are, for obvious reasons, unknown. The admiral went down with his flagship *Yamashiro*, which broke up rapidly in a tremendous explosion after torpedo hits in the Battle of Surigao Strait. It would be a blind partisanship that would question the bravery of any man who took that small force up the strait on the night of the 25th. The admiral has been criticised by survivors of the battle for his tactics in the action, one critic going so far as to say that "there are some people who think Nishimura was very fortunate not to have returned from this battle." As it is, the case rests between the admiral and his ancestors.

The case of Admiral Kurita presents more difficulties. Kurita evidently made a reasonable case for himself in Tokyo, since Admiral Toyoda, when asked for his opinion of Kurita's decision to turn back from Leyte Gulf, said that he "would not criticize." On the other hand, one of Kurita's fellow officers is content with a simple judgment: "He should have been braver and gone on to Leyte." Perhaps that is true, but the question would appear to be more complicated.

During the war it was a common expedient among Americans to attribute any puzzling or erratic conduct on the part of their eastern enemy to "Oriental mentality." In this case, however, it would seem that one is dealing with that type of mind which in a crisis envisions unseen dangers and sees too many alternatives, and while hesitating among them evades a commitment to the obvious course of action—one who hesitates to act regardless of the necessity for action. Hamlet was no Oriental. There were circumstances, even in this battle, when the Hotspur temperament probably misguided a commander, but the crisis off Samar Island was not one of them. What was needed on the flag bridge of the *Yamato* on the morning of the 25th was not a Hamlet but a Hotspur—a Japanese Halsey instead of a Kurita.

It would be a distortion of history to fix upon the short comings of a personality to explain a failure of this magnitude. But in his confused and hesitant maneuvers off Samar, in his obstinate and dogged advance in the face of odds and in his weak vacillation of purpose, as well as in the suicidal self-sacrifice of men and ships in Surigao Strait and off Cape Engaño, is written the deterioration of command and morale and the ultimate downfall of the Imperial Fleet.

ABOUT THE AUTHOR

C. Vann Woodward, associate Professor of History at John Hopkins University, served during the war as an Intelligence Officer in the Office of Chief of Naval Operations. Before the war he taught at Scripps College, the University of Virginia, and the University of Florida. Professor Woodward is also the author of *Tom Watson, Agrarian Rebel*.